This book is dedicated to Judith D. Zuk, president emeritus of Brooklyn Botanic Garden, whose leadership made the Garden's pioneering books on invasive plants possible.

Native Alternatives to Invasive Plants

By C. Colston Burrell

Janet Marinelli and Bonnie Harper-Lore
Editors

Janet Marinelli
SERIES EDITOR

Sigrun Wolff Saphire
SENIOR EDITOR

Gerry Moore
SCIENCE EDITOR

Elizabeth Ennis
ART DIRECTOR

Joni Blackburn
COPY EDITOR

Elizabeth Peters
DIRECTOR OF
PUBLICATIONS

Steven Clemants
VICE-PRESIDENT,
SCIENCE &
PUBLICATIONS

Scot Medbury
PRESIDENT

Elizabeth Scholtz
DIRECTOR
EMERITUS

Judith D. Zuk
PRESIDENT
EMERITUS

Handbook #185

Copyright © 2006, 2007
by Brooklyn Botanic Garden, Inc.

All-Region Guides, formerly *21st-Century Gardening
Series,* are published three times a year at
1000 Washington Ave., Brooklyn, NY 11225.

Subscription included in Brooklyn Botanic Garden
subscriber membership dues ($35 per year;
$45 outside the United States).

ISBN 13: 978-1-889538-74-7
ISBN 10: 1-889538-74-4

Printed by OGP in China.
Printed on recycled paper.

Acknowledgments

Many thanks to the Chanticleer Foundation, the Federal Highway Administration,
the Bureau of Land Management, and the Center for Plant Conservation, without
whose financial support this book would not have been possible.

Cover: American bittersweet is a vigorous and large-berried alternative to the invasive Oriental bittersweet.
Above: Rock clematis, a showy native vine, is a good alternative to Japanese honeysuckle.

Native Alternatives to Invasive Plants

Preventing Plant Invasions

Janet Marinelli

As the old saying goes, an ounce of prevention is worth a pound of cure. This is especially true of the struggle to control invasive species. In the New York metropolitan area, where I live, roadsides have been overtaken by solid stands of purple loosestrife, and forest understories are thick with Japanese barberry. Biologists consider invasive species such as these to be one of the two greatest threats to native plants and animals, second only to the outright loss of habitat to suburban sprawl, agriculture, and industrial development. Land managers fight a daily battle to remove invasives from important natural areas.

The conventional wisdom, at least in horticultural circles, used to be that most invasive plants were introduced accidentally—in agricultural seed stocks, say, or even on the bottom of some unsuspecting tourist's shoes. But during the course of researching Brooklyn Botanic Garden's influential 1996 handbook *Invasive Plants: Weeds of the Global Garden*, my colleagues and I were dismayed to discover that about half of the worst invasive plants currently degrading natural habitats from coast to coast were brought here intentionally, for horticultural use.

While the vast majority of species planted on highway rights-of-way, in public landscapes, and in home gardens are not invasive, a small percentage have adapted too well and escaped cultivation. These plants have become established, or naturalized, in the wild. Not every naturalized plant is a threat to native ecosystems, however. This handbook is concerned with those nonnative plants that not only establish viable populations in but also alter the structure and/or functioning of those ecosystems.

Many invasive plants are still being sold as garden specimens or for wildlife plantings and erosion control, despite their documented ability to degrade natural areas. And although no system is in place to effectively screen them for potential invasiveness, new plants from around the world are constantly being introduced to satisfy the preoccupation with the new and exotic that has characterized horticulture for at least the past hundred years. The more we learn about invasive plants, the more we realize how difficult they are to control, much less eradicate. The most prudent course of action clearly is to avoid planting these species in the first place.

Since BBG's original handbook on invasive plants was published, we have received numerous requests for a companion volume featuring ecologically safe alternatives. The Encyclopedia of Native Alternatives to Invasive Plants, at the heart of this book, recommends a variety of beautiful, regionally native species that fill the same needs as the worst nonnative invasive plants commonly used in horticulture. If you select these species, it is highly unlikely that you will be unleashing North America's next invasive menace. Regional natives aren't the only ecologically responsible choices; nonnatives that have been planted in gardens for decades without demonstrating any signs of invasiveness are good candidates for landscaping as well. But by selecting regional natives you will be preserving the natural character of your area. You will also be preserving the complex interrelationships between the native plants and the butterflies, birds, and myriad other creatures with which they have coevolved.

Allegheny serviceberry, right, native to the eastern states, is a beautiful alternative to the invasive callery pear, left. The lovely white flowers are followed by purple-black berries that are relished by birds.

The Role of Roadside Managers
Bonnie Harper-Lore

Native wildflowers planted along the Taconic State Parkway in New York delight travelers and provide food and shelter for wildlife.

Highway corridors crisscross North America, connecting neighboring parkland, farmland, and your land. Totaling over 12 million acres in the U.S. alone, the rights-of-way that border the highway pavement are highly disturbed landscapes, beginning with the original construction and continuing with upgrades, mowing, spraying, snowplowing, grading, and the placement of signs and utility lines. The plants likely to establish on disturbed lands are invasive. And so highway agencies across the country are often blamed for increasing the spread of invasive plants.

State departments of transportation (DOTs) do bear some of the responsibility, because they became a conduit for invasives by often relying on plants perceived as problem solvers. During construction, the quick establishment of groundcover to stabilize slopes and ditches is a critical concern. Revegetation not only controls erosion but also minimizes runoff and sedimentation of nearby waters. When highway departments began revegetation they adopted an agricultural approach, routinely using mixes of legumes and grasses. What we did not know then was that many of these easy-to-grow and quick-establishing problem solvers would soon become invasive. During the past few decades, transportation policy and lessons learned from the 1970s energy crunch have encouraged an ecological approach to vegetation management, including the planting of native species along roadsides.

While it has become clear that invasive plants should no longer be used, finding alternate problem solvers has not been easy. This volume is designed to provide DOTs, as well as other land managers, designers, and gardeners, with a range of regionally native alternatives.

Invasive Plants
Questions and Answers

What is an invasive species?

The U.S. government defines an invasive species as one "that is not native to the ecosystem under consideration and whose introduction causes or is likely to cause economic or environmental harm or harm to human health."

How do plants become invasive?

Simple physics dictates that two plants cannot occupy the same spot, so when a nonnative plant settles into a new ecosystem, it displaces a native. Invasive plants may grow faster, taller, or wider and shade out native species. Many stay green later into the season or leaf out earlier, giving them an advantage over natives. Nonnative plants can change the vertical and horizontal structure of ecosystems, alter hydrology, and disrupt nutrient cycles—all with devastating effects on native plants and animals.

How much damage do invasive species cause?

According to a paper by Cornell ecologist David Pimentel and others, invasive species cause major environmental damage amounting to almost $120 billion per year. About 42 percent of the species on the U.S. List of Endangered and Threatened Species are at risk primarily because of nonnative invasives. (See *Ecological Economics*, Volume 52, Issue 3, 1 February 2005, pages 273–288.)

Is it possible to predict whether a plant will be invasive?

A foolproof system for predicting invasiveness has proven elusive, but a few traits should raise red flags. For example, nonnative species bearing fleshy fruits dispersed by birds are at the top of the suspect list. Declining to plant—or recommend—such species can help prevent plant invasion. However, the most prudent prevention measure is to choose a regionally native species. For more information on invasive plants, see page 206.

The multiflora rose is lovely looking, but its rampant spread has made it an outlaw in several states.

Native Plants
Questions and Answers

What is a native plant?

The federal Plant Conservation Alliance defines a native plant species as one that occurs naturally in a particular region, ecosystem, and/or habitat without direct or indirect human intervention. A plant endemic to Europe and introduced to North America is not native to this continent. Likewise, a plant native to one region of North America is not native to another region unless it originated there without help from us.

Ecologically speaking, political boundaries such as national or state lines have no bearing on plant distribution. Plant ecologists have divided North America into 15 plant provinces (see opposite page). The species in these distinct vegetation regions are determined by such regional factors as high and low temperatures in summer and winter, total annual precipitation, timing and nature of precipitation, elevation, and soil type.

What is local provenance, and why is it important?

Provenance refers to the specific place from which a plant or seed originated. Plants of local provenance—those whose native origin is close to where they will be planted—are apt to be better adapted, and therefore perform better, than plants of more distant origin because temperature, precipitation, and other factors vary within each plant province.

Growing plants that are not of local provenance can also affect the gene pool of a native species. The genetic makeup, or genotype, of a plant may vary from place to place. When a nonlocal genotype is planted, it can mix with the local plants and alter the local gene pool in a way that

---

North America's natural vegetation is divided into plant provinces, or regional vegetation types.

Key to Map

A Ice
B Arctic Tundra
C Boreal Forests
D Pacific Coastal & Cascade Mountain Forests
E Palouse Prairies
F Great Basin Desert
G California Forests & Alpine Vegetation
H California Grasslands, Chaparral & Woodlands

I Mojave and Sonoran Deserts
J Rocky Mountain Forests & Alpine Vegetation
K Central Prairies & Plains
L Eastern Deciduous Forests
M Chihuahuan Desert
N Coastal Plain Forests
O Tropical Forests

Adapted from *North American Terrestrial Vegetation*, edited by Michael G. Barbour and William Dwight Billings (New York: Cambridge University Press, 1988).

Plant Provinces of North America

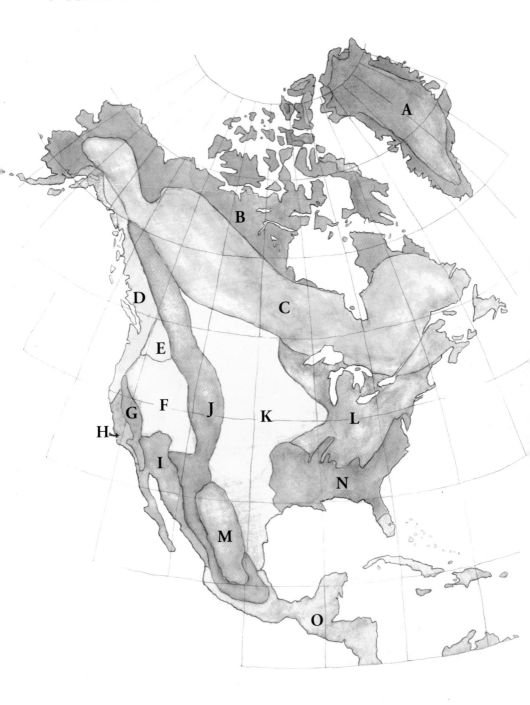

Purple loosestrife, of Eurasian origin, is displacing native wetland plants across much of North America.

Fireweed is a long-blooming native named for its tendency to colonize burned and disturbed sites.

decreases the plant's ability to survive in the area.

Can a cultivar of a native plant be considered native?

Technically, a cultivar is a plant that has been selected for cultivation because of a particular attribute or group of attributes—a particular flower color, say. To ensure that these characteristics are retained, cultivars typically are propagated by cloning via rooted cuttings. A cultivar produced by cloning a wild plant may be described as native, but it is not necessarily of local provenance. So, whenever possible, avoid selecting cultivars of native species, unless they have been propagated from local plant stock. What's more, look for local genotypes produced from seed rather than by cloning, because they maintain the maximum genetic diversity.

Can native plants be invasive?

Yes, but they rarely are. Some species display invasive growth tendencies in their native regions in response to disturbances caused by us—for example, native grapevines may grow vigorously after timber cutting creates an opening in the forest canopy, flooding once shaded areas with sunlight. However, this aggressive growth spurt usually slows down as trees and other plants fill the gap in the canopy. The vast majority of the most severe and persistent invasives are not native to the region.

Encyclopedia of Native Alternatives to Invasive Plants

C. Colston Burrell

The encyclopedia that follows is organized by horticultural plant group: trees, shrubs, vines, herbaceous plants, and grasses. To find an alternative to purple loosestrife, for example, look in the section on herbaceous plants; it will be in alphabetical order under its botanical name, *Lythrum salicaria.*

For each invasive species, between one and four regional natives are profiled, and a list of several others is provided on the Brooklyn Botanic Garden website at www.bbg.org/nativealternatives. Ideally, the alternative matches most or all of the invasive plant's desirable characteristics, such as flowers, fruit, fall color, and ease of care. However, in some cases it was possible to match only one or two of the attributes. The following checklist was used to select the recommended alternatives that most closely match the corresponding invasive species:

- Is the plant locally or regionally native?
- Are the flowers or fruit the same color?
- Is the inflorescence the same shape and size?
- Does the plant bloom at the same time?
- Is the foliage similar in form, texture, and color?
- Is the overall shape and size of the plant similar?
- Does the plant have multiple seasons of interest?
- Is the root system similar?
- Is the plant easy to establish and maintain?
- Will it grow in the same hardiness zone and under the same site conditions?

Invasive Tree
Acacia auriculiformis • Earleaf Acacia
Current Invaded Range: Florida

Native Alternative
Quercus virginiana
Virginia Live Oak

Native Habitat and Range Woodland edges, clearings, and shores from coastal regions of Virginia, south to Florida and west to Texas and Mexico

Hardiness Range Zones 8 to 10

Ornamental Attributes and Uses This picturesque species has a broadly oval to rounded crown 40 to 80 feet tall and 60 to 100 feet wide; it is usually single-stemmed and low-branching, but it may be multistemmed. Dark evergreen leaves with silvery undersides densely clothe the rounded, umbrella-like crown of this familiar southern tree. Small black acorns add to the ornamental appeal. Use it as a specimen or shade tree, windbreak or screen.

Growing Tips Plant this long-lived tree in average to humus-rich, well-drained acidic soil in full sun. It is adaptable and tolerates sand or clay as long as the soil is well drained. It is best moved when young. Oak wilt is rare in this species but has been reported, so prune only in the winter months.

More Native Alternatives For a list of additional native trees, visit www.bbg.org/nativealternatives.

Attributes at a Glance
Quercus virginiana

Huge, mounding tree

40 to 80 feet tall and 60 to 100 feet wide

Leathery, evergreen foliage

Invasive Tree
Acer tataricum var. *ginnala* • Amur Maple

Current Invaded Range: Maine to Manitoba, south to North Carolina and Iowa

Native Alternative
Stewartia malacodendron
Silky Stewartia

Native Habitat and Range Woodlands, woodland edges, and streambanks of the coastal plain from Virginia, south to Florida, west to Louisiana

Hardiness Range Zones 6 (with protection) to 9

Ornamental Attributes and Uses This tree is upright oval to mounding in habit, 8 to 20 feet tall and wide. Its delicate white, cup-shaped early-summer flowers resemble those of camellia. The mid-green pointed, broadly oval foliage ignites in orange, red, and yellow hues in fall, and its bark is attractive in winter. It is an elegant specimen, patio tree, or screen.

Growing Tips Plant in evenly moist, well-drained, humus-rich acidic soil in full sun or partial shade. The tree is heat tolerant but has limited cold hardiness. It is slow to establish and may grow slowly, especially in northern regions. Remove root suckers to maintain a tree form, as its natural habit is a large, multistemmed shrub.

Related Native Alternative *Stewartia ovata*, mountain stewartia, is a hardier (Zone 5) cousin similar in most respects but shrubbier. It is native to the Appalachians from northern Virginia to Kentucky and Alabama.

Attributes at a Glance
Stewartia malacodendron

Upright or mounding habit

8 to 20 feet tall and wide

White satiny flowers in summer

Orange to red autumn color

Irregular winter silhouette

Attributes at a Glance
Cotinus obovatus

Upright oval to rounded, irregular tree

10 to 30 feet tall and 10 to 20 feet wide

Bold, sea-green foliage

"Smoky" plumes in summer

Orange to red autumn color

Native Alternative
Cotinus obovatus
American Smoke Tree

Native Habitat and Range Woodland edges, clearings, glades, and rock outcroppings from Tennessee and Missouri, south to Alabama, Oklahoma, and Texas

Hardiness Range Zones 4 to 8

Ornamental Attributes and Uses This upright oval to rounded small tree reaches 10 to 30 feet tall and 10 to 20 feet wide; it grows as a clump or is low branching. Mature trees are beautifully formed with eccentric, twisted branches. Sea-green, paddlelike leaves with glowing orange to red autumn color crowd the tips of older stems and line fresh growth. In summer, hairs on the stalks surrounding the insignificant flowers resemble billowing plumes of smoke that light up the tree from . Use smoke tree as a unique specimen or in a mixed border provided it is coppiced (cut back to the ground) regularly. It can also serve as a screen or hedge.

Growing Tips Plant in average to humus-rich, well-drained, near-neutral soil in full sun or light shade. Smoke tree tolerates drought and alkaline soil. It is fast growing when young and often shows a coarse texture; mature plants are irregular in form and less rank looking. It can take severe pruning and is often coppiced in late winter to promote straight, lush growth for maximum foliage impact with minimum bulk.

Native Alternative
Cornus alternifolia
Pagoda Dogwood

Native Habitat and Range Woodland understory, clearings, and roadsides from Cape Breton highlands of Nova Scotia, west to Minnesota, south to Georgia and Missouri.

Hardiness Range Zones 3 to 7

Ornamental Attributes and Uses
Tiers of horizontal branches tapering in size toward the top give rise to the common name pagoda dogwood. The unique form, coupled with beautiful domed white flower clusters in late spring, blue-black fall berries, and brilliant red autumn color make this a highly prized ornamental tree. Choose it for a terrace, as a specimen, or for an allee or hedge. It reaches 20 to 35 feet at maturity and lives 40 to 60 years.

Growing Tips Plant in rich, evenly moist soil in light to partial shade for optimum growth. Though established plants are slightly drought tolerant, moisture is critical for long-term survival. In hot regions, the foliage will burn in too much sun. Wide crowns and shallow roots make it subject to being blown over in high winds. Keep an eye out for canker in stressed trees.

Attributes at a Glance
Cornus alternifolia

Small tree with horizontal branching habit

20 to 35 feet tall and wide

White flower clusters in spring

Blue-black berries

Fiery red autumn color

Native Alternative
Carpinus caroliniana
Musclewood

Native Habitat and Range Low woods, streamsides, and riverbanks from Maine and Florida, west to Minnesota and Texas

Hardiness Range Zones 4 to 9

Attributes at a Glance
Carpinus caroliniana

Small tree with a broadly oval to rounded crown

15 to 25 feet tall and wide; may reach 50 feet tall

Sinuous, silver-gray bark

Pointed-oval, toothed foliage

Orange, burgundy, or mauve autumn color

Ornamental Attributes and Uses This underutilized small tree has an elegant, often multistemmed oval crown and grows 15 to 25 feet tall and wide; occasionally it reaches 50 feet tall. Young trees are upright, but the crown broadens with age. Silvery-gray sinuous, twisted trunks and branches account for the very appropriate common name musclewood. The quilted, oval leaves with fine marginal teeth and pointed tips turn mauve to orange in autumn. The clustered dry, nutlike fruits have ragged wings. Use musclewood to shade a patio or as a specimen; it is also good in planters in urban situations.

Growing Tips Plant this tree in evenly moist, rich, preferably acidic soil in full sun or light shade. Musclewood tolerates soggy soils for short periods, as well as moderate drought. It grows at a moderate rate when young but slows with age.

More Native Alternatives *Cladrastis kentukea*, yellowwood (page 20)—North Carolina and West Virginia, south to Florida and Mississippi. *Hamamelis virginiana*, witch hazel (page 105)—Nova Scotia to Minnesota, south to Florida and Texas. *Oxydendrum arboreum*, (page 131)—Pennsylvania to Indiana, south to Florida and Louisiana. For a list of additional native trees, visit www.bbg.org/nativealternatives.

Invasive Trees

Acer platanoides • Norway Maple; *A. pseudoplatanus*
Large Maple, Sycamore Maple

Current Invaded Range: Maine to Ontario, south to North Carolina and Tennessee; *A. platanoides* also in Washington, Idaho, and Oregon

Native Alternative
Acer rubrum
Red Maple

Native Habitat and Range Lowland or upland forests, swamps, and disturbed areas from Newfoundland to Manitoba, south to Florida and Texas

Hardiness Range Zones 3 to 9

Ornamental Attributes and Uses Red maple is a versatile shade tree with a full crown of tidy, three- to five-lobed leaves with silvery undersides; its autumn color is scarlet to burgundy, sometimes yellow to orange. It produces bright red flower clusters on bare winter branches, followed by red samaras that ripen early. The winter silhouette varies from eccentric to uniformly branching, and upper branches retain the smooth, gray bark even as the trunk fissures with age. The mature tree has an upright, occasionally rounded crown with a single or multiple trunks. It grows 50 to 80 feet tall and 30 to 50 feet wide.

Growing Tips Plant in average to rich, moist to well-drained soil in sun or partial shade. This maple is easily established, fast growing, and heat and drought tolerant. It is shallow-rooted and robs water from shrubs and perennials where the soil dries in summer. The dense crown can be thinned to allow ample light to filter through.

Related Native Alternative *Acer saccharum,* sugar maple, is a tree for cooler regions in deep, rich, near-neutral soils. It produces a rounded, finely branched crown. The five-fingered leaves turn flaming orange in fall and are a tourist attraction where sugar maples grow in profusion. It is native from Nova Scotia to Minnesota, south to Virginia and Missouri; Georgia in the mountains.

Attributes at a Glance
Acer rubrum

Shade tree with upright to rounded crown

50 to 80 feet tall and 30 to 50 feet wide

Smooth gray bark when young

Red samaras in spring

3- to 5-lobed leaves

Red autumn color

Native Alternative
Nyssa sylvatica
Black Gum

Native Habitat and Range Low woods, swamps, dry upland forests, and roadsides from Maine to Minnesota, south to Florida and Texas

Hardiness Range Zones 4 (with protection) to 9

Ornamental Attributes and Uses Attractive enough in summer, this tree turns into a column of fire when late summer slips to early autumn. The foliage is flaming scarlet to glowing purple-red, colors seldom attained by other trees. Tiny flowers cluster on new growth in early spring, followed in mid- to late summer by small blue-black berries. The crown is pyramidal when young but broadens with age, often producing gnarly, erratic branching that is quite decorative in winter. The tree reaches 30 to 60 feet and occasionally 80 feet tall, and 20 to 35 feet wide. The furrowed bark is decorative in winter.

Growing Tips Plant in rich, evenly moist soil in full sun or light shade. The tree colors best in full sun. An adaptable species in the wild, black gum grows in seasonally flooded woods in soggy soils or in leaner, dry uplands; best growth occurs with ample moisture and soil fertility. Black gum is tap-rooted and difficult to transplant: Look for balled and burlapped stock to minimize root disturbance and soil incompatibility.

Attributes at a Glance
Nyssa sylvatica

Upright oval to pyramidal tree

Unusual form when mature

Glossy oval leaves

Brilliant red autumn color

Small blue-black fruit

Native Alternative
Acer macrophyllum
Big-Leaf Maple

Native Habitat and Range Lowland or upland forests, floodplains from Alaska, south to California

Hardiness Range Zones 6 to 8

Ornamental Attributes and Uses
Big-leaf maple is a versatile tree with a wide, full crown of huge five- to seven-lobed leaves with pale undersides. Chartreuse flower clusters appear before the leaves come out. The upper branches retain their smooth, dark bark as the trunk fissures with age, but they are often wrapped in moss and ferns.

Growing Tips Plant this tree in average to rich, moist, well-drained soil in sun or partial shade. This maple is easily established and fast growing, but it is only slightly drought tolerant. The crown can be thinned to allow light to filter through.

Related Native Alternative *Acer circinatum*, vine maple, is a smaller tree with elegant rounded, lobed leaves that turn red to orange in fall. It is often multistemmed and grows 10 to 20 feet tall and 8 to 12 feet wide. It is naturally found in British Columbia to northern California.

More Native Alternatives
Gymnocladus dioica, Kentucky coffee-tree (page 47)—New York to Minnesota, south to Virginia and South Dakota and Oklahoma. For a list of additional native trees, visit www.bbg.org/nativealternatives.

Attributes at a Glance
Acer macrophyllum

Shade tree with a broad, rounded crown

50 to 80 feet tall and 20 to 50 feet wide

Smooth gray bark when young

Huge round lobed leaves

Yellow autumn color

Invasive Tree
Ailanthus altissima • Tree of Heaven

Current Invaded Range: Maine to Michigan, Nebraska and Oregon, south to Florida and California

Native Alternative
Cladrastis kentukea
Yellowwood

Native Habitat and Range Open woods, bottomlands, and bluffs in scattered sites from Kentucky and North Carolina, west to Missouri and Arkansas

Hardiness Range Zones 3 to 8

Ornamental Attributes and Uses Yellowwood is a rounded to broadly oval medium to large tree that grows 20 to 60 feet tall and 20 to 40 feet wide. Elegant, pendent clusters of white pea-shaped flowers grace the horizontal to gracefully ascending branches in late spring. Pinnately divided leaves with five to nine broadly oval leaflets turn clear yellow in autumn. The smooth gray bark is attractive in every season, especially in winter when the zigzag twigs lend interest. Use as a patio tree, specimen tree, or slow-growing shade tree.

Growing Tips Plant in rich, evenly moist soil in full sun or light shade. Once established, the tree is somewhat drought tolerant, but the foliage will scorch during prolonged dry, hot weather. In warmer zones, avoid plant-ing sites with excessive reflected heat such as parking lots and the south or west sides of tall buildings.

Attributes at a Glance
Cladrastis kentukea

Medium to large tree with rounded to spreading form

20 to 60 feet tall and 20 to 40 feet wide

Branched drooping clusters of white flowers

Pinnately divided foliage

Native Alternative
Carya illinoinensis
Pecan

Native Habitat and Range Floodplains, bottomlands, and open woods from Indiana to Iowa, south to Louisiana, Texas and Mexico; widely cultivated elsewhere

Hardiness Range Zones 5 to 10

Ornamental Attributes and Uses A common lawn and shade tree on old farmsteads in the south, pecan is widely cultivated for its delectable nuts. The full, rounded crown and delicate foliage make it a handsome ornamental in its own right. Pinnately divided leaves have 9 to 11 broadly lance-shaped leaflets that turn yellow in autumn. The gray bark becomes furrowed to ragged with age.

Growing Tips Plant in rich, moist, neutral to acidic soil in full sun or light shade. The tree tolerates drought and neglect once established. Pecan is easy to establish and relatively fast growing. It colors early and drops its foliage quickly, leaving the clustered nuts to decorate the autumn landscape.

Related Native Alternative Native from Maine to Minnesota, south to northern Florida and Texas, *Carya cordiformis*, bitternut, is a forest giant, reaching 70 to 100 feet tall in rich bottomland soils. The tree's elegant, fine-textured leaves have lance-shaped leaflets of rare beauty.

Attributes at a Glance
Carya illinoinensis

Large tree with an upright oval crown

60 to 90 feet tall and 30 to 50 feet wide

Ragged bark

Fine-textured pinnately divided leaves

Yellow autumn color

Edible nuts

Native Alternative
Sorbus sitchensis
Sitka Mountain Ash

Native Habitat and Range Open woods, rock outcropping, seepage slopes, and bog margins from Alaska and Yukon, south to Montana and California

Attributes at a Glance
Sorbus sitchensis

Small upright to rounded tree

10 to 20 feet tall and 6 to 10 feet wide

Smooth, glossy bark

Domed clusters of creamy-white summer flowers

Red berries in autumn

Hardiness Range Zones 3 to 6

Ornamental Attributes and Uses
Showy white spring flowers in domed clusters and colorful trusses of large waxen red berries make Sitka mountain ash a desirable ornamental. The pinnately divided foliage with yellow to purple autumn color adds to the show. It is good as a patio, lawn, or specimen tree as well as in naturalistic plantings. Birds savor the berries.

Growing Tips Plant in moist, rich soil in full sun or partial shade. Sitka mountain ash performs best when grown within its native range on appropriate soils. It often succumbs in areas with high nighttime temperature and humidity.

Related Native Alternative *Sorbus scopulina*, Greene's mountain ash, is similar but with greater stature and foliage of finer texture. It is more widely distributed, growing from Alaska south to South Dakota, New Mexico, and California.

More Native Alternatives *Amelanchier laevis*, Allegheny serviceberry—Nova Scotia and Ontario, south to Georgia and Iowa (see page 42). *Cercis canadensis*, redbud—Pennsylvania and Nebraska, south to Florida and Texas (see page 23). For a list of additional native trees, visit www.bbg.org/nativealternatives.

Invasive Tree
Albizia julibrissin • Mimosa, Silk Tree

Current Invaded Range: New York and Illinois, south to Florida and west to California

Native Alternative
Cercis canadensis
Redbud

Native Habitat and Range Open woodlands, woodland edges, meadows, and roadsides from Pennsylvania and Nebraska, south to Florida and Texas

Hardiness Range Zones 4 to 8

Ornamental Attributes and Uses Rosy-purple flowers in dense axillary clusters on bare branches are followed by bold, heart-shaped gray-green leaves with yellow autumn color. Its winter twigs have a medium-textured, attractive zigzag pattern. Use the tree as a specimen, in groupings in a lawn or at the edge of a woodland, or as a shade tree in a small garden. It may be single-stemmed or clumping in form.

Growing Tips Plant in average to humus-rich moist soil in full sun or partial shade. Redbud thrives in both acid and limy soils and is drought tolerant once established. It is very sensitive to salt and may be susceptible to canker. This short-lived tree lasts an average of 30 to 50 years.

More Native Alternatives For a list of additional native trees, visit www.bbg.org/nativealternatives.

Attributes at a Glance
Cercis canadensis

Tree with a broad, vase-shaped crown when mature

20 to 35 feet tall and 20 to 40 feet wide

Zigzag branching pattern

Rose-purple, pink, or white flowers in spring

Decorative heart-shaped foliage

Yellow autumn color

Invasive Tree
Alnus glutinosa • European Alder
Current Invaded Range: Quebec and Ontario, south to Delaware, Tennessee, and Iowa

---

Native Alternative
Alnus incana subsp. *rugosa*
Speckled Alder

Native Habitat and Range Native to wet woods, pond and stream margins, and ditches from Labrador to Alaska and British Columbia, south to Virginia, Iowa, New Mexico, and California

Attributes at a Glance
Alnus incana

10 to 15 feet tall and wide

Multistemmed large shrub or single-stemmed tree

Silvery-gray bark

Quilted oval leaves

Small woody cones

Hardiness Range Zones 2 to 7

Ornamental Attributes and Uses Speckled alder generally grows as a thicket of fine branches with a rounded crown 10 to 15 feet tall and wide, but it may grow treelike with a few main trunks that reach 30 feet. Luscious quilted leaves cover the twiggy stems of this fast-growing species. The foliage seldom colors well in fall: It may turn to yellow, but more often it browns. The smooth trunks and brown stems speckled with lenticels are attractive in winter. Use the tree as a specimen, patio tree, or screen or to soften the edge of a pond.

Growing Tips Plant in wet to consistently moist, rich soil in full sun or light shade. The plant tolerates flooding but is surprisingly drought tolerant as well. Alders can be aggressive in the wild, quickly forming a thicket around a pond or in a ditch. In the garden, it seldom reseeds if the soil is not wet. Prune it into tree form by removing all but a few trunks and all the lower branches.

Related Alternatives *Alnus serrulata*, smooth alder, has a more southern distribution (Nova Scotia, south to Florida, and west to Nebraska and Texas) and is more heat tolerant. Often a multistemmed shrub when young, this species is easily trained to tree form by removing lower branches and thinning the crown to three main trunks. *A. rubra*, red alder, is usually a forest or wetland tree reaching 50 to 80 feet; it grows in Alaska south to central California.

Native Alternative
Betula nigra
River Birch

Native Habitat and Range Low woods, stream and river edges from Massachusetts and southeastern Minnesota, south to northern Florida and east Texas

Hardiness Range Zones 4 to 9

Ornamental Attributes and Uses Exfoliating bark that is cream- to peach-colored when young, finely textured branches, and toothed, triangular leaves with yellow fall color make river birch an all-around favorite. Use this single-stemmed or clump-forming tree as a specimen, shade tree, or tall hedge if pruned or sheared.

Growing Tips Plant in average to humus-rich acidic soil in full sun or partial shade. River birch is intolerant of alkaline soils but can take drought, soil compaction, and flooding. Its heat tolerance makes it much more suitable for warm regions than other birch species. It is fast growing when young and slows with age; it lives only 60 to 75 years. This tree is resistant to many pest and diseases that plague other birches but is weak wooded and may be damaged by ice.

Related Alternative *Betula papyrifera*, paper birch, is a robust northern species with snow-white bark and pointed oval foliage that turns rich, clear yellow in autumn. It is intolerant of hot nights and high humidity. It is native from Newfoundland to Alaska, south to New Jersey, Indiana, and Washington.

More Native Alternatives For a list of additional native trees, visit www.bbg.org/nativealternatives.

Attributes at a Glance
Betula nigra

Medium to large, oval tree

40 to 60 feet tall and 20 to 30 feet wide

Exfoliating bark

Toothed triangular leaves

Yellow autumn color

Invasive Tree
Bischofia javanica • Bishopwood
Current Invaded Range: Florida (also Hawaii)

Native Alternative
Ptelea trifoliata
Wafer Ash, Hop Tree

Native Habitat and Range Open woods, floodplains, and uplands from Ontario to Minnesota, south to Florida and northern Mexico

Attributes at a Glance
Ptelea trifoliata

Large shrub to small tree

10 to 20 feet tall and wide

Rounded, open crown

Compound leaves

Fragrant flowers

Yellow autumn color

Hardiness Range Zones 3 to 9

Ornamental Attributes and Uses This is an easy-care, hardy small tree that has languished in undeserved obscurity. Fragrant green flowers cluster like nosegays above tufts of deep green trifoliate leaves that turn yellow in autumn. The foliage has a pungent aroma when crushed. The flowers are followed by flattened, circular winged fruits that give rise to the plant's many descriptive common names. Use wafer ash as a specimen, patio tree, or screen. This rounded, slow-growing large shrub to small tree reaches 10 to 20 feet tall and wide. Shrub forms are more common than tree forms in the northern reaches of this plant's native range.

Growing Tips Plant in moist, humus-rich soil in full sun or partial shade. Wafer ash grows well in full shade, though the crown is more open and it flowers sparsely. Prune as necessary to shape the crown; it is easily pruned into tree form.

More Native Alternatives *Simarouba amara,* paradise tree—Florida (page 30). For a list of additional native trees, visit www.bbg.org/nativealternatives.

Invasive Tree
Broussonetia papyrifera • Paper Mulberry
Current Invaded Range: Massachusetts to Kansas, south to
Florida and Texas (also Hawaii)

Native Alternative
Morus rubra
Red Mulberry

Native Habitat and Range Open
woods, clearings, and roadsides from
Massachusetts to Michigan, south to
Florida and Texas

Hardiness Range Zones 5 to 9

Ornamental Attributes and Uses
Red mulberry is seldom grown, which is
a pity because the foliage is bold and
nearly tropical in appearance, and the
form is distinctive, with horizontal or
ascending branches creating a rounded,
broad crown. The single-stemmed,
often low-branching tree grows 20 to 60
feet tall and 20 to 40 feet wide. The
stems and buds are mahogany colored,
and similarly hued bark exfoliates in
long, fibrous strips. The quilted, heart-
shaped leaves are six to eight inches
long and turn yellow to straw colored in
autumn. Red to purple fruits like knobby
caterpillars ripen on the female trees of
this dioecious species in mid- to late
summer. Use it as a patio tree, specimen, or in naturalized settings.

Growing Tips Plant in rich, moist soil in
full sun or partial shade. Fast growing and
tough, the plants need little care. Choose
a mature plant in flower if you want a
male, which will produce no fruit.

More Native Alternatives *Catalpa speciosa* (page 39)—western Tennessee and
adjacent Arkansas, north to Indiana
and Illinois. *Cercis canadensis*, redbud

(page 23)—Pennsylvania and Nebraska,
south to Florida and Texas. *Hydrangea
quercifolia*, oak-leaf hydrangea (page
110)—Georgia to Florida and Mississippi.
For a list of additional native trees, visit
www.bbg.org/nativealternatives.

Attributes at a Glance
Morus rubra

Small- to medium-sized tree

**20 to 60 feet tall and 20 to 40
feet wide**

Rounded crown

**Sparsely branched winter
silhouette**

Bold, heart-shaped leaves

Purple fruit

Invasive Tree
Casuarina equisetifolia • Australian Pine

Current Invaded Range: Florida (also Hawaii and Puerto Rico)

Attributes at a Glance
Juniperus virginiana

Upright, pyramidal to columnar tree

25 to 50 feet tall and 10 to 20 feet wide

Soft blue-green to olive-green needles

Knobby gray fruit

Exfoliating bark

Native Alternative
Juniperus virginiana
Eastern Redcedar

Native Habitat and Range Woodland edges, old fields, meadows, and rocky ground from Nova Scotia and Ontario, south to Florida and Texas

Hardiness Range Zones 4 to 9

Ornamental Attributes This small- to medium-sized conifer can take a conical upright shape or an oval to rounded shape and is densely clothed in deep green fine- to medium-textured soft awl-like needles. The foliage varies in color from olive to deep green, sometimes gray-green, and it often darkens or yellows in winter. The scented bark exfoliates in long, ragged strips. This species is dioecious, with female plants producing copious attractive blue-gray berries. Eastern redcedar grows 25 to 50 (sometimes 60) feet tall and 10 to 20 feet wide and may be used as a specimen, topiary, screen, windbreak, or tall hedge, either sheared or unpruned. It is also appropriate for naturalistic plantings.

Growing Tips Plant in average to humus-rich, well-drained, near-neutral soil in full sun or partial shade. The tree has a moderate growth rate when young, to 15 or 20 feet. This tough, underappreciated tree tolerates drought, heat, wind, salt, alkaline soil, acidic soil, and moderate air pollution. It may be susceptible to cedar-apple rust, which produces globular orange growths on the branches.

Native Alternative
Pinus clausa
Sand Pine

Native Habitat and Range Sandy ridges, barrens, and dunes in Florida, Georgia, and Alabama

Hardiness Range Zones 8 to 9

Ornamental Attributes and Uses Sand pine has paired (occasionally three) deep green, waxy needles held at the tips of spurs. The red-brown bark is relatively smooth when young and becomes platelike with age. The overall appearance of the tree is picturesque: Use it as a specimen, screen, or windbreak near the beach. This upright to oval tree grows 30 to 40 feet tall and 10 to 15 feet wide. Plants growing in poor sandy soils or near the beach are smaller and more dramatically distorted than those in richer or deeper soils.

Growing Tips Plant sand pine in average sandy or loamy acidic soil in full sun. Good drainage is essential. Transplant it in spring or late summer, not in autumn.

More Native Alternatives For a list of additional native trees, visit www.bbg.org/nativealternatives.

Attributes at a Glance
Pinus clausa

Upright to mounding tree

30 to 40 feet tall and 10 to 15 feet wide

Irregular winter silhouette

Deep green, waxy needles held at the tips of spurs

Invasive Tree
Cupaniopsis anacardioides • Carrotwood
Current Invaded Range: Florida

Attributes at a Glance
Simarouba amara

Elegant medium-sized tree

30 to 50 feet tall and 20 to 30 feet wide

Upright, rounded crown

Pinnately divided foliage

Yellow flowers

Purple fruit

Native Alternative
Simarouba amara
Paradise Tree

Native Habitat and Range Forested hammocks in south Florida

Hardiness Range Zones 9 to 10

Ornamental Attributes and Uses The smooth, pale gray trunk of paradise tree supports an open crown 30 to 50 feet tall and 20 to 30 feet wide. Large, pinnately divided evergreen leaves with 10 to 16 leathery obovate leaflets crowd the ends of the branches of this attractive and underutilized native tree. Emerging foliage is tinged with red and turns deep green and lustrous with maturity. Pendent panicles of small yellow flowers dangle below the crowns of foliage. Scarlet fruits ripen to deep purple on female trees of this dioecious species. Use paradise tree as a specimen, lawn tree, screen, or in naturalized settings.

Growing Tips Plant in sandy humus-rich, well-drained soil in full sun to partial shade. Mycorrhizal fungal associations allow this plant to exploit difficult sites. It is drought and salt tolerant. Since it can be messy in landscaped settings, choose male trees for patios and near walkways and other hard surfaces.

More Native Alternatives For a list of additional native trees, visit www.bbg.org/nativealternatives.

Invasive Tree
Eucalyptus globulus • Tasmanian Blue Gum

Current Invaded Range: California (also Hawaii)

Native Alternative
Quercus engelmannii
Engelmann Oak

Native Habitat and Range Open woods and chaparral in foothills of southern California

Hardiness Range Zones 8 to 10

Ornamental Attributes and Uses A gorgeous foliage plant with small acorns, Engelmann oak is a monumental shade tree for dry sites. The evergreen, sometimes deciduous leaves are gray-green with shallow lobes rather than sharp points like those of many California species. This upright to rounded, medium to large tree grows 40 to 60 feet tall and 40 to 50 feet wide.

Growing Tips Plant in average to rich, well-drained soil in full sun or light shade. Established trees are moderately heat and drought tolerant. Though evergreen, the tree sheds old leaves in spring, as new growth is emerging, and may shed early when stressed. Do not prune while the tree is actively growing.

Related Native Alternative *Quercus garryana*, Garry oak, is a tall, upright species that grows 40 to 80 feet tall. The lustrous, elongated leaves have blunt lobes. It has a more northern distribution, from British Columbia, south to southern California mountains.

> ### Attributes at a Glance
> *Quercus engelmannii*
>
> **Medium to large tree with upright to rounded crown**
>
> **40 to 60 feet tall and 40 to 50 feet wide**
>
> **Evergreen, oval foliage with shallow lobes**

Native Alternative
Arbutus menziesii
Pacific Madrone

Native Habitat and Range Open woods, streambanks, and outcroppings from British Columbia south to Baja California

Hardiness Range Zones 7 to 9

Attributes at a Glance
Arbutus menziesii

Medium-sized upright oval tree

20 to 50 feet tall and 15 to 30 feet wide

Cinnamon-colored exfoliating bark

Glossy evergreen foliage

Branched clusters of creamy-white flowers

Ornamental Attributes and Uses This coveted, medium-sized upright oval tree grows 20 to 50 feet tall (to 100 in the wild) and 15 to 30 feet wide. Sprays of white bell-shaped flowers give way to edible red berries set off by a collar of glossy, evergreen leaves. The narrow oval leaves are a rich green and turn burgundy to yellow when they are shed in spring.

Growing Tips Plant in average to rich, well-drained acidic soil in full sun or partial shade. Pacific madrone is slow growing and long-lived. It is difficult to transplant; young balled and burlapped stock is the best bet. Protect the tree from wind and extremely wet weather; excellent drainage is essential. Prolonged drought stress weakens the tree, and it is subject to a fungal canker disease, which has killed many beautiful, mature specimens in urban and natural environments.

Native Alternative
Cupressus arizonica (*C. glabra*) Arizona Cypress

Native Habitat and Range Woodland edges, clearings, rock outcroppings from Texas west to Utah and California, south to central Mexico

Hardiness Range Zones 7 to 9

Ornamental Attributes This pyramidal, gray-blue conifer has a beautiful form and fine-textured needles in all seasons. The richly colored bark is shaggy or exfoliating. Mature plants reach 40 to 60 feet tall and 25 to 30 feet wide. Use this conifer as a specimen tree, screen, windbreak, or tall hedge.

Growing Tips Plant in average to humus-rich, very well drained neutral soil in full sun. Established trees are drought tolerant, but they are intolerant of high humidity and heavy soil.

Arizona cypress may be susceptible to canker under environmental stress. The tree keeps a regular form and seldom needs pruning.

More Native Alternatives For a list of additional native trees, visit www.bbg.org/nativealternatives.

Attributes at a Glance
Cupressus arizonica

Tall, conical conifer

40 to 60 feet tall and 25 to 30 feet wide

Blue-green foliage

Globe-shaped, often glaucous cones

Invasive Trees
Ficus microcarpa, F. altissima, F. benghalensis • Figs
Current Invaded Range: Florida (also Hawaii and Puerto Rico)

Native Alternative
Persea borbonia
Redbay

Native Habitat and Range Sandy low woods, swamps, pond margins, and pine savannas from North Carolina and Arkansas, south to Florida and Texas; spotty distribution in the Mississippi Valley.

Hardiness Range Zones 7 (with protection) to 10

Ornamental Attributes and Uses Bay-scented evergreen foliage, narrowly elliptical to lance shaped in outline, is the primary charm of this plant. The foliage clusters toward the tips of the stems, creating a lush, tropical look. Axillary clusters of small greenish-yellow flowers in June give way to blue-black fruit. The reddish-brown bark is smooth in youth, irregularly furrowed with maturity.

Growing Tips Plant in average to rich, sandy or loamy soil in full sun or partial shade. Redbay grows best in sun but can take considerable shade. It tolerates wet soil and drought. The tree's foliage is subject to windburn at the northern edge of its range. Remove any dead or damaged twigs in spring.

Related Alternatives *Persea palustris*, swamp bay, is similar, but the foliage is narrower and quite elegant. It is hardier and has a wider, denser range, though it is rare at the northern end of its distribution, which is coastal regions from Delaware, south to Florida, and west to Texas. *Persea humilis*, silk bay (page 57), is another Florida native.

Attributes at a Glance
Persea borbonia

Medium-sized upright oval tree

20 to 50 feet tall and 15 to 20 feet wide

Fragrant evergreen foliage

Native Alternative
Magnolia virginiana
Sweetbay

Native Habitat and Range Low woods, swamps, and streambanks from Massachusetts to Florida, west to Texas

Hardiness Range Zones 6 to 9

Ornamental Attributes and Uses Lemon-scented creamy-white chalicelike flowers open in late spring and early summer. The lush, elongated oval leaves are sea green and leathery, turning russet to yellow in autumn. This upright oval to rounded, small to medium-sized tree, 20 to 40 feet tall and 10 to 15 feet wide, may be single-stemmed or clump-forming. Use it as a specimen tree, patio tree, screen, or in containers.

Growing Tips Plant in evenly moist, humus-rich acidic soil in full sun or shade. This versatile species tolerates flooding, soil compaction, salt, and moderate air pollution. No serious pests.

Related Alternatives *Magnolia virginiana* var. *virginiana,* swamp magnolia, found from Massachusetts to Florida, west to Texas, is fully deciduous in the northern reaches of its territory to semievergreen in the South. It is multistemmed, often with an irregular crown that may need shaping. In the same range is *Magnolia virginiana* var. *australis,* southern sweetbay, which is usually single-stemmed and upright, with evergreen foliage (semievergreen in its northern reaches).

More Native Alternatives *Bucida buceras,* black olive (page 52)—southern Florida (also Puerto Rico). For a list of additional native trees, visit www.bbg.org/nativealternatives.

Attributes at a Glance
Magnolia virginiana

Upright to broadly oval tree

20 to 40 feet tall and 10 to 15 feet wide

Deciduous or semievergreen

Smooth winter bark

Fragrant white flowers

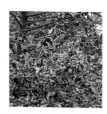

Invasive Tree
Ilex aquifolium • English Holly
Current Invaded Range: British Columbia to California

Native Alternative
Lithocarpus densiflorus
Tan Oak

Native Habitat and Range Dry, rocky slopes and chaparral in Oregon and California

Attributes at a Glance
Lithocarpus densiflorus

Handsome evergreen shrub or small tree

10 to 60 feet tall and 20 to 30 feet wide

Deep green leathery leaves

Upright spikes of white male flowers

Large acorns with fringed caps

Hardiness Range Zones 7 to 10

Ornamental Attributes and Uses
Broadly elliptical dark green toothed leaves with featherlike venation clothe the dense, upright crown of this tough and adaptable small tree. Erect terminal clusters of small creamy-white male flowers arrive in late spring and summer. The inconspicuous female flowers give rise to acorns with pointed bases and fringed caps. The crown of this upright evergreen tree (*Lithocarpus densiflorus* var. *densiflorus*) or shrub (*Lithocarpus densiflorus* var. *echinoides*) reaches 10 to 60 feet tall and 20 to 30 feet wide. Use it as a specimen, hedge, screen, or in xeriscape gardens and borders.

Growing Tips Plant in moist, sandy or loamy soil in full sun or light shade. Good drainage is essential for the success of this native of summer-dry areas; it is drought tolerant and can also survive extreme heat. Its regular crown seldom needs pruning.

More Native Alternatives
Arctostaphylos columbiana, hairy manzanita (page 96)—British Columbia to California. *Arbutus menziesii*, Pacific madrone (page 32)—British Columbia south to Baja California. For a list of additional native trees, visit www.bbg.org/nativealternatives.

Invasive Tree
Melia azedarach • Chinaberry

Current Invaded Range: Virginia, Missouri, and California, south to Florida, Texas, and Mexico (also Hawaii and Puerto Rico)

Native Alternative
Aralia spinosa
Devil's Walking Stick

Native Habitat and Range Open woods, edges of meadows, and along roadsides from Delaware and Pennsylvania to Indiana, south to Florida and Texas; naturalized elsewhere

Hardiness Range Zones 4 to 9

Ornamental Attributes and Uses This curious tree rises to 25 feet or more, and forms large colonies from fast-spreading underground stems. Huge spherical to domed clusters of tiny round, white flower heads are followed by a dramatic display of purple-black berries. The huge, tripinnate leaves have dozens of two- to three-inch pointed oval leaflets. Sharp spines move right up the stems and onto the petioles of the four- to six-foot leaves, so be careful when handling this plant. Seldom employed in ornamental settings, the stunningly beautiful species makes a formidable barrier if you wish to exclude or confine someone or something. It excels in naturalistic settings along the edges of woodlands or as a focal point at the back of a pond. Birds relish the purple-black fruit.

Growing Tips Plant in humus-rich, moist, neutral or acidic soil in full sun to partial shade. Established plants are drought tolerant. Set out young plants in their permanent spot. If planting more than one specimen, leave at least four feet between each plant to allow for mature spread. Suckers must be pulled to check this colonial species.

Attributes at a Glance
Aralia spinosa

Suckering woody shrub or small tree

25 feet tall and 5 to 10 feet wide

Large, tripinnately divided leaves

Spherical clusters of small white flowers

Yellow autumn foliage

Dark purple berries

Native Alternative
Fraxinus dipetala
Flowering Ash

Native Habitat and Range Found in open woods, ravines, chaparral slopes, and streambanks from Utah to California and Arizona

Hardiness Range Zones 8 to 10

Ornamental Attributes and Uses An anomaly among ashes, this species has

showy, long racemes of large fragrant white flowers. The bright green pinnate leaves have three to five broad, oval leaflets and set off the billowing flowers to good advantage. Use the tree as a specimen, patio tree, screen, or in informal settings.

Growing Tips Plant in moist, sandy or loamy, neutral to acidic soil in full sun or light shade. This tree tolerates temporary flooding and periodic drought but does best with constant moisture.

Related Alternative *Fraxinus velutina*, leatherleaf ash, forms an attractive, upright tree of the same size. It is found in Texas west to Utah and California.

More Native Alternatives *Carya illinoinensis*, pecan (page 21)—Indiana to Iowa, south to Louisiana, Texas, and Mexico. For a list of additional native trees, visit www.bbg.org/nativealternatives.

Attributes at a Glance
Fraxinus dipetala

Deciduous multistemmed small tree

30 to 50 feet tall and 20 to 30 feet wide

Pinnate light green leaves

White flower clusters

Yellow to golden autumn color

Invasive Tree
Paulownia tomentosa • Princess Tree
Current Invaded Range: Massachusetts and Illinois, south to Florida and Texas

Native Alternative
Catalpa speciosa
Northern Catalpa

Native Habitat and Range Bottomlands and river terraces in a narrow band at the junction of the Ohio and Mississippi rivers from western Tennessee and adjacent Arkansas, north to Indiana and Illinois; widely naturalized throughout eastern and central North America but considered invasive only in California

Hardiness Range Zones 4 to 8

Ornamental Attributes and Uses The catalpa is a large, commanding shade tree with bold, heart-shaped leaves in whorls. Flowers emerge in early summer, and the profusion of bloom against the tower of greenery is stupendous. Long, narrow pendulous pods follow the flowers and dry to brown as the foliage turns straw yellow and drops in late fall. The older it becomes, the more character the tree develops in its branching structure. Use it as a specimen or lawn tree.

Growing Tips Plant in moist to dry, rich acidic or neutral soil in full sun. Though widely tolerant of different soil and moisture conditions, the tree develops its best form in deep, rich soil. It is fast growing and precocious; flowers appear within a few years. Self-sows freely.

More Native Alternatives *Gymnocladus dioicus*, Kentucky coffeetree (page 47)—New York to Minnesota, south to Virginia and South Dakota and Oklahoma. For a list of additional native trees, visit www.bbg.org/nativealternatives.

Attributes at a Glance
Catalpa speciosa

Large tree with a tall, upright but irregular shape

60 feet tall or more and 20 to 40 feet wide

Dark brown, ragged bark

Large, showy trusses of tubular white flowers in late spring and early summer

Bold, heart-shaped leaves

Yellow autumn foliage color

Long pods that look like tinsel in winter

Invasive Tree
Populus alba • White Poplar
Current Invaded Range: Most of North America

Native Alternative
Populus grandidentata
Bigtooth Aspen

Native Habitat and Range Open woods, edges of clearings, roadsides, and disturbed sites from Newfoundland and Manitoba, south to Virginia, Kentucky, and Iowa

Hardiness Range Zones 3 to 7

Ornamental Attributes and Uses The tall, slender trunk of bigtooth aspen is usually single-stemmed, but the tree also may be clump forming. It has smooth, beige to green bark with dark nodes. Copious rhombic to ovate scalloped leaves turn clear yellow in autumn. The leaves have long, flattened petioles that allow the leaves to tremble freely in the wind. Use this elegant tree as a specimen tree, shade tree, patio tree, screen, or windbreak.

Growing Tips Plant in average to humus-rich, well-drained neutral to acidic soil in full sun or partial shade. This tree is fairly short-lived—30 to 40 years, occasionally longer.

Related Alternative *Populus tremuloides*, quaking aspen (page 48), is a less heat-tolerant cousin.

Attributes at a Glance
Populus grandidentata

Medium-sized tree

30 to 60 feet tall or more and 20 to 30 feet wide

Upright oval form

Rhomboid leaves

Yellow autumn color

Native Alternative
Betula lenta
Sweet Birch

Native Habitat and Range Dry woods, rocky slopes, and streambanks from Maine and Ontario, south to Georgia and Mississippi

Hardiness Range Zones 4 to 7

Ornamental Attributes and Uses This single or rarely multistemmed tree with smooth charcoal-gray bark is seldom seen in gardens but should be. Toothed, oval leaves are pleated and turn clear yellow in autumn. The crown of sweet birch forms an upright oval 40 to 60 feet tall and 10 to 25 feet wide. Use the tree as a specimen, shade tree, tall screen, or to create an airy grove.

Growing Tips Plant in average to humus-rich acidic soil in full sun or partial shade. Sweet birch is intolerant of alkaline soils. Its fast growth in youth moderates with age, and it is relatively short-lived, to 60 or 70 years. It shows moderate resistance to many pests and diseases that plague other birches and is drought tolerant.

More Native Alternatives For a list of additional native trees, visit www.bbg.org/nativealternatives.

Attributes at a Glance
Betula lenta

Upright oval, medium to large tree

40 to 60 feet tall and 10 to 25 feet wide

Toothed oval leaves

Yellow autumn color

Smooth, charcoal-gray bark

Invasive Tree
Pyrus calleryana • Callery Pear

Current Invaded Range: Maryland and Illinois, south to Florida and Texas

Native Alternative
Amelanchier laevis
Allegheny Serviceberry

Native Habitat and Range Woodland edges, rock outcroppings, and roadsides from Nova Scotia and Ontario, south to Georgia and Iowa

Hardiness Range Zones 4 to 9

Ornamental Attributes and Uses Allegheny serviceberry offers a fleeting display of clustered white flowers in early spring, followed by edible red berries ripening to dark blue in early summer. It has orange to red fall foliage and silver to charcoal-gray bark. The crown may be single-stemmed or clumping. Use it as a specimen, shade tree, or tall hedge when pruned or sheared.

Growing Tips Plant in average to humus-rich, neutral to acidic soil in full sun or partial shade. Serviceberry is drought tolerant once it is established. Fast growing when young, serviceberry quickly reaches 15 to 20 feet, and unlike Callery pear, it has strong branch unions and seldom falls apart at maturity.

Related Native Alternatives *Amelanchier arborea*, shadbush, has downy new growth. Multistemmed *Amelanchier canadensis*, shadblow serviceberry, grows 10 to 20 feet tall and wide.

Attributes at a Glance
Amelanchier laevis

Upright to rounded medium-sized flowering tree

20 to 40 feet tall and 10 to 12 feet wide

Silver-gray bark

Airy white flowers in early to mid-spring

Elliptical gray-green foliage

Red to purple-black edible fruit beloved by birds in early summer

Orange autumn foliage

Native Alternative
Chionanthus virginicus
Fringe Tree

Native Habitat and Range Woodland edges, rock outcroppings, and roadsides from New Jersey, Kentucky, and Missouri, south to Florida and Texas

Hardiness Range Zones 4 to 9

Ornamental Attributes and Uses This tree is low branching or clump forming, with an upright and oval to rounded form. It is small to medium sized, growing 20 to 35 feet tall and 10 to 20 feet wide. Fragrant trusses of nodding white flowers with thin, twisted, fringelike petals smother the tree in late spring. Broadly lance-shaped foliage clusters at the tips of the branches and presents a clear yellow autumn color. It is dioecious, and females produce abundant showy blue-black fruit. Use this beauty as a specimen tree, patio tree, in a container, or as an informal screen.

Growing Tips Plant in moist, humus-rich, neutral to acidic soil in full sun or partial shade. This tree flowers best in the sun, but it tolerates considerable shade. Once established, it is fairly drought tolerant. It grows into a shrubby, densely branched clump but is easily pruned into tree form. Transplant it in spring.

Attributes at a Glance
Chionanthus virginicus

Small- to medium-sized tree with rounded to horizontal form

20 to 35 feet tall and 10 to 20 feet wide

Flat clusters of creamy-white flowers in spring

Attractive pleated summer foliage

Red autumn leaf color

Blue-black berries in winter

Native Alternative
Crataegus viridis
Green Hawthorn

Native Habitat and Range Clearings, glades, woodland borders, and roadsides from Maryland and Illinois, south to Florida and Texas

Attributes at a Glance
Crataegus viridis

Small- to medium-sized tree with rounded to horizontal form

20 to 35 feet tall with an equal or greater spread

Flat clusters of creamy-white flowers in spring

Attractive pleated summer foliage

Red autumn leaf color

Red berries in winter

Hardiness Range Zones 4 to 7

Ornamental Attributes and Uses Underappreciated and often maligned, green hawthorn is an easy-care plant with elegant form and branching habit, copious creamy-white flowers in domed clusters, brilliant fall fruit, and scarlet to wine-red, sometimes yellow, fall leaf color. It flowers in late spring to early summer, and the fruit colors in early autumn and persists through winter. An upright tree when young, it spreads with age. Use it as a specimen or in open groupings at the edge of a lawn or by a pond; it also thrives in containers and planters.

Growing Tips Green hawthorn is a tough and adaptable tree that thrives in average to rich soil in full sun to partial shade. It tolerates drought and alkaline soils.

Related Native Alternatives *Crataegus viridis* 'Winter King' is a disease-resistant cultivar with large fruit and a rounded crown. It is recommended where rust is a problem or in regions with hot, humid summers. *Crataegus crus-galli* var. *inermis*, thornless cock-spur hawthorn, is a good choice for anyone who doesn't want to tangle with thorns. *Crataegus phaenopyrum*, Washington hawthorn, forms an upright rounded crown 25 to 30 feet tall and 20 to 30 feet wide, with ragged, deep green oval leaves and delicate clusters of red fruit. It is native from Pennsylvania and Illinois, south to Missouri and Alabama.

Native Alternative
Halesia diptera var. *magniflora*
Two-Winged Silverbell

Native Habitat and Range Moist woodland edges, streamsides, and swales from South Carolina and Tennessee, south to Florida and Texas

Hardiness Range Zones 5 to 9

Ornamental Attributes and Uses This is one of the most beautiful native flowering trees, with elegant form and pretty pendulous snow-white bell-shaped flowers that dangle in clusters from bare spring branches. The lush, broadly oval summer foliage turns yellow in fall. The brown seedpods have two papery wings. Use the tree as a specimen, patio tree, or in informal groupings.

Growing Tips Plant this understory tree in moist, humus-rich neutral to acidic soil in full sun or partial shade. It doesn't transplant easily, so set it out in spring as containerized stock or balled and burlapped. To maintain a single trunk form, remove suckers from the base as needed. To convert a single-stemmed plant to a multistemmed clump, cut it to the ground in winter when young and allow the root ball to resprout. Choose three to five strong stems and remove the rest to encourage strong growth.

Related Native Alternative *Halesia tetraptera*, Carolina silverbell, is more upright and grows to 80 feet or more. It lives in mountain forests from North Carolina and West Virginia, south to Florida and Mississippi.

More Native Alternatives *Cladrastis kentukea*, yellowwood (page 20)—North Carolina and West Virginia, south to Florida and Mississippi. *Oxydendrum arboreum*, sourwood (page 131)—Pennsylvania to Indiana, south to Florida and Louisiana. For more native trees, visit www.bbg.org/nativealternatives.

Attributes at a Glance
Halesia diptera var. *magniflora*

Oval to rounded medium-size tree

20 to 40 feet tall and wide

Pendulous bell-shaped flowers in spring

Yellow fall foliage color

Invasive Tree
Quercus acutissima • Sawtooth Oak
Current Invaded Range: Mid-Atlantic region; Louisiana

Native Alternative
Quercus imbricaria
Shingle Oak

Native Habitat and Range Upland forests and wooded slopes from Pennsylvania to Minnesota, south to North Carolina and Kansas

Hardiness Range Zones 4 to 8

Attributes at a Glance
Quercus imbricaria

Pyramidal to round-crowned tree

50 to 60 feet tall and 30 to 40 feet wide

Smooth gray-brown bark when young

Lance-shaped, unlobed foliage

Yellow to russet autumn color

Ornamental Attributes and Uses
Elegant, laurel-like glossy green foliage sets this oak apart from most others. The broad lance-shaped leaves are not lobed, and their autumn color is mostly russet to brown, sometimes yellow. The bark is smooth in youth and grows furrowed with age. The form is pyramidal when young, becoming rounded with maturity. Use shingle oak as a street tree, shade tree, or screen; it is even suitable for small gardens.

Growing Tips Plant in rich, moist soil in full sun or light shade. Like most oaks, this species is long-lived and drought tolerant when established. It grows moderately to fast when young and slows with age. An easy oak to transplant, it should be more widely used.

Related Native Alternatives
Quercus nigra, water oak, is a larger tree (50 to 80 feet tall) with spatula-shaped semievergreen leaves. The wide crown makes it a perfect shade tree. It is found from New Jersey, south to Florida, and west to the central Mississippi valley and Texas. *Quercus phellos,* willow oak, is another large species, to 80 feet tall and wide, with narrow, willow-like leaves that create a soft, graceful look. It grows from New York, south to Florida, and west to Texas.

More Native Alternatives For a list of additional native trees, visit www.bbg.org/nativealternatives.

Invasive Tree
Robinia pseudoacacia • Black Locust
Current Invaded Range: North America outside its native range from Pennsylvania and Indiana, south to Georgia, Louisiana, and Oklahoma

Native Alternative
Gymnocladus dioica
Kentucky Coffeetree

Native Habitat and Range Woodlands, floodplains, old fields, and clearings from New York to Minnesota, south to Virginia, South Dakota, and Oklahoma; naturalized elsewhere but not considered invasive

Hardiness Range Zones 4 to 8

Ornamental Attributes and Uses This tall, stout dioecious tree is sparsely branched to accommodate enormous tripinnate leaves that turn clear yellow in autumn and drop early. The flowers are insignificant, but the female tree produces large, flat mahogany-colored seedpods covered in a bluish waxy bloom. The winter silhouette is irregular and distinctive. It has an upright oval crown, sometimes with a split leader. It is 60 to 75 feet tall and 30 to 50 feet wide. Like all legumes, Kentucky coffeetree fixes nitrogen. Use the tree as a specimen or shade tree.

Growing Tips Plant in average to humus-rich, well-drained, neutral to acidic soil in full sun or partial shade. This tree is tolerant of alkaline soil, drought, wind, and cold. Older plants with split leaders have narrow branch unions and may suffer ice damage.

Attributes at a Glance
Gymnocladus dioica

Large upright oval dioecious tree

60 to 75 feet tall and 30 to 50 feet wide

Huge compound leaves

Yellow autumn color

Waxy brown pods in autumn

Attributes at a Glance
Populus tremuloides

Medium-sized tree

30 to 60 feet tall and 20 to 30 feet wide

Upright oval form

Rhomboid leaves that quake in the wind

Yellow autumn color

Native Alternative
Populus tremuloides
Quaking Aspen

Native Habitat and Range Woodland edges, old fields, and clearings from Newfoundland across the subarctic to Alaska and British Columbia, south to Pennsylvania and Iowa; mountains of New Mexico and California

Hardiness Range Zones 1 to 7

Ornamental Attributes and Uses Quaking aspen is a narrow, upright oval, small- to medium-sized tree, 30 to 60 (sometimes to 90) feet tall and 20 to 30 feet wide. It is usually single-stemmed, but it may grow as a clump. This tall, slender tree has rhombic to ovate leaves that turn clear yellow in autumn. The leaves have long, flattened petioles that let the leaves move freely, quaking or trembling in the wind. The bark is smooth and tan to creamy white with dark nodes. Use the tree as a specimen, shade, or patio tree, or as a screen or windbreak.

Growing Tips Plant in average to humus-rich, well-drained, neutral to acidic soil in full sun or partial shade. The tree is moderately drought tolerant and extremely tolerant of wind and cold. This early successional species is very fast growing when young and grows at a moderate pace with age. It has weak wood and generally lives only 40 to 60 years. Canker and mildew are problems that occur mostly when the tree is grown outside its native range.

Native Alternative
Parkinsonia (*Cercidium*) *florida*
Blue Palo Verde

Native Habitat and Range Intermittent streams, arroyos, and riverbanks of the Sonoran desert of southeastern California, Arizona, and Mexico

Hardiness Range Zones 8 to 10

Ornamental Attributes and Uses Showy yellow flowers smother this small to medium tree's lithe branches in early spring. The small, scalelike leaves drop as summer heats up, revealing green branches, and on younger trees, green trunks. Thin, beanlike pods form in summer. Use the tree as a screen or remove lower limbs for use as a specimen or patio tree.

Growing Tips Plant in average to sandy, well-drained, neutral to alkaline soil in full sun. Blue palo verde is extremely tough and drought tolerant.

Related Native Alternative *Parkinsonia* (*Cercidium*) *microphyllum*, little-leaf palo verde, is a densely branched large shrub to small tree, 12 feet tall and wide. It is very drought tolerant and blooms in late spring and early summer. It is native to California, Arizona, and Mexico.

More Native Alternatives For a list of additional native trees, visit www.bbg.org/nativealternatives.

Attributes at a Glance
Parkinsonia florida

Small to medium tree with wide oval crown

20 to 25 feet tall and 25 to 30 feet wide

Yellow flowers in spring

Small, bright green leaves

Green winter twigs

Invasive Tree
Salix × sepulcralis (*Salix babylonica*) • Weeping Willow
Current Invaded Range: New Hampshire to Michigan and Iowa, south to North Carolina and Louisiana; California and Utah, south to Arizona and New Mexico

Native Alternative
Salix nigra
Black Willow

Native Habitat and Range Low woods, floodplains, pond margins, and ditches from New Brunswick to Minnesota, south to Florida and Texas

Hardiness Range Zones 4 to 8

Ornamental Attributes and Uses Rather than a graceful weeping form, this native willow has a billowing, soft shape that is passed over for exotic relatives. The linear, pointed leaves are silvery on the undersides and shimmer in the breeze. The young twigs are green and flexible and may droop at the tips. Deeply furrowed bark and an irregular form add to the tree's appeal. At maturity, this species may reach 40 to 60 feet tall and 40 to 50 feet wide. Use it as a focal point at the edge of a pond or as a screen. Coppice it if you want to keep it small.

Growing Tips Plant in constantly moist, rich soil in full sun or light shade. The tree tolerates waterlogged soil and periodic flooding. It is fast growing, and like all willows, somewhat weak-wooded, so prune as needed to remove damaged growth. It is a short-lived tree best replaced before it starts to fall apart.

More Native Alternatives For a list of additional native trees, visit www.bbg.org/nativealternatives.

Attributes at a Glance
Salix nigra

Medium-sized tree

40 to 60 feet tall and 40 to 50 feet wide

Furrowed bark

Elegant, narrowly lance-shaped foliage

Green, flexible twigs

Invasive Tree
Sapium sebiferum (*Triadica sebifera*)
Chinese Tallow Tree
Current Invaded Range: North Carolina and Texas, south to Florida and Mexico

Native Alternative
Sassafras albidum
Sassafras

Native Habitat and Range Open woods, meadows, rocky uplands, and roadsides from Maine to Ontario, south to Florida and Texas

Hardiness Range Zones 4 to 9

Ornamental Attributes and Uses The sweet scent of fresh sassafras is merely a memory for most of us. The lovely and familiar tree is often ignored in favor of trendier ornamentals, but few can rival sassafras for season-long interest. Globelike clusters of sweet-scented chartreuse flowers open in early spring on bare branches. Soon following are the oval to mitten-shaped leaves, which are a favorite of larval swallowtail butterflies. In late summer, females of this dioecious species bear blue-black fruit on scarlet stalks, but it isn't long before they disappear, devoured by birds and other wildlife. The fall foliage color is variable, ranging from yellow with hints of orange to fiery red and burgundy. Use this great tree as a specimen, patio tree, screen, or in naturalized settings. It may form dense thickets from root suckers.

Growing Tips Plant in average to rich, evenly moist soil in full sun or light shade. The tree tolerates abuse, including heat and drought, even some salt.

More Native Alternatives *Cercis canadensis* var. *canadensis*, redbud

(page 23)—Pennsylvania and Nebraska, south to Florida and Texas. For a list of additional native trees, visit www.bbg.org/nativealternatives.

Attributes at a Glance
Sassafras albidum

Upright oval medium-sized tree

30 to 60 feet tall and 25 to 40 feet wide

Green, horizontal branches

Fragrant yellow flowers

Mitten-shaped leaves

Orange to red autumn color

Invasive Tree
Schefflera actinophylla • Umbrella Tree
Current Invaded Range: Florida (also Hawaii and Puerto Rico)

Native Alternative
Bucida buceras
Black Olive

Native Habitat and Range Brackish marshes in southern Florida (also Puerto Rico)

Hardiness Range Zones 9 to 11

Ornamental Attributes and Uses The small, obovate, leathery evergreen leaves of black olive are clustered in whorls at the tips of stout branches. The upper surfaces are blue-green, and the leaf undersides are chartreuse, creating a handsome effect. In the wild, the main trunk of the tree may grow horizontally, producing a series of upright trunks that may reach 90 feet tall. In a landscape setting, the tree produces a single, upright trunk 20 to 40 feet tall and 20 to 30 feet wide. Use it as a lawn or shade tree, in municipal settings, or as a screen or windbreak.

Growing Tips Plant in average to rich, most soil in full sun or light shade. The tree thrives in a variety of landscape settings in moist or dry sites.

More Native Alternatives For a list of additional native trees, visit www.bbg.org/nativealternatives.

Attributes at a Glance
Bucida buceras

Large, upright to rounded tree

20 to 40 feet tall and 20 to 30 feet wide

Leathery evergreen leaves

Invasive Tree
Sorbus aucuparia • European Mountain Ash
Current Invaded Range: Northern North America, south to West Virginia, Illinois, and California

Native Alternative
Sorbus americana
American Mountain Ash

Native Habitat and Range Open woods, rocky slopes and outcroppings, and mixed coniferous woods from Newfoundland to Manitoba, south to Maryland, Illinois, and Minnesota; in the mountains to Georgia

Hardiness Range Zones 2 to 7

Ornamental Attributes and Uses Large domed clusters of creamy-white spring flowers and colorful trusses of large waxen red berries make American mountain ash every bit as attractive as its invasive European cousin. Pinnately divided foliage with 11 to 13 narrow elliptical leaflets turns yellow to purple in autumn, creating quite a show. Use this elegant single or multistemmed tree as a patio or lawn tree, as a specimen, or in naturalistic plantings. Birds savor the berries.

Growing Tips Plant in moist, rich soil in full sun or partial shade. The species performs best when grown on appropriate soils within its native range. It often succumbs in areas with high nighttime temperatures and humidity. Fire blight may kill the tips of branches of stressed trees.

Related Native Alternatives *Sorbus scopulina*, Greene's mountain ash, and *S. sitchensis*, western mountain ash, are similar species native to the West Coast.

More Native Alternatives *Amelanchier laevis*, Allegheny Serviceberry (page 42)—Nova Scotia and Ontario, south to Georgia and Iowa. *Viburnum opulus* var. *americanum*, high-bush cranberry (page 126)—Newfoundland and South to British Columbia, Indiana, and Washington. For a list of additional native trees, visit www.bbg.org/nativealternatives.

Attributes at a Glance
Sorbus americana

Small tree with a rounded crown

20 to 40 feet tall and 10 to 30 feet wide

Elegant pinnately divided leaves

Large, domed flower clusters

Scarlet berries

Yellow autumn color

Invasive Trees
Ulmus pumila • Siberian Elm; *U. parvifolia* Chinese Elm

Current Invaded Range: Most of North America south of the boreal forest

Native Alternative
Ulmus alata
Winged Elm

Native Habitat and Range Open woods, floodplains, rocky slopes, and dry uplands from Maryland to Kansas, south to Florida and Texas

Hardiness Range Zones 5 to 9

Ornamental Attributes and Uses Fine-textured, small foliage that turns yellow in autumn and an eccentric branching habit make winged elm an attractive specimen in gardens and larger landscapes. Unlike many elms, the leaves are widely lance-shaped with nearly equal bases. The branches are lined with decorative and curious-looking corky wings. The lower branches often droop, and in old age the effect is picturesque. The tree's mature size is 30 to 60 feet tall (sometimes to 100 feet in the wild) and wide.

Growing Tips Plant in average to rich, well-drained soil in full sun or light shade. This tough elm often grows in inhospitable soils and is readily adaptable in landscape settings.

Related Alternatives *Ulmus thomasii*, rock elm, is a larger, coarser-textured tree with pointed oval leaves and an oval crown 60 to 80 (sometimes to 100) feet tall and wide. It is found from Quebec to Minnesota, south to Tennessee and Nebraska.

Attributes at a Glance
Ulmus alata

Medium to large tree with irregular crown

60 to 80 feet tall and wide

Winged branches

Small pointed oval foliage

Yellow autumn color

Native Alternative
Celtis occidentalis
Hackberry

Native Habitat and Range Floodplains, rocky uplands, waste sites, and roadsides from Quebec to Manitoba and North Dakota, south to Florida and New Mexico

Hardiness Range Zones 3 to 9

Ornamental Attributes and Uses Hackberry is a picturesque and underutilized large tree with a wide, irregular crown. Pointed, narrow oval leaves have uneven bases like those of elms. They turn yellow late in fall. Hard black fruits ripen in late summer and are enjoyed by a variety of birds. The bark is smooth and silvery gray in youth but becomes attractively knobby with age. Use hackberry as a specimen or shade tree, or as a tough street tree.

Growing Tips Plant in average to rich, well-drained soil in full sun or light shade. This tree is tough and drought tolerant. It is susceptible to nipple gall, which creates hard cysts in the foliage, but though somewhat unattractive, it does no harm to the tree. Witches' broom and powdery mildew are other occasional maladies.

Related Native Alternatives *Celtis laevigata*, sugarberry, is finer in texture, with smaller foliage but no less massive a trunk. It reaches 40 to 60 feet tall and wide. There are several botanical varieties and a wide native range from Maryland, Illinois, and British Columbia, south to Florida, Texas, and Baja California.

More Native Alternatives *Gymnocladus dioica*, Kentucky coffeetree (page 47)— New York to Minnesota, south to Virginia, South Dakota, and Oklahoma. For a list of additional native trees, visit www.bbg.org/nativealternatives.

Attributes at a Glance
Celtis occidentalis

Large tree with a massive, irregular crown

40 to 80 feet tall and wide

Knobby bark

Pointed, narrow oval foliage

Yellow autumn color

Invasive Shrub
Ardisia elliptica • Shoebutton Ardisia
Current Invaded Range: Florida (also Hawaii and Puerto Rico)

Native Alternative
Ardisia escallonioides
Marlberry

Native Habitat and Range Pinelands, marl ridges, and hummocks in central and southern Florida (also Puerto Rico)

Attributes at a Glance
Ardisia escallonioides

Mounded shrub to small tree

10 to 15 feet tall and 10 feet wide

Evergreen elliptical leaves

White flower clusters in winter

Dark purple fruit

Hardiness Range Zones 9 to 11

Ornamental Attributes and Uses
Marlberry's terminal panicles of small white flowers open against glossy, deep green five- to six-inch elliptical leaves in winter. In spring, dark purple fruits ripen in showy upright to drooping clusters that last several months. Though edible, the fruits are often passed over by birds in favor of more tasty fare. The upright oval to rounded crown reaches 10 to 15 feet tall and 10 feet wide and is easily trained into a single- or multi-stemmed tree. This decorative shrub to small tree is inderutilized, which is a shame, as it makes an attractive landscape plant. Use it as a foundation shrub, specimen, screen, or hedge. It also works well in seaside and dune plantings.

Growing Tips Plant in average to rich, sandy or loamy soil in full sun or partial shade. Marlberry thrives in sun but will tolerate considerable shade. It can also take drought and salt and remain deep green and attractive. Prune it as needed to control size or shape.

Native Alternative
Persea humilis
Silk Bay

Native Habitat and Range Sandy low woods and margins of swamps and ponds in peninsular Florida

Hardiness Range Zones 8 to 10

Ornamental Attributes and Uses
Persea humilis has silky, bay-scented narrowly elliptical to lance-shaped evergreen foliage. Small greenish-yellow flowers cluster in the leaf axils and give way to blue-black fruit. The reddish-brown bark is smooth in youth and becomes irregularly furrowed with maturity. This delicate tree has an upright to rounded crown 20 to 30 feet tall and 10 to 20 feet wide. The foliage clusters toward the tips of the stems, creating a lush, tropical look.

Growing Tips Plant in average to rich, sandy or loamy soil in full sun or partial shade. Silk bay grows best in sun but tolerates considerable shade. It also tolerates wet soil and drought. The foliage is subject to windburn at the northern edge of the tree's range. Remove any dead or damaged twigs in spring.

Related Alternatives *Persea borbonia*, redbay, and *P. palustris*, swamp bay, are also species native to Florida.

More Native Alternatives For a list of additional native shrubs, visit www.bbg.org/nativealternatives.

Attributes at a Glance
Persea humilis

Medium-sized upright oval tree

20 to 30 feet tall and 10 to 20 feet wide

Fragrant, evergreen foliage

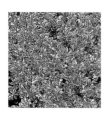

Invasive Shrub
Berberis thunbergii • Japanese Barberry
Current Invaded Range: Maine to Manitoba, south to Georgia and Kansas

Native Alternative
Fothergilla gardenii
Witch Alder

Native Habitat and Range Pine flatwoods, savannas, and pond margins from North Carolina, south to Florida and Alabama

Attributes at a Glance
Fothergilla gardenii

Small shrub with rounded to mounding form

3 to 5 feet tall and wide

Fuzzy white terminal flower clusters in early spring

Oval, scalloped foliage

Orange to burgundy fall color

Hardiness Range Zones 5 to 8

Ornamental Attributes and Uses The fragrant white bottlebrush flowers of witch alder are borne in early spring at the tips of wispy branches. The softly hairy, gray-green foliage turns flaming orange to burgundy in autumn, and the twiggy, zigzag stems provide winter interest. This upright oval to rounded shrub can be used as a hedge, in mass plantings, foundations, and as an underplanting for shade and flowering trees in naturalized settings. It grows three to five feet tall and wide. Older plants are more open and spreading.

Growing Tips Plant in humus-rich, well-drained acidic soil in full sun or partial shade. Witch alder is intolerant of limy soils as well as waterlogged conditions; it is drought tolerant once established. Its foliage develops its best color in full sun. This shrub is slow growing and maintains an even, symmetrical shape and seldom needs pruning. Don't shear it or you will destroy the form.

Related Alternative *Fothergilla major*, mountain witch alder, is a larger species in every respect, with stout stems reaching 6 to 15 feet tall and wide. The broad, oval foliage has exceptional beauty and excellent autumn color. It is found in the mountains from North Carolina to Georgia and Alabama.

Native Alternative
Ceanothus americanus
New Jersey Tea

Native Habitat and Range Open woods, rocky slopes, barrens, prairies, and roadsides from Quebec and Minnesota, south to Florida and Texas

Hardiness Range Zones 3 to 9

Ornamental Attributes and Uses This subtle but attractive and very adaptable shrub has tight, elongated terminal clusters of small white flowers in late spring and summer. The flowers are magnets to insects. The quilted oval leaves with finely toothed margins—once used as a substitute for tea—turn clear yellow in autumn. Use New Jersey tea in meadows, prairies, and borders or en masse on slopes. The stems are upright to somewhat sprawling and form a mounding crown one to three feet tall and two to four feet wide.

Growing Tips Plant in moist, sandy or loamy soil in full sun or light shade. The plant's deep, water-seeking roots bestow amazing adaptability, enabling it to tolerate extreme drought and heat. It is sometimes rangy or irregular in form; trim it as needed to maintain the desired shape and size.

Attributes at a Glance
Ceanothus americanus

Mounding to spreading form

One to three feet tall and two to four feet wide

Terminal white flower clusters in late spring and summer

Deep green foliage

Yellow autumn color

Attributes at a Glance
Itea virginica

Arching to round form

Fragrant white flower clusters

Flaming autumn color

Green or red winter twigs

Native Alternative
Itea virginica
Virginia Sweetspire

Native Habitat and Range Streams and pond margins, swamps, and low woods from New Jersey and Missouri, south to Florida and Louisiana

Hardiness Range Zones 5 to 9

Ornamental Attributes and Uses Virginia sweetspire is an upright, arching to rounded shrub four to eight feet tall and wide. It is deciduous to semievergreen, with leaves that persist well into the winter before dropping. In early to midsummer, fragrant white bottlebrush flowers open at a time when few other shrubs are blooming. The lustrous green leaves, up to four inches long, line arched green stems. When grown in a sunny location, the shrub shows fiery fall color in shades of crimson, burgundy, and purple. In part to full shade, it has autumn hues of orange, gold, and scarlet. It is best used in mass plantings along creek and stream edges, as an informal but tight hedge, in beds and borders, and on slopes.

Growing Tips Plant in full sun to partial shade in evenly moist, organic, rich acidic soil. It can adapt to neutral and slightly alkaline soils. It tolerates flooding but is equally adaptable to dry situations.

Native Alternative
Diervilla lonicera
Bush Honeysuckle

Native Habitat and Range Open deciduous or mixed coniferous woods, rocky slopes, and roadsides from Newfoundland to Saskatchewan, south to Virginia and Minnesota, and mountains to Tennessee

Hardiness Range Zones 3 to 7

Ornamental Attributes and Uses Bush honeysuckle's clustered yellow flowers open throughout the summer at the tips and in the axils of arching stems clothed with opposite, pointed oval leaves. The deep green foliage emerges tinged with bronze in spring and turns clear yellow to apricot or scarlet in autumn. Use this shrub as a low screen, in mass plantings, or for erosion control.

Growing Tips Plant in evenly moist, rich soil in full sun or light shade. Bush honeysuckle is moderately drought tolerant once established. The arching crown keeps a fairly regular form. Prune to control size and shape, and remove sprouting runners if necessary.

Related Alternative *Diervilla sessilifolia*, southern bush honeysuckle, is more delicate. It grows in Virginia and West Virginia, south to Georgia and Alabama.

More Native Alternatives *Clethra alnifolia*, summersweet (page 63)—Maine south to Florida, and west to Texas. *Ilex verticillata*, winterberry holly (page 98)—Nova Scotia to Minnesota, south to Florida and Arkansas. *Morella* (*Myrica*) *pensylvanica*, bayberry (page 73)—Newfoundland, south along the coast to North Carolina; west along the Saint Lawrence and the eastern Great Lakes to Ohio. For a list of additional native shrubs, visit www.bbg.org/nativealternatives.

Attributes at a Glance
Diervilla lonicera

Small shrub with arching, vaselike form

2 to 4 feet tall and 3 to 5 feet wide

Yellow flowers all summer

Yellow to burgundy autumn color

Invasive Shrub
Buddleja davidii and Hybrids • Butterfly Bush
Current Invaded Range: Massachusetts, Ontario, and Michigan, south to Florida and Texas; west to California, north to British Columbia

---

Native Alternative
Cephalanthus occidentalis
Buttonbush

Native Habitat and Range Swamps, marshes, riverbanks, and floodplains from New Brunswick and Minnesota, south to Florida and Mexico, west to California

Hardiness Range Zones 4 to 11

Ornamental Attributes and Uses The sweet-scented, fuzzy white globes of buttonbush are familiar to anyone who spends time fishing or lounging along a river or pond. This widespread plant is so common that it is often overlooked. In the garden, blooms appear throughout the summer against a backdrop of glossy oval leaves. Butterflies adore the sweet flowers and flock in great numbers to partake of the bounty. The foliage turns yellow in autumn, and the dried clusters of hard nutlets remain into winter. This rounded, open shrub grows 6 to 10 feet tall and wide and occasionally reaches 15 feet.

Growing Tips Though a denizen of swamps, buttonbush is tolerant of wide soil and moisture conditions once established. For best growth, plant in average to rich soil in full sun to partial shade. It is fast growing and quickly reaches four to six feet unless pruned. Like *Buddleja,* buttonbush can be heavily pruned to control height and spread. The foliage emerges late in spring, and tip dieback often occurs. Reshape the shrub in spring and remove any dead growth.

Attributes at a Glance
Cephalanthus occidentalis

Rounded, irregular form

6 to 10 feet tall and wide

Attractive winter silhouette

Fuzzy white summertime flowers popular with butterflies

Deep glossy green foliage

Yellow autumn color

Native Alternative
Clethra alnifolia
Summersweet, Sweet Pepperbush

Native Habitat and Range Swamps, low woods, floodplains, and pond margins on the coastal plain and outer piedmont from Maine south to Florida, west to Texas

Hardiness Range Zones 4 to 9

Ornamental Attributes and Uses Summersweet has intensely scented, creamy-white summer flowers adored by butterflies. The upright spikes resemble the flower form of butterfly bush more closely than those of buttonbush. The elongate spikes of dry capsules are decorative throughout the winter. Many named selections vary in size and flower color. Summersweet is an upright to rounded, twiggy shrub four to eight feet tall and wide that often suckers to form broad colonies. Use it in borders, as a hedge, or in a butterfly garden.

Growing Tips Plant in sandy or loamy, evenly moist soil in full sun or shade. This shrub blooms best with some direct sun. It tolerates short periods of drought but prefers even moisture. Suckers are common on some selections, enabling clumps to spread to form large colonies.

Attributes at a Glance
Clethra alnifolia

Upright to irregular form

4 to 8 feet tall and wide

Tawny to chestnut-colored bark

Deep green quilted foliage

Spikes of sweet-scented white flowers in summer

Yellow autumn foliage color

Charcoal-gray seed heads

Native Alternative
Ceanothus thyrsiflorus
Wild Lilac, Blue Blossom

Native Habitat and Range Open woods and chaparral in coastal mountains from southern California, north to southern Oregon

Hardiness Range Zones 7 (with protection) to 10

Ornamental Attributes and Uses Wild lilac sports clouds of medium to deep blue flowers that float above dark green, quilted foliage in spring and early summer. Use it as a specimen or hedge, or prune out lower branches to make a tree for a small garden or patio.

Growing Tips Plant in well-drained, average to rich soil in full sun or partial shade. Wild lilac tolerates drought and heat and blooms for an extended time. Prune the crown as needed to maintain an even shape. To encourage good growth, take old stems down to major branches within the crown.

Related Alternatives *Ceanothus griseus,* Carmel mountain lilac, *C. purpureus,* holly-leaf ceanothus; and *C. tomentosus,* Ramona lilac, are three other California natives.

More Native Alternatives For a list of additional native shrubs, visit www.bbg.org/nativealternatives.

Attributes at a Glance
Ceanothus thyrsiflorus

Dense mounding evergreen shrub

4 to 12 feet tall and wide

Clusters of fragrant blue flowers in spring and early summer

Quilted evergreen foliage

Invasive Shrub
Caragana arborescens • Siberian Pea Shrub
Current Invaded Range: Nova Scotia to British Columbia, south to Maryland, Colorado, and California

Native Alternative
Ribes aureum
Clove Currant

Native Habitat and Range Open woods, streambanks, desert washes, and pine flats from Saskatchewan to British Columbia, south to New Mexico and California

Hardiness Range Zones 4 to 8

Ornamental Attributes and Uses The clove-scented star-shaped flowers of this shrub cluster in the nodes of stiff branches before the ragged, deeply lobed leaves emerge. Occasionally it produces red berries. Where summers are cool, it remains leafy throughout the season, but in hot, dry weather, the branches will be bare by midsummer. The foliage colors to medium yellow in late summer and drops soon after. This versatile shrub has an upright, rounded to oval form three to six feet tall and wide with stiff, erect branches. Use clove currant as a specimen, hedge, or screen. Consider planting clematis to intertwine with the crown for color later in the season.

Growing Tips Plant in evenly moist, humus-rich neutral to alkaline soil in full sun to light shade. Summer defoliation is common and not an indication of disease. In warm, humid zones, the plant is susceptible to diseases such as fire blight.

Attributes at a Glance
Ribes aureum
Upright rounded form

Fragrant yellow flowers

Twiggy upright to vase-shaped winter silhouette

Native Alternative
Leucophyllum frutescens,
Texas Ranger

Native Habitat and Range Open canyons, arroyos, and scrub in Texas and northern Mexico

Hardiness Range Zones 8 to 9

Ornamental Attributes Texas ranger's shimmering silver stems and silver-gray leaves overlaid with white hairs add a ghostly air to the landscape. Small lavender-purple flowers are borne in the leaf axils, flowering after rainfall. An arching to rounded, compact shrub to six feet tall and eight feet wide, it is excellent for mass and foundation plantings, rock gardens, xeriscapes, hedges, and shelterbelts.

Growing Tips Plant in full sun in a sheltered location in sandy, well-drained loam. Texas ranger is extremely heat tolerant but needs good drainage and some supplemental water until established. Planted in a garden setting, the shrub tends to become rangy over time from too much water and fertilizer; it withstands hard pruning to control size and shape.

Attributes at a Glance
Leucophyllum frutescens

Medium-sized shrub with arching to rounded crown

Purple flowers

Silvery foliage

Irregular, twiggy winter aspect

Native Alternative
Forestiera pubescens var. *pubescens* (*F. neomexicana*)
Desert Olive

Native Habitat and Range Desert slopes, canyons, and flats from Colorado and Utah, south to Texas and California

Hardiness Range Zones 4 to 9

Ornamental Attributes and Uses Bright green leaves contrast with the chalky bark of this tidy, versatile, vase-shaped shrub or small tree. It reaches 8 to 12 feet tall and wide when mature and properly pruned. Small, greenish-yellow flowers open along the naked branches in late winter or spring. Toothed, oblong leaves cloth the lithe stems and turn bright yellow in autumn, accenting the shrub's fleshy, blue-black fruit. Use desert olive as a specimen or patio tree or as a trimmed or natural, wildlife-attracting hedge.

Growing Tips Plant in average to rich, well-drained soil in full sun. Desert olive is drought and heat tolerant. It is easily sheared as a hedge or pruned into an attractive, multistemmed tree.

Attributes at a Glance
Forestiera pubescens

Vase-shaped large shrub or small tree

Greenish-yellow flowers in late winter

Blue-black fruit attractive to wildlife

Bright yellow foliage in autumn

Native Alternative
Purshia tridentata
Antelope Brush

Native Habitat and Range Open woods, streambanks, rocky slopes, and pine forests from Alberta to British Columbia, south to New Mexico and California

Hardiness Range Zones 4 to 9

Attributes at a Glance
Purshia tridentata

Upright rounded to mounding form with stiff, erect branches

Small evergreen leaves

Yellow flowers

Twiggy upright winter silhouette

Ornamental Attributes and Uses This versatile shrub has an upright, rounded to oval crown with stiff, erect branches. Five-petaled stars with a boss of fuzzy yellow stamens are borne singly at the tips of stiff spur branches in spring and early summer. The flowers are surrounded by small, quilted three-lobed oval evergreen leaves that emit a resinous smell in the hot sun. Use antelope brush as a specimen, hedge, or screen, or in mass plantings and shelterbelts.

Growing Tips Plant in evenly moist, humus-rich neutral to alkaline soil in full sun to light shade. This slow-growing but long-lived shrub is tolerant of extreme heat and drought; however, it grows best where night temperatures are cool.

Related Alternative *Purshia glandulosa*, desert bitterbrush, is similar to *P. tridentata* in appearance and use but differs botanically in the glandular hairs present on the foliage. Its native range is restricted to California, Nevada, Utah, and Arizona.

More Native Alternatives *Ericameria nauseosa* (*Chrysothamnus nauseosus*), rubber rabbitbrush (page 76)—Alberta, south to Texas, Mexico, and California. *Jamesia americana*, waxflower, cliffbush (page 75)—Wyoming to California, south to New Mexico and Arizona. *Prosopis glandulosa* var. *glandulosa*, honey mesquite (page 118)—Kansas and Texas west to New Mexico and Mexico. For a list of additional native shrubs, visit www.bbg.org/nativealternatives.

Invasive Shrub
Cotoneaster apiculatus, C. franchetii, C. microphyllus, C. pannosus, C. lacteus • Cotoneaster

Current Invaded Range: Great Lakes states; California and Pacific Northwest

Native Alternative
Heteromeles arbutifolia
Toyon

Native Habitat and Range Chaparral and rocky canyon slopes from California to Baja

Hardiness Range Zones 8 to 10

Ornamental Attributes and Uses The upright oval to rounded crown of this large shrub or small tree reaches 7 to 35 feet tall and 10 to 25 feet wide. Domed terminal clusters of small lacy white flowers open against leathery, elliptical evergreen leaves edged with sharp teeth. The flowers open in early summer, followed by large trusses of brilliant red-orange persistent fruit. Use toyon as a foundation shrub, specimen, hedge, or screen; it is excellent for wildlife gardens. It reaches maximum size in the wild on rich soils with ample water. In the garden, the plant is much smaller.

Growing Tips Plant in well-drained, loamy or sandy soils in full sun or light shade. Toyon is heat and drought tolerant but prefers ample summer moisture for best growth. Prune it as needed to shape the crown or to harvest branches for holiday decorations.

SHRUBS

Attributes at a Glance
Heteromeles arbutifolia

Large upright oval shrub to small tree

Lustrous evergreen leaves

White flower clusters

Trusses of red berries

Native Alternative
Arctostaphylos nevadensis
Pinemat Manzanita

Native Habitat and Range Open montane woods and rocky slopes from British Columbia, south to Nevada and California

Hardiness Range Zones 4 (with protection) to 8

Ornamental Attributes and Uses This handsome groundcover—a spreading to mounding evergreen shrub one to two feet tall and two to six feet wide—is favored by dryland gardeners because of its adaptability. Terminal clusters of

waxy, pale pink spring flowers give way to reddish-brown berries that often persist into winter. The elliptical, leathery evergreen leaves are held erect and thickly clothe the mahogany-colored stems. Pinemat manzanita is excellent used as a weed-free groundcover, cascading down decorative stone or timber walls, or for erosion control.

Growing Tips Plant in well-drained neutral sandy or loamy soils in full sun or partial shade. The plant tolerates full shade but seldom flowers without sun. It is also heat and drought tolerant but prefers ample summer moisture for best growth. Prolonged sogginess will kill it. This shrub can be slow to establish but is worth the trouble.

Related Alternative *Arctostaphylos densiflora,* vinehill manzanita, is a low, mounding shrub with white to pink flowers and red berries. It is found in central California.

Attributes at a Glance
Arctostaphylos nevadensis

Spreading groundcover shrub

Small elliptical evergreen foliage

Waxy, bell-shaped flowers

Large reddish-brown berries

Native Alternative
Symphoricarpos orbiculatus
Coralberry

Native Habitat and Range Open woods, floodplains, and rocky slopes from New Jersey to South Dakota, south to Georgia and Texas

Hardiness Range Zones 2 to 8

Ornamental Attributes and Uses This suckering, colonizing shrub grows one to three feet tall and three to six feet wide. Paired elliptical leaves line the stems, obscuring the axillary clusters of greenish-white to pale pink flowers in high summer. Rosy-red berries cluster in the leaf axils of the arching stems of this unobtrusive shrub in fall, as the foliage turns yellow or shrivels with frost. Use it as a tall groundcover, a foundation shrub, in naturalized settings, or for erosion control.

Growing Tips Plant in average to rich, evenly moist soil in full sun or partial shade. Coralberry tolerates abuse, including heat, drought, and deep shade. Prune it as needed before new growth begins. Remove the suckers to control spread and reduce the size of the clump. The foliage is subject to powdery mildew, which may disfigure the plant. Once the leaves fall, the berries come into their own and make the plant worth the effort.

Related Alternatives *Symphoricarpos albus*, snowberry, is a larger shrub, to six feet, with large white berries on arching stems. It is found from Nova Scotia to Alberta, south to Virginia and Minnesota. *Symphoricarpos* var. *laevigatus*, shrub snowberry, is similar but grows in the West, from British Columbia to Arizona and California.

More Native Alternatives For a list of additional native shrubs, visit www.bbg.org/nativealternatives.

Attributes at a Glance
Symphoricarpos orbiculatus

Mounding, suckering deciduous shrub

Small greenish-white to pink flowers

Rosy-red fruit

Twiggy winter silhouette

Invasive Shrub
Crataegus monogyna • English Hawthorn

Current Invaded Range: New Brunswick to Ontario, south to Virginia and Arkansas; Utah, Montana, and Pacific Northwest

Native Alternative
Crataegus crus-galli
Cock-Spur Hawthorn

Native Habitat and Range Woodland borders, rocky slopes, savannas, and clearings from Nova Scotia to Ontario, south to Florida and Texas

Hardiness Range Zones 3 to 8

Ornamental Attributes and Uses The horizontal branching structure of this alluring tree seems to echo the lines of the open landscapes it favors. In spring the branches are tipped with domed clusters of showy, slightly ill-scented white flowers that give way to waxy red berries in late summer. Lustrous, elongated oval to broadly lance-shaped foliage turns flaming red to burgundy in fall. The clustered berries often persist until spring, though winter cold may blacken them. This broad oval, single- to multi-stemmed large shrub or small tree is 15 to 25 feet tall and 20 to 30 feet wide. In garden settings, especially where children play, beware of the plant's menacing thee-inch thorns. It is best used as a specimen or in small groups.

Growing Tips Plant in average to rich, well-drained soil in full sun. The plant tolerates acidic or alkaline soil, heat, and drought. It is resistant to fire blight and most other pests that plague this genus.

More Native Alternatives *Chionanthus virginicus*, fringe tree (page 43)—New Jersey, Kentucky, and Missouri, south to Florida and Texas. *Viburnum prunifolium*, black-haw viburnum (page 93)—Connecticut to Michigan, south to Florida and Texas. For a list of additional native shrubs, visit www.bbg.org/nativealternatives.

Attributes at a Glance
Crataegus crus-galli

Large shrub or small tree with broad oval crown

15 to 25 feet tall and 20 to 30 feet wide

Domed clusters of white flowers

Glossy deep green leaves

Red fruit

Red to burgundy autumn color

Invasive Shrub
Cytisus scoparius • Scotch Broom

Current Invaded Range: Maine to Alabama; California north to British Columbia

Native Alternative
Morella (Myrica) pensylvanica
Bayberry

Native Habitat and Range Dunes, swamps, marshes, bog margins, and roadsides from Newfoundland, south along the coast to North Carolina; west along the Saint Lawrence; eastern Great Lakes to Ohio

Hardiness Range Zones 4 to 7

Ornamental Attributes and Uses The aroma of bayberry is most often associated with holiday candles. When you live near the coastal marshes where this elegant shrub is native, however, bayberry is the scent of summer. The pungent oil that imparts the classic scent is present in the broadly lance-shaped to narrow oval deciduous leaves. The berries of this species are the commercial source of bayberry oil. Bayberries are dioecious, so only female plants produce berries, which cluster on short spurs. Use them as a salt-tolerant hedge or low screen, in beds and borders, or in naturalistic and seaside plantings. This open-crowned, rounded to mounding shrub reaches two to eight feet tall and wide.

Growing Tips Plant in moist, humus-rich or sandy acidic soil in full sun or light shade. Bayberry makes a good trimmed hedge but is best when left to grow unclipped. Plants can get quite large, so removing older stems down to a branch union within the crown is recommended to reduce the height of the plant. If necessary, cut plants to the ground to renew the growth. Plants tolerate fire, drought, and salt, as well as blistering daytime heat. This species performs best in the North.

Related Native Alternative *Morella cerifera*, southern wax myrtle (page 81), is a good choice for gardens from New Jersey south to Florida and west to the lower Mississippi Valley and Texas.

Attributes at a Glance
Morella pensylvanica

Salt-tolerant medium-sized shrub

2 to 8 feet tall and wide

Rounded crown

Deep green oval scented foliage

Blue-gray waxy berries

Attributes at a Glance
Lupinus arboreus

Rounded, leafy crown

3 to 5 feet tall and wide

Dense spikes of yellow flowers

Sea-green, divided foliage

Native Alternative
Lupinus arboreus
Tree Lupine

Native Habitat and Range Coastal bluffs and open woods in central California

Hardiness Range Zones 8 to 9

Ornamental Attributes and Uses Fragrant spikes of yellow, occasionally blue legume flowers tip multiple stems, covering the dense crowns with long-lasting blooms. Peak bloom occurs in winter and spring, though plants flower sporadically throughout the year. The twiggy crown is studded with leathery, sea-green leaves with 5 to 12 segments arranged like fingers on a hand. Use the shrub in borders singly or in drifts, or as a low hedge. The rounded to mounding crown of this evergreen shrub is three to five feet tall and wide.

Growing Tips Plant in well-drained, rich soil in full sun or light shade. Avoid soggy soils, as tree lupine is subject to root rot. It is tolerant of various soil conditions and airborne salt. Trim spent inflorescences to keep the plant in flower. Prune as necessary to maintain an attractive shape. This species is an aggressive seeder and may invade disturbed sites; plant with caution. It is also considered a noxious weed outside its restricted native range.

Native Alternative
Jamesia americana
Waxflower, Cliffbush

Native Habitat and Range Mountains, canyons of pinyon, and juniper woodland in mountains of Wyoming to California, south to New Mexico and Arizona

Hardiness Range Zones 3 to 8

Ornamental Attributes and Uses Waxflower gets its name from the fragrant five-petaled, star-shaped, waxy white flowers that appear in terminal panicles in late spring and early summer. The bright green, rough-textured foliage turns to brilliant red, orange, and pink with the onset of fall. Flaking cinnamon-colored bark is noticeable in winter. The medium-sized, upright rounded to mounding deciduous shrub grows six feet tall and wide. Choose waxflower for a rock garden, shrub border, hedge, or foundation planting.

Growing Tips Plant in average to rich, moist but well-drained soil in full sun or light shade. Waxflower is drought tolerant, but until it is established, provide supplemental water. After the flowers fade, prune old canes to the ground to maintain good branching structure.

Attributes at a Glance
Jamesia americana

Rounded to mounding shrub

6 feet tall and wide

Fragrant white flowers

Red autumn color

Irregular winter form

Native Alternative
Ericameria (Chrysocoma) nauseosa
Rubber Rabbitbrush

Native Habitat and Range Desert washes, open hillsides, and high plains from Alberta, south to Texas, Mexico, and California

Hardiness Range Zones 6 to 9

Ornamental Attributes and Uses Radiant yellow asterlike flowers smother plants in late summer and autumn, followed by bristly seed clusters. Blue-gray to sea-green needlelike deciduous to semievergreen leaves clothe the pliable bottle-brush stems. Use rubber rabbitbrush in foundation plantings, borders, mass plantings, informal hedges, or as an accent. This variable species has a huge natural range, with two subspecies and numerous varieties. Buy from a local source to assure regional adaptability.

Growing Tips Plant in well-drained, poor to average sandy, gravelly, or clay neutral to alkaline soil in full sun. The plant prefers cool summer nighttime temperatures. In hot regions, provide afternoon shade. Soggy soil is sure death, as is high humidity. Prune as needed to maintain fresh growth and good form.

Related Native Alternative *Ericameria parryii*, Parry's rabbitbrush, is a more compact, floriferous species native to the upper slopes of desert mountains from Saskatchewan, south to New Mexico and California.

More Native Alternatives *Oemleria cerasiformis*, Indian plum (page 80)— British Columbia south to California. *Prunus maritima*, beach plum— Newfoundland to Ontario, south to Maryland and Michigan. *Purshia tridentata*, antelope brush (page 68)— Alberta to British Columbia, south to New Mexico and California. *Ribes aureum*, golden currant (page 65)— Saskatchewan to British Columbia, south to New Mexico and California. For a list of additional native shrubs, visit www.bbg.org/nativealternatives.

Attributes at a Glance
Ericameria nauseosa

Mounded, multistemmed shrub

3 to 4 feet tall and wide

Blue-gray needlelike leaves

Yellow flowers in late summer and fall

Invasive Shrub
Elaeagnus angustifolia • Russian Olive
Current Invaded Range: Northern North America, south to Virginia, Texas, and California

Native Alternative
Salix sericea
Silky Willow

Native Habitat and Range Pond margins, streambanks, ditches, and springs from Nova Scotia to Michigan, south to Georgia and Missouri

Hardiness Range Zones 3 to 8

Ornamental Attributes and Uses The silvery lance-shaped leaves on supple stems of silky willow add light and motion to the garden. The rounded crown grows 6 to 12 feet tall and wide. Use this attractive plant as a specimen, screen, or en masse at the edge of a pond.

Growing Tips Plant in evenly moist to wet, rich soil in full sun or light shade. Silky willow tolerates flooding and is moderately drought tolerant. It is not as tough as Russian olive but still good for most landscape settings. To control its size, cut it to the ground in winter as needed.

Related Native Alternative *Salix scouleriana*, Scouler's willow, is an elegant species with showy pussy-willow catkins in late winter. The narrow leaves are set off against the green stems. It has a rounded, full crown 8 to 15 feet tall and wide. It is found from Alberta and British Columbia, south to New Mexico and Texas.

Attributes at a Glance
Salix sericea
Rounded large shrub to small tree

6 to 12 feet tall and wide

Silvery lance-shaped foliage

Twiggy winter silhouette

Attributes at a Glance
Elaeagnus commutata

Small, mounded shrub

2 to 7 feet tall and 4 to 8 feet wide

Silvery oval foliage

Small yellow flowers

Fleshy red berries

Native Alternative
Elaeagnus commutata
Silverberry

Native Habitat and Range Riverbanks, dry plains, slopes, and rocky shores from Ontario to Alaska, south to Iowa; in the Rockies to Colorado; British Columbia

Hardiness Range Zones 2 to 6

Ornamental Attributes and Uses The artfully twisted, bright silver leaves of this suckering shrub add light to the garden. The small yellow tubular flowers offer sweet fragrance in summer. Red berries follow that are relished by birds and other wild animals. Silverberry is an open-crowned, mounding shrub two to seven feet tall and four to eight feet wide. The constant suckering limits its use to informal settings. The best uses for this tough northerner are as a screen, in mass plantings for erosion control, or as wildlife food.

Growing Tips Plant in moist, average to poor, neutral to alkaline soil in full sun or light shade. The established plant is extremely cold and drought tolerant. Prune it to maintain a tidy form if necessary.

Native Alternative
Shepherdia argentea
Silver Buffaloberry

Native Habitat and Range Prairies, dry plains, slopes, and rocky shores from Minnesota and Saskatchewan to British Columbia, south to Iowa and California

Hardiness Range Zones 3 to 7

Ornamental Attributes and Uses This open-crowned, upright shrub to small tree grows 6 to 18 feet tall and 8 to 12 feet wide. The blunt, lance-shaped, bright silver deciduous leaves of this upright thorny shrub reflect the sun and shimmer in the evening. Small yellow tubular flowers open in late spring, followed by red berries on female plants of this dioecious species. The berries are devoured by birds and other creatures. Choose this shrub for a screen, for mass erosion control plantings, or as wildlife food.

Growing Tips Plant in moist, average to rich soil in full sun or light shade. Established plants are extremely drought tolerant. Bacteria that live in nodules on the root system enable this species to fix nitrogen, which allows it to grow on very poor soils. Prune as needed, taking care to avoid the short spines at the nodes.

Related Native Alternative *Shepherdia canadensis,* russet buffaloberry, is a thornless, green-leaved shrubby species with a huge native range from Newfoundland to Alaska, south to New York, Indiana, and Arizona. The sea-green leaves are oval, and the fruits are larger but inedible.

Attributes at a Glance
Shepherdia argentea
Mounded shrub to small tree

6 to 18 feet tall and 8 to 12 feet wide

Silvery oval foliage

Small yellow flowers

Scarlet fruit

Native Alternative
Oemleria (Osmaronia) cerasiformis
Indian Plum

Native Habitat and Range Chaparral, forest clearings, low woods, streambanks and moist seepage slopes from British Columbia, south to California

Hardiness Range Zones 5 (with protection) to 8

Ornamental Attributes and Uses Indian plum's fragrant white flowers in drooping racemes open precociously on erect polished red stems. The oblong leaves with short petioles taper at both ends and turn yellow in autumn. Purple-black cherrylike fruit ripen in summer but are quickly consumed by wildlife. The upright crown is 15 to 20 feet tall and wide. Use Indian plum as a specimen, hedge or screen, in mixed borders, or in naturalized settings.

Growing Tips Plant in moist, rich soil in full sun or light shade. Established plants are somewhat drought tolerant. Indian plum is somewhat stoloniferous and may form thickets in time.

More Native Alternatives *Carpinus caroliniana*, musclewood (page 16)—Maine and Florida, west to Minnesota and Texas. For a list of additional native shrubs, visit www.bbg.org/nativealternatives.

Attributes at a Glance
Oemleria cerasiformis

Upright, stiff shrub

15 to 20 feet tall and wide

Drooping white flower spikes in early spring

Purplish cherrylike fruit

Invasive Shrub
Elaeagnus umbellata • Autumn Olive
Current Invaded Range: Maine to Michigan and Nebraska, south to Florida and Louisiana

Native Alternative
Morella (Myrica) cerifera
Southern Wax Myrtle, Bayberry

Native Habitat and Range Dunes, swamps, marshes, bog margins, and roadsides from New Jersey south to Florida, west to the lower Mississippi Valley and Texas

Hardiness Range Zones 7 to 10

Ornamental Attributes and Uses
Near the coastal marshes where this elegant shrub is native, bayberry scents the hot summer air. The pungent oil that imparts the classic scent is present in the lance-shaped, evergreen leaves with ragged tips as well as the grainy, wax-coated berries. Bayberries are dioecious, so only female plants produce berries, which ring the older stems in tight clusters. Use this large shrub as a pruned hedge or natural screen, as a specimen, or in naturalized settings.

Growing Tips Plant in moist, humus-rich or sandy, acidic soil in full sun or light shade. Southern wax myrtle can get quite large, so control its height by removing older stems. If necessary, cut the plant to the ground to renew growth. It tolerates fire, drought, salt, and heat. This species is less hardy than *Morella pensylvanica*, northern bayberry (page 73).

Attributes at a Glance
Morella cerifera

Salt-tolerant large shrub

10 to 20 feet tall and wide

Rounded crown

Toothed, lance-shaped evergreen foliage

Waxy, blue-gray berries

Native Alternative
Styrax americanus
American Snowbell

Native Habitat and Range Open low woodlands, streamsides, swamps, and pond margins from Virginia and Missouri, south to Florida and Louisiana.

Attributes at a Glance
Styrax americanus

Broadly oval to rounded shrub or small tree

20 to 30 feet tall and wide

Pendulous white flowers

Fine-textured foliage and branching

Hardiness Range Zones 5 to 8

Ornamental Attributes and Uses This broadly oval to rounded large shrub to small tree, 20 to 30 feet tall and wide, is usually single-stemmed and low-branching. It produces elegant pendent clusters of five-petaled white bells in late spring. The bright green elliptic leaves turn pale yellow in autumn; winter reveals smooth gray bark that fissures with age. American snowbell is best as a specimen or patio tree.

Growing Tips Plant in moist, well-drained, fertile, neutral to acidic soil in full sun or partial shade. Once established, American snowbell is moderately drought tolerant and requires little care. Transplant it only in spring.

Native Alternative
Baccharis halimifolia
Groundsel Tree

Native Habitat and Range Coastal marshes, dunes, roadsides, and waste places from Massachusetts south to Florida, west to Texas

Hardiness Range Zones 5 to 9

Ornamental Attributes and Uses This large, rounded to mounding, often irregular shrub grows 6 to 12 feet tall and wide. Like clouds rising on a hot summer afternoon, the fuzzy seed heads create a billowing white mass in late summer and autumn. The ragged, wedge-shaped foliage is sea-green to silvery gray. Groundsel tree is semievergreen and loses some or all of its foliage, depending on the severity of the winter.

Growing Tips Plant in moist or dry, average loamy or sandy soil in full sun or light shade. The plant tolerates a wide variety of soils and moisture regimes, as well as soil-borne and air-borne salt. Tip dieback is common in winter. Reshape the shrub in spring before fresh growth emerges.

More Native Alternatives *Carpinus caroliniana*, musclewood (page 16)—Maine and Florida, west to Minnesota and Texas. *Hamamelis virginiana*, witch hazel (page 105)—Nova Scotia to Minnesota, south to Florida and Texas. For a list of additional native shrubs, visit www.bbg.org/nativealternatives.

Attributes at a Glance
Baccharis halimifolia

Rounded to mounding shrub

6 to 12 feet tall and wide

Attractive cottonlike seed heads

Gray-green to silvery foliage

Invasive Shrub
Euonymus alatus • Winged Euonymus

Current Invaded Range: New Hampshire to Michigan, south to
South Carolina, Tennessee, and Iowa; Montana

Native Alternative
Aronia melanocarpa
Black Chokeberry

Native Habitat and Range Swamps,
woodland clearings, wetland forests, and
outcroppings from Newfoundland to
Ontario, south to Georgia and Arkansas

Attributes at a Glance
Aronia melanocarpa

**Mounding to rounded small to
medium-sized shrub**

4 to 6 feet tall and wide

**Domed clusters of white spring
flowers**

Glossy, broad oval foliage

Clusters of black berries

**Brilliant red to burgundy
autumn color**

Hardiness Range Zones 3 to 9

Ornamental Attributes and Uses
White flowers with pink anthers open in
mid-spring as the deep green foliage
unfurls. Glossy black fruit color in mid-
to late summer and persist into winter
long after the crimson to burgundy-red
leaves have fallen. This upright to broad-
spreading, deciduous shrub reaches four
to six feet tall and wide; multistemmed
clumps may sucker. Use this exception-
ally beautiful wildlife plant for mass
plantings, informal hedges, pond plantings, and to add a spot of brilliant
autumn color to the mixed border.

Growing Tips Plant in full sun or partial
shade in rich neutral to acidic soil. This
shrub tolerates wet or dry conditions but
not alkaline soils. The best fruit set and
autumn color occur in the full sun. To
regenerate growth, remove a third of the
old shoots to the ground after flowering.

Native Alternative
Vaccinium corymbosum
Highbush Blueberry

Native Habitat and Range Swamps, clearings, low woods, and outcroppings from Nova Scotia to Michigan, south to Florida and Texas

Hardiness Range Zones 3 to 8

Ornamental Attributes and Uses This parent of commercial blueberries is an upright to broad-spreading, deciduous shrub that reaches four to ten feet tall and wide; multistemmed clumps may sucker. White to pink-blushed bell-shaped flowers nod in clusters on bare stems in spring before the deep green foliage unfurls. The glossy oval leaves turn fiery red in autumn. Edible, waxy blue-black fruit color in mid- to late summer. Use this overlooked native food plant for mass plantings, informal hedges, pond plantings, and to add a spot of brilliant autumn color to the mixed border.

Growing Tips Plant in humus-rich to sandy, evenly moist acidic soil in full sun or part shade. Highbush blueberry is intolerant of alkaline soils. Once established, it is drought tolerant and can also withstand periodic flooding. The best fruit set and autumn color occur in full sun. The plant forms a tight crown and seldom needs pruning.

Attributes at a Glance
Vaccinium corymbosum

Mounding to rounded medium-sized shrub

4 to 10 feet tall and wide

Clusters of nodding white spring flowers

Glossy, oval foliage

Edible blue berries

Brilliant red to burgundy autumn color

Native Alternative
Rhus aromatica
Fragrant Sumac

Native Habitat and Range Forest edges, rock outcroppings, shale barrens, and dry uplands from Vermont to Minnesota, south to Florida and Louisiana

Hardiness Range Zones 4 to 8

Ornamental Attributes and Uses The glossy, three-lobed leaves of this plant are unlike other sumacs in shape and are pungently fragrant. Yellow flowers are carried in tight clusters at the tips of the stems above new growth. The flowers give way to large red berries. The fine-textured crown is perfect for mass plantings, foundations, screens, and naturalized settings.

Growing Tips Plant in moist or dry, average humusy, loamy, or sandy soil in full sun or light shade. This plant tolerates a wide variety of soils and moisture regimes, as well as airborne salt. Like all sumacs, this species suckers, but due to its smaller size it romps less. Remove wayward suckers with a sharp spade, or site it where the plant's colonial nature is an asset.

Related Native Alternatives Also attractive are *Rhus copallina*, winged sumac (page 114), and *R. glabra*, smooth sumac.

More Native Alternatives For a list of additional native shrubs, visit www.bbg.org/nativealternatives.

Attributes at a Glance
Rhus aromatica

Rounded, densely branched shrub

3 to 6 feet tall and wide

Small yellow flower clusters

Glossy, three-lobed leaves

Red berry clusters

Brilliant red autumn color

Invasive Shrub
Euonymus fortunei • Fortune's Euonymus
Current Invaded Range: Massachusetts to Michigan, south to
South Carolina and Mississippi

Native Alternative
Arctostaphylos uva-ursi
Bearberry, Kinnikinnick

Native Habitat and Range Dunes, outcroppings, lakeshores, and open woods from Labrador and British Columbia, south to Virginia, New Mexico and California

Hardiness Range Zones 2 to 8

Ornamental Attributes and Uses A spreading to mounding evergreen shrub two to six inches tall and one to six feet wide, this tidy, ruglike groundcover is revered by all who know it. Generally considered a plant for seaside conditions, it thrives in a variety of garden situations as long as it is free from smothering vegetation. The terminal clusters of white to pale pink flowers give way to oversized red berries that often persist into winter. It is excellent for erosion control, as a weed-free groundcover, or cascading down decorative stone or timber walls.

Growing Tips Plant bearberry in well-drained acidic sandy, loamy, or clay soils in full sun or partial shade. It toleratess full shade but seldom flowers. It can take drought, salt. and occasional flooding, but prolonged sogginess will kill it. This shrub can be difficult to establish but is worth the trouble. With age, the plant mounds up at the center.

SHRUBS

> ## Attributes at a Glance
> ### *Arctostaphylos uva-ursi*
> **Spreading groundcover shrub**
>
> **2 to 6 inches tall and 1 to 6 feet wide**
>
> **Small elliptical evergreen foliage**
>
> **Waxy, bell-shaped flowers**
>
> **Large red berries**

Native Alternative
Decumaria barbara
Wood Vamp, Climbing Hydrangea

Native Habitat and Range Low woods, swamps, and pond margins from Virginia, south to Florida, west to Louisiana

Hardiness Range Zones 6 to 9

Ornamental Attributes and Uses This native climbing hydrangea vine is most often seen as a dramatic vertical accent on tall tree trunks, walls, or trellises, but if planted away from supports, it will run over the ground to form an open groundcover. Glossy, elliptical semievergreen leaves create a lush backdrop for the domed clusters of white flowers in late spring and early summer. The autumn foliage turns yellow late in the season or after the start of the new year. The plant reaches 10 to 30 feet into the canopy of host trees and may form a skirt that reaches 6 to 8 feet out from the trunk.

Growing Tips Plant in evenly moist, humus-rich soils in full sun or shade. Wood vamp tolerates full deciduous shade and will even flower in it. It also tolerates drought if well established, as well as occasional flooding, but prolonged sogginess will drown it.

Attributes at a Glance
Decumaria barbara

Climbing woody vine suitable as a groundcover

6- to 8-foot spread

Glossy, elliptical semievergreen foliage

Clusters of white flowers

Native Alternative
Vaccinium crassifolium
Creeping Blueberry

Native Habitat and Range Open woods, pine flats, and thickets from Virginia to Georgia

Hardiness Range Zones 7 to 9

Ornamental Attributes and Uses The glossy oval leaves of creeping blueberry alternate on creeping stems that form a tidy, elegant groundcover. Terminal clusters of white to red-stained flowers give way to oversized blue-black berries. The foliage turns bronzy in winter. This plant is excellent as a delicate ground-cover or as underplanting with larger shrubs.

Growing Tips Plant in well-drained acidic sandy or loamy soil in full sun or partial shade. This plant will grow in full shade but will seldom flower. It tolerates drought and salt but is susceptible to root rot in heavy or wet soils. This shrub can be difficult to establish, but it is worth the trouble.

Related Native Alternative *Vaccinium elliottii*, Elliott's blueberry, is a low, spreading shrub to 12 inches tall with pointed oval leaves and nodding white to pink flowers followed by black berries. It is found from Virginia, south to Florida, west to Texas and Arkansas.

More Native Alternatives *Xanthorrhiza simplicissima*, shrub yellowroot (page 137)—mostly in the Appalachians from New York, south to Florida and Louisiana. For a list of additional native shrubs, visit www.bbg.org/nativealternatives.

Attributes at a Glance
Vaccinium crassifolium

Trailing groundcover shrub

2 to 6 inches tall and 1 to 4 feet wide

Small elliptical evergreen foliage

Waxy, bell-shaped flowers

Blue-black berries

Invasive Shrub
Ficus carica • Edible Fig

Current Invaded Range: California, Florida

Native Alternative
Calycanthus occidentalis
Western Sweetshrub

Native Habitat and Range Streambanks and in seeps in scattered localities throughout California

Hardiness Range Zones 8 to 10

Ornamental Attributes and Uses The deep maroon to reddish-brown spring flowers of this shrub resemble strap-petaled water-lilies and smell of ripe fruit. Bold, lustrous pointed oval leaves are paired on slender stems. Use western sweetshrub as an accent, screen, or hedge, as well as in naturalized settings.

Growing Tips Plant in moist, humus-rich to loamy soil in full sun to partial shade. Western sweetshrub is quite shade-tolerant, but without direct sun it is open crowned and flowers more sparsely. In warmer regions, however, a little shade is advisable. This plant is fast growing—prune as needed to control its size or to reshape.

Related Native Alternative *Calycanthus floridus*, eastern sweetshrub, is more compact and floriferous. It grows from Quebec, south to Florida and Louisiana.

More Native Alternatives For a list of additional native shrubs, visit www.bbg.org/nativealternatives.

Attributes at a Glance
Calycanthus occidentalis

Multistemmed, rounded shrub

4 to 10 feet tall and wide

Bold, lustrous foliage

Fragrant, spidery flowers

Yellow autumn color

Invasive Shrub
Hibiscus syriacus • Rose of Sharon

Current Invaded Range: New York to Missouri, south to Georgia and Texas; Utah

Native Alternative
Hibiscus coccineus
Scarlet Mallow

Native Habitat and Range Swamps, marshes, and pond margins in Georgia and Florida

Hardiness Range Zones 6 to 10

Ornamental Attributes and Uses Enormous, saucer-shaped scarlet flowers with the texture of quilted crepe open for just a day atop tall, leafy stems. A succession of buds keeps this beautiful shrub-sized perennial in bloom for several months in mid- to late summer. The attractive foliage has three to five elongated, fingerlike lobes. The flowers give way to showy brown capsules that split to release rounded seeds. Plant scarlet mallow as a seasonal hedge or screen; use it in borders, or as a specimen.

Growing Tips Plant in rich, evenly moist soil in full sun or light shade. Scarlet mallow tolerates wet soil and is surprisingly drought tolerant once the fleshy roots are well established. It forms huge woody crowns with age. Cut the stout stems to the ground in winter or spring. New growth emerges late in the season.

Related Native Alternatives *Hibiscus grandiflorus,* swamp rosemallow, has pink flowers carried on six- to eight-foot stems clothed in bold, soft, hairy sea-green leaves. It grows in the wild from Georgia and Florida, west to Texas. *Hibiscus moscheutos,* marsh mallow, is a widespread and variable species with several botanical varieties. It grow three to six feet tall and has huge white to pink, red-eyed flowers on leafy stems. It is found from Quebec to Minnesota, south to Florida and New Mexico.

More Native Alternatives For a list of additional native shrubs, visit www.bbg.org/nativealternatives.

Attributes at a Glance
Hibiscus coccineus

Tall, sparsely branched stems

6 to 12 feet tall and wide

Huge scarlet flowers

Bold, hand-shaped leaves

Decorative woody seed capsules

Invasive Shrub
Lantana camara • Lantana
Current Invaded Range: Florida (also Hawaii)

Native Alternative
Erythrina herbacea
Coral Bean

Native Habitat and Range Low woods, savannas, and swamp and pond margins in North Carolina, south to Florida and west to Texas

Attributes at a Glance
Erythrina herbacea

Multistemmed shrub to small tree

5 to 10 feet tall and 3 to 5 feet wide

Flaming red flowers

Distinctive pointed foliage

Green winter stems

Hardiness Range Zones 7 to 10

Ornamental Attributes and Uses Brilliant scarlet flowers to three inches long in fantastic plumes crown the stems of coral bean in mid- to late summer and continue for months. The compound leaves have three broad leaflets with long, narrow pinched tips. The species is deciduous but retains its foliage late into the season. In dry sites it may flower on bare stems. It can reach 20 feet tall, but the stems are weak and are often winter-killed at the northern reaches of its natural distribution. Most plants are small to medium-sized multistemmed shrubs that reach five feet in a season.

Growing Tips Plant in sandy or loamy, moist soil in full sun or light shade. Coral bean will form a trunk in subtropical zones but is killed to the ground by freezing temperatures. Remove damaged growth in spring and the plant will rebound. Constantly coppice it to keep it low and encourage fresh growth from the base.

More Native Alternatives For a list of additional native shrubs, visit www.bbg.org/nativealternatives.

Invasive Shrubs
Ligustrum amurense, L. japonicum, L. lucidum, L. obtusifolium, L. ovalifolium, L. sinense, L. vulgare • Privets

Current Invaded Range: Maine to Michigan, south to Florida and Texas; Montana and Oregon, south to Utah and California

Native Alternative
Viburnum prunifolium
Black Haw

Native Habitat and Range Woodlands, meadows, streamsides, and road cuts from Connecticut to Michigan, south to Florida and Texas

Hardiness Range Zones 3 to 9

Ornamental Attributes and Uses This large shrub to small tree is 8 to 25 feet tall and 6 to 12 feet wide with an upright oval crown when young, often becoming irregular with drooping lower branches. Handsome, deep green oval leaves are paired along the thin stems. Creamy-white flowers in paired, flat-tened clusters give way to edible pink berries that ripen to deep blue-black. The autumn foliage is flaming red to burgundy. Use black haw as a hedge, screen, specimen, or at the edge of woods in naturalized situations.

Growing Tips Plant in most, humus-rich to loamy soil in full sun to partial shade. Black haw grows best in deep soils, but it also grows well, if slowly, in leaner and drier sites. It is moderately drought and salt tolerant. Foliage may succumb to powdery mildew in hot, dry weather.

SHRUBS

Attributes at a Glance
Viburnum prunifolium

Large shrub to small tree

8 to 25 feet tall and 6 to 12 feet wide

Flat clusters of creamy flowers

Drooping blue-black fruit

Irregular, somewhat weeping winter silhouette

Native Alternative
Osmanthus americanus
Devilwood

Native Habitat and Range Low woodland, swamps, streambanks, and pond margins from southern Virginia, south to Florida and west to Louisiana

Hardiness Range Zones 7 to 10

Ornamental Attributes and Uses Small, greenish-white, tubular flowers held in clusters are abundant in winter and early spring. Although the flowers are small, they give off a very heady sweet fragrance. Blue-purple fruit follow and are gobbled up by birds. The dark, lance-shaped evergreen leaves are four to five inches long. Use devilwood in naturalized settings, as a specimen, or clipped into a hedge.

Growing Tips Plant in moist, fertile, well-drained neutral to acidic soil in full sun or partial shade protected from hot afternoon sun and strong winds. Devilwood thrives in high shade situations and tolerates heavy clay soil and moderate salt. It is very disease and pest resistant. Prune it to maintain size and shape and to promote a strong branching structure.

Related Alternative *Osmanthus americanus* var. *megacarpus*, scrub tea olive, has larger fruit and leaves and is native to the scrub of central Florida.

Attributes at a Glance
Osmanthus americanus

Upright, open shrub or small tree

10 to 30 feet tall and 6 to 15 feet wide

Evergreen, lance-shaped leaves

Fragrant spring flowers

Showy purple fruit

Native Alternative
Prunus caroliniana
Carolina Cherry Laurel

Native Habitat and Range Woods, thickets, and hedgerows from eastern Virginia, south to Florida, and west to Louisiana, often in dense stands

Hardiness Range Zones 7 to 9

Ornamental Attributes and Uses Handsome, dark evergreen narrow, oval leaves alternate along the thin green stems of this familiar southern shrub. Fragrant white flowers in erect spikes are carried at the nodes in spring. They give way to edible blue-black fruit in late summer. This small tree is 20 to 30 feet tall and 15 to 25 feet wide and has an upright oval crown when young; it often becomes vase-shaped with age. Use it as a hedge, screen, specimen, or at the edge of woods in naturalized plantings.

Growing Tips Plant in moist, fertile, well-drained acidic soil in full sun or partial shade. Carolina cherry laurel thrives in high shade and tolerates heavy clay. It is very disease and pest resistant. Prune it hard to maintain size and shape and to promote a strong branching structure when using it as a hedge. Shape it as needed when open grown. This plant self-sows freely and is sometimes considered a nuisance. Birds love the berries.

Attributes at a Glance
Prunus caroliniana

Upright, open small tree

20 to 30 feet tall and 15 to 25 feet wide

Evergreen, oval leaves

Fragrant spring flower spikes

Showy black fruit

Native Alternative
Arctostaphylos columbiana
Hairy Manzanita

Native Habitat and Range Open woods, chaparral, and outcroppings from British Columbia to California

Hardiness Range Zones 8 to 9

Ornamental Attributes and Uses Few shrubs form tight, evergreen mounds with foliage all the way to the ground, but hairy manzanita does. The small,

Attributes at a Glance
Arctostaphylos columbiana

Large mounding shrub

6 to 10 feet tall and wide

Small elliptical evergreen foliage

Waxy, bell-shaped flowers

Red berries

hairy blue-green elliptical leaves stand erect while the showy terminal clusters of white to pale pink bell-shaped flowers nod. The decorative red berries often persist into winter. The bark is smooth and mahogany- to chestnut-colored. Use it as a specimen, hedge, screen, or for erosion control.

Growing Tips Plant in moist, sandy or loamy soil in full sun or light shade. Deep, water-seeking roots make this shrub tough, adaptable, and tolerant of extreme heat. The regular crown seldom needs pruning.

Related Native Alternative *Arctostaphylos patula*, greenleaf manzanita, has smooth, bright green leaves and smaller clusters of pink flowers. It is found in desert canyons and scrublands, on rocky mountainsides, and in open woods from Alberta and British Columbia, south to Colorado, Arizona and California.

Native Alternative
Ceanothus velutinus
Redroot

Native Habitat and Range Open pine woods, rocky slopes, barrens, and road-sides from South Dakota to British Columbia, south to Colorado and California

Hardiness Range Zones 4 to 8

Ornamental Attributes and Uses This tough, adaptable shrub bears tight, elongated clusters of small creamy-white flowers in late spring and summer. The oval evergreen leaves with finely toothed margins are coated with fragrant, sticky resin, which helps them retain moisture and discourages browsing by insects and mammals. The resin also burns hot in brushfires, reportedly to help eliminate competition from fire-sensitive species. Use redroot in xeriscape gardens and borders or en masse on slopes.

Growing Tips Plant in moist, sandy or loamy soil in full sun or light shade. Deep, water-seeking roots bestow amazing adaptability to this species. It tolerates extreme heat. The regular crown seldom needs pruning.

More Native Alternatives *Aronia arbutifolia*, red chokeberry (page 123)—New England and Florida, west to Missouri and Texas. *Aronia melanocarpa*, black chokeberry—Newfoundland to Ontario, south to Georgia and Arkansas. *Lindera benzoin*, spicebush (page 99)—Maine and Ontario, south to Florida and Texas. *Morella californica*, California wax myrtle—British Columbia, south to California. *Morella cerifera*, southern wax myrtle (page 81)—New Jersey south to Florida, west to the lower Mississippi Valley and Texas. For a list of additional native shrubs, visit www.bbg.org/nativealternatives.

Attributes at a Glance
Ceanothus velutinus
Mounding to spreading form

2 to 5 feet tall and wide

Terminal white flower clusters

Deep green resinous foliage

Invasive Shrubs
Lonicera tatarica • Tartarian Honeysuckle; *L. maackii*
Amur Honeysuckle; *L. morrowii* • Morrow's
Honeysuckle; *L. xylosteum* • Dwarf Honeysuckle

Current Invaded Range: Most of North America

Native Alternative
Ilex verticillata
Winterberry

Native Habitat and Range Low woods, swamps, and wetland margins from Nova Scotia to Minnesota, south to Florida and Arkansas

Hardiness Range Zones 3 to 9

Ornamental Attributes and Uses The vivid scarlet berries of winterberry mature in late August and September, contrasting with the glossy green foliage, which turns yellow to brown in autumn. The berries persist well into winter and are food for birds and other wildlife. Use this versatile and attractive shrub in mass plantings, as a deciduous screen, or as a specimen or accent at the edges of ponds and bogs.

Growing Tips Plant in full sun or partial shade in moist, fertile, well-drained acidic soil. Plants located in alkaline soil are subject to stunted growth and chlorotic foliage. Established plants tolerate compacted soil, moderate drought, and periodic flooding. For effective berry set, situate one male of this dioecious plant in close proximity with a group of females. Older plants become leggy in shade and form colonies by suckering.

Attributes at a Glance
Ilex verticillata

Medium to large shrub with a rounded crown

6 to 12 feet tall and wide

Quilted green foliage

Brilliant red berries

Twiggy winter silhouette

Native Alternative
Lindera benzoin
Spicebush

Native Habitat and Range
Floodplains, bottomlands, streamsides, and cove forests from Maine and Ontario, south to Florida and Texas

Hardiness Range Zones 4 to 9

Ornamental Attributes and Uses The small, fragrant yellow flowers of spicebush cluster at the nodes of bare stems in late winter. This plant is dioecious; females produce single-seeded berries that ripen to scarlet in late summer. The foliage turns clear, rich yellow in autumn. This medium-sized shrub has a rounded to vase-shaped crown 6 to 15 feet tall and wide. The smooth, gray-brown bark with prominent lenticels is attractive in winter. Use spicebush in naturalistic plantings and wildflower gardens or as a specimen, hedge, or screen.

Growing Tips Plant in humus-rich, evenly moist, neutral to acidic soil in sun or shade. This plant tolerates a wide range of soil, moisture, and light conditions in cultivation. Unlike many shrubs, spicebush tolerates deep shade.

Attributes at a Glance
Lindera benzoin

Medium-sized shrub

Rounded to oval crown

6 to 15 feet tall and wide

Gray-brown, smooth bark

Yellow flowers

Sea-green oval leaves

Red berries

Native Alternative
Cornus sericea
Red Osier Dogwood

Native Habitat and Range Woodland riparian zones, swamps, and low-lying meadows, floodplains, and wetlands in the northeastern United States

Attributes at a Glance
Cornus sericea

Upright, mounded shrub

Flame-red stems and twigs

6 to 8 feet tall and wide

White flowers in flat clusters

Red to burgundy autumn color

White berries

Hardiness Range Zones 2 to 9

Ornamental Attributes and Uses This upright, rounded deciduous shrub, six to eight feet tall and wide, has opposite, oval, bright green leaves. The carmine stems and twigs of this dogwood add much-needed color to the winter garden. In spring, small white flowers are displayed in flat-topped clusters and produce white berries. The leaves turn orange-red to burgundy in the autumn. Use red osier dogwood for the edges of ponds, streamside, along forest or woodland verges, in mixed beds or borders, as informal hedging, or as mass plantings in informal areas.

Growing Tips Red osier dogwood thrives in rich, moist soils in partial to full sun. It tolerates wet soils and flooding but not prolonged drought. To rejuvenate it and encourage maximum winter color, coppice or cut all stems back to 12 to 18 inches in early spring every two to three years. This plant tends to sucker, producing many-stemmed wide clumps.

Related Native Alternative *Cornus amomum*, silky dogwood, looks similar and often shares the same habitat but has a more open crown, thinner stems, and silken hairs in the leaf veins, visible if you pull a leaf in half. The winter stems are deep red to burgundy. It grows in low woods, bottomlands, and along streams and rivers from Massachusetts and New York, south to Georgia and Tennessee.

Native Alternative
Lonicera involucrata
Twinberry

Native Habitat and Range Open deciduous or mixed coniferous woods, rocky slopes, and roadsides from Ontario to Alaska, south to Michigan, Minnesota, New Mexico, and California

Hardiness Range Zones 3 to 7

Ornamental Attributes and Uses Clustered yellow flowers surrounded by cuplike bracts open throughout summer in the axils of upright stems clothed with opposite, pointed oval leaves. Black fruit follow, accented by the reflexed bracts, which turn brilliant scarlet. The quilted, deep green foliage is tinged with bronze in spring and turns clear yellow in fall. Use twinberry as a low screen, in mass plantings, or for erosion control.

Growing Tips Plant in evenly moist, rich soil in full sun or light shade. Twinberry is moderately drought tolerant once established but grows best with consistent moisture. Prune to control size and shape, and remove spreading runners as needed.

Related Native Alternatives *Lonicera canadensis*, fly honeysuckle, is a more delicate-looking species with an upright habit and smaller, sea-green oval leaves. The flowers are paired at the tips of the branches and open in midsummer. The flowers produce red fruit. Fly honeysuckle is found from Nova Scotia and Saskatchewan, south to North Carolina, Tennessee, and Iowa.

More Native Alternatives *Aronia melanocarpa*, black chokeberry (page 84)—Newfoundland to Ontario, south to Georgia and Arkansas. *Viburnum dentatum*, arrowwood—Massachusetts south to Florida, west to Texas. For a list of additional native shrubs, visit www.bbg.org/nativealternatives.

Attributes at a Glance
Lonicera involucrata

Small shrub with arching, vaselike form

2 to 6 feet tall and 3 to 5 feet wide

Yellow flowers all summer

Yellow to burgundy autumn color

Invasive Shrub
Myoporum laetum • Myoporum
Current Invaded Range: California

Native Alternative
Carpenteria californica,
Tree Anemone, Carpenteria

Native Habitat and Range Moist ravines in the foothills of central California; rare plant listed as threatened

Hardiness Range Zones 8 to 9

Ornamental Attributes and Uses Tree anemone's showy, five-petaled roselike flowers with golden stamens cover the tips of new branches in early summer above pointed, elliptical evergreen leaves. The flowers smell of citrus, a link to its next of kin, mock orange. Use tree anemone as a specimen, foundation plant, screen, or in containers.

Growing Tips Plant in evenly moist but well-drained soil in full sun or light shade. This shrub is widely cultivated in Europe, but it is rare in American gardens outside its native range. The plant has a narrow range of temperature and moisture requirements. It needs a Mediterranean climate that in summer is dry with cool nights and in winter is is frost free. Tree anemone dislikes humidity and is subject to root rot in heavy soils.

More Native Alternatives *Arctostaphylos columbiana*, hairy manzanita (page 96)—British Columbia to California. For a list of additional native shrubs, visit www.bbg.org/nativealternatives.

Attributes at a Glance
Carpenteria californica

Upright to mounding shrub

3 to 8 feet tall and 3 to 4 feet wide

Showy, fragrant white flowers

Lustrous evergreen leaves

Invasive Shrub
Nandina domestica • Heavenly Bamboo

Current Invaded Range: Southeastern states from Virginia to Texas

Native Alternative
Agarista populifolia
Florida Leucothoe

Native Habitat and Range Open woods, pond margins, and savannas from South Carolina to Florida

Hardiness Range Zones 6 to 10

Ornamental Attributes and Uses This multistemmed, vase-shaped shrub is 6 to 12 feet tall and wide. The elegant, ascending branches of Florida leucothoe form a wide vase of vibrant green foliage accented in spring by small axillary clusters of white, bell-shaped flowers. The evergreen foliage darkens in winter. Use this serviceable beauty as a backdrop for bold flowering shrubs or perennials, as a mass planting or screen, or as a specimen.

Growing Tips Plant in average to rich, sandy or loamy soil in sun or shade. Planted in poorer soils, the shrub will grow more slowly and stay more compact. Winter burn sometimes occurs when days are warm and the roots are frozen. In spring, remove any brown or damaged branches. Do not shear this shrub or you will ruin its form. Keep plants small by pruning out tall, two- to three-year-old canes from the base. Renew overgrown plants by cutting them to the ground in late winter.

Attributes at a Glance
Agarista populifolia

Medium to large vase-shaped evergreen shrub

6 to 12 feet tall and wide

Glossy, awl-shaped leaves

Axillary clusters of white flowers

Native Alternative
Ilex vomitoria
Yaupon

Native Habitat and Range Low woodland edges, fields, and marshy spots from coastal Virginia west to Missouri, south to Florida and Texas

Hardiness Range Zones 7 to 10

Ornamental Attributes and Uses This underutilized upright evergreen may be oval to rounded in shape and single-stemmed or clump-forming. There are also weeping and dwarf forms. Yaupon has small, rich green leaves and graceful branches lined with copious scarlet berries from late summer through winter. The fine-textured foliage makes it a perfect screen or tall hedge to contrast with bold plants. Use it as a specimen tree, patio tree, or espalier.

Growing Tips Plant in average to humus-rich neutral to acidic soil in full sun or partial shade. Like all hollies, yaupon is dioecious. Male and female plants are needed for fruit set, but this species is cross-fertile with other hollies. It is widely tolerant of soil types and moisture levels, as well as salt and pollution.

More Native Alternatives For a list of additional native shrubs, visit www.bbg.org/nativealternatives.

Attributes at a Glance
Ilex vomitoria

Tall upright, spreading, or pendulous shrub or small tree

15 to 20 (occasionally 30) feet tall and wide

Fine-textured, dark evergreen foliage

Brilliant red berries

Invasive Shrub
Rhamnus cathartica • Buckthorn

Current Invaded Range: New Brunswick and Alberta, south to Virginia and Wyoming

Native Alternative
Hamamelis virginiana
Witch Hazel

Native Habitat and Range Rocky uplands, streambanks, and forested slopes from Nova Scotia to Minnesota, south to Florida and Texas

Hardiness Range Zones 5 to 8

Ornamental Attributes and Uses This small- to medium-sized, horizontal oval, rounded, or spreading vase-shaped tree may have a multistemmed clump or low-branching form. Unlike other *Hamamelis* species, this witch hazel blooms in autumn rather than in winter. Twisted, spider-like fragrant flowers illuminate the landscape in pale yellow. Broadly oval, scalloped leaves turn yellow to pale orange in autumn. Use witch hazel as a specimen tree, patio tree, or in a container.

Growing Tips Plant in average to humus-rich, well-drained neutral to acidic soil in full sun or partial shade. Witch hazel prefers full sun to partial shade and protection from constant wind. If planted in deep shade, it will seldom bloom. Once established it tolerates considerable drought, but it grows best with consistent moisture. It has no serious pests, though Japanese beetles may munch the leaves.

Attributes at a Glance
Hamamelis virginiana

Large shrub or small tree

15 to 20 feet tall and wide

Scalloped oval leaves

Yellow autumn flowers

Yellow to pale orange fall foliage

Native Alternative
Cornus racemosa
Gray Dogwood

Native Habitat and Range Open woods, clearings, roadsides, and rocky uplands from Maine to Manitoba, south to Virginia, Illinois, and Missouri

Hardiness Range Zones 3 to 8

Attributes at a Glance
Cornus racemosa

Open, mounding crown

4 to 8 feet tall and 6 to 10 feet wide

Pleated oval leaves

White flower clusters

White fruit on red stalks

Red to orange autumn color

Ornamental Attributes and Uses Often overlooked in favor of the red-stemmed species, gray dogwood has a quiet charm. The irregular branches bear pleated, oval gray-green leaves that are paired toward the tips of the stems. Domed clusters of starry white flowers give way to white fruit on showy, glowing red stalks. Its red to orange fall color develops best in sun. Use as a specimen, in naturalized plantings, or pruned into a hedge.

Growing Tips Plant in average to rich soil in full sun or partial shade. Once established, gray dogwood is drought tolerant and blooms well in considerable shade. It tolerates intermittent sogginess but not waterlogging. Renew old clumps by cutting them to the ground. Remove suckers to control spread.

Related Alternative *Cornus drummondii,* rough-leaf dogwood, is similar but forms a small, multistemmed tree at maturity. It grows from New York and Quebec to South Dakota, south along the western Appalachians to Georgia and Texas.

More Native Alternatives *Aronia melanocarpa,* black chokeberry (page 84)—Newfoundland to Ontario, south to Georgia and Arkansas. *Rhamnus (Frangula) caroliniana,* Carolina buckthorn (page 107)—New Jersey to Missouri, south to Florida and Texas. *Viburnum prunifolium,* blackhaw (page 93)—Connecticut to Michigan, south to Florida and Texas. For a list of additional native shrubs, visit www.bbg.org/nativealternatives.

Invasive Shrub
Rhamnus frangula (*Frangula alnus*)
Tall Hedge Buckthorn

Current Invaded Range: New Brunswick and Ontario, south to West Virginia and Iowa

Native Alternative
Rhamnus caroliniana
Carolina Buckthorn

Native Habitat and Range Low woods, streambanks, floodplains, and wooded slopes from New Jersey to Missouri, south to Florida and Texas

Hardiness Range Zones 5 to 9

Ornamental Attributes and Uses This open-crowned, rounded to broadly oval tree is 10 to 15 (occasionally to 30) feet tall and 10 to 20 feet wide. The foliage clusters toward the tips of the branches, especially when grown in shade. The autumn foliage turns clear yellow. Glossy, deep green oval, quilted leaves accented by red berries that ripen to black make this underutilized shrub a perfect substitute for tall hedge buckthorn. The two are so similar that they are often confused. Use Carolina buckthorn as a hedge, trimmed or natural; as a tall screen; or in wildlife plantings.

Growing Tips Plant in moist, humus-rich soil in sun or shade. This versatile species is drought tolerant. It fruits heavily and colors well in sun or light shade. Birds relish the berries, and the plant may self-sow. Shade-grown plants are open crowned.

Attributes at a Glance
Rhamnus caroliniana

Upright to broadly oval small tree

10 to 15 feet tall and 10 to 20 feet wide

Lustrous, bright green foliage

Red berries that ripen to black

Yellow autumn color

Native Alternative
Viburnum nudum var. *cassinoides*
Witherod

Native Habitat and Range Low woods, swamps, floodplains, and stream edges from Newfoundland and Michigan, south in the mountains to Georgia; coastal population from Florida to Louisiana

Hardiness Range Zones 2 to 8

Ornamental Attributes and Uses Domed clusters of creamy-white flowers show off against glossy, deep green oval foliage in late spring. The flowers are followed by multicolored fleshy berries—relished by birds—that ripen unevenly in shades of yellow and red to deep powdery blue. The ovate, finely toothed foliage starts out green and in autumn turns orange and then to deep purple. Use witherod as a hedge, foundation shrub, in mass plantings, or in mixed borders.

Growing Tips Plant in rich, evenly moist soil in full sun or partial shade. Witherod tolerates periodic flooding but not prolonged drought. It keeps a fairly regular form but may need light pruning to maintain an even shape; it can be limbed up to form a multistemmed small tree.

More Native Alternatives *Aronia melanocarpa*, black chokeberry (page 84)—Newfoundland to Ontario, south to Georgia and Arkansas. *Ilex verticillata*, winterberry (page 98)—Nova Scotia to Minnesota, south to Florida and Arkansas. *Lindera benzoin*, spicebush, page 99—Maine and Ontario, south to Florida and Texas. *Viburnum nudum* var. *nudum*, smooth witherod (page 128)—Massachusetts south to Florida, west to Texas. For a list of additional native shrubs, visit www.bbg.org/nativealternatives.

Attributes at a Glance
Viburnum nudum var. *cassinoides*

Broad, rounded shrub or small tree

6 to 12 feet tall and wide

Domed clusters of creamy-white flowers in late spring

Deep green foliage

Blue-black berries

Invasive Shrub
Rhodotypos scandens • Jetbead
Current Invaded Range: New England and Wisconsin, south to South Carolina and Alabama

Native Alternative
Physocarpus opulifolius
Ninebark

Native Habitat and Range Open woods, lakeshores, streambanks, rock outcroppings, and prairies from New Brunswick to Ontario, south to Georgia and Arkansas

Hardiness Range Zones 3 to 8

Ornamental Attributes and Uses Domed clusters of creamy-white flowers smother the even, rounded crowns of ninebark in late spring and early summer, and the resulting red seed capsules dry to brown and remain all winter. In autumn, the foliage varies from yellow to orange or burgundy. Exfoliating bark and dried seed heads add to the winter landscape. This durable upright oval to rounded, mounding multistemmed shrub grows 4 to 8 feet tall and 6 to 12 feet wide. It works well in beds and borders, as an informal hedge or screen, or in naturalized settings.

Growing Tips Plant in rich, evenly moist soil in full sun to partial shade. Ninebark grows in diverse situations in the wild and tolerates drought once established. Renew the crown of an established plant by removing old canes at the base. Though it is tolerated by the shrub, shearing destroys the shape of the crown. Cut oversized plants to the ground in late winter and they will resprout.

Attributes at a Glance
Physocarpus opulifolius

Rounded to mounding shrub

4 to 8 feet tall and 6 to 12 feet wide

Creamy-white flower clusters in late spring

Yellow to orange autumn color

Exfoliating bark

Native Alternative
Hydrangea quercifolia
Oakleaf Hydrangea

Native Habitat and Range Wooded slopes and shaded, rocky outcroppings from Georgia to Florida and Mississippi

Hardiness Range Zones 5 to 9

Ornamental Attributes and Uses The show of large conical panicles of white sepals and fertile flowers begins in June.

Attributes at a Glance
Hydrangea quercifolia

Rounded to broad mounded shrub

6 to 8 feet tall and wide

Huge trusses of white flowers

Brilliant red autumn color

Dried flower heads in winter

As the flowers mature they are suffused with pink, and the dried flower heads remain attractive all winter. The leaves have three to seven lobes and are up to eight inches long. They turn red to burgundy in fall and often persist into winter. Use this shrub in mass plantings, naturalized at a woodland edge, in borders, and as foundation plantings.

Growing Tips Oakleaf hydrangea performs best in moist, humus rich, well-drained soil in full sun to part shade. The brightest fall color develops in sun. The plant is drought tolerant once established.

More Native Alternatives For a list of additional native shrubs, visit www.bbg.org/nativealternatives.

Invasive Shrub
Rosa multiflora • Multiflora Rose;
R. rugosa • Beach Rose

Current Invaded Range: New Brunswick and Ontario, south to Florida and Texas; Pacific Northwest

Native Alternative
Rosa setigera
Climbing Prairie Rose

Native Habitat and Range Low woods, edges of swamps, thickets, and ditches from Ontario to Kansas, south to Florida and Texas

Hardiness Range Zones 4 to 9

Ornamental Attributes and Uses The weak canes of our only native climbing rose sprawl over rocks and fences or rise through the branches of shrubs and trees. The canes reach 6 to 8 feet tall, and clumps spread 8 to 12 feet wide. The canes are armed with large prickles, so beware. The bold leaves have three quilted oval leaflets and cluster below the tight groups of five to seven fragrant pink flowers that last for nearly a week. Use this rose in hedgerows or in naturalistic plantings.

Growing Tips Plant in average to rich, moist soil in full sun or light shade. This rose is a rampant grower and quickly forms a broad clump with many prickly canes. Renew it every two to three years by removing old canes to the ground.

More Native Alternatives *Clethra alnifolia*, summersweet (page 63)—Maine south to Florida, and west to Texas. *Prunus virginiana*, choke cherry—most of North America. For a list of additional native shrubs, visit www.bbg.org/nativealternatives.

Attributes at a Glance
Rosa setigera

Open crown of arching stems

Single pink flowers in tight groups of 5 to 7

Neat, quilted pinnate foliage

Invasive Shrub
Scaevola sericea var. *taccada* • Beach Naupaka
Current Invaded Range: Florida

Native Alternative
Scaevola plumieri
Inkberry

Native Habitat and Range Florida, Louisiana, and Texas (also Puerto Rico)

Hardiness Range Zones 10 to 11

Ornamental Attributes and Uses This mounding, colonial shrub grows two to three feet tall and three to six feet wide. The dense succulent stems of inkberry bear deep green, fleshy obovate evergreen leaves clustered at the tips of the branches on fresh growth. Inconspicuous axillary flowers give way to conspicuous, glossy black fruit. Choose inkberry for dune and beach plantings, for erosion control, or as a foundation shrub; it also works as a screen and in mass plantings.

Growing Tips Plant in sandy, well-drained soil in full sun or light shade. This beachfront native is extremely heat, drought, and salt tolerant. It spreads by runners that are easily removed to control the plant's spread or for propagation. In landscape settings, light, fast-draining soil is essential.

More Native Alternatives *Morella cerifera*, southern wax myrtle (page 81)—New Jersey south to Florida, west to the lower Mississippi Valley and Texas. For a list of additional native shrubs, visit www.bbg.org/nativealternatives.

Attributes at a Glance
Scaevola plumieri

Small mounding shrub

2 to 3 feet tall and 3 to 6 feet wide

Evergreen foliage

Glossy black berries

Invasive Shrub
Schinus terebinthifolius • Brazilian Pepper Tree
Current Invaded Range: Florida, Texas, and California (also Hawaii and Puerto Rico)

Native Alternative
Psychotria nervosa
Wild Coffee

Native Habitat and Range Marl ridges and hummocks throughout peninsular Florida

Hardiness Range Zones 8 to 10

Ornamental Attributes and Uses The glowing red berries of wild coffee contrast beautifully with the deep green varnished oval leaves that taper at both ends. The leaves have conspicuous, impressed veins that give the plant a quilted look and are often likened to those of gardenia or true coffee, which share the family tree. Small white flowers are carried in the axils of the upper portions of the stems. The plant forms an upright crown 6 to 15 feet tall and 4 to 8 feet wide. Use wild coffee as a foundation shrub, specimen, or in mass plantings.

Growing Tips Plant in average to rich, sandy or loamy more or less neutral soil in full sun or partial shade. This plant grows best in sun but will tolerate considerable shade. It also tolerates drought and salt. Though usually shrub-sized in the landscape, wild coffee may grow into a small tree. In full sun, it stays shorter and the foliage may blanch. Prune as needed to control size or shape.

Attributes at a Glance
Psychotria nervosa

Upright evergreen shrub

6 to 15 feet tall and 4 to 8 feet wide

Glossy, quilted leaves

Brilliant red berries

Native Alternative
Rhus copallina
Winged Sumac

Native Habitat and Range Forest edges, fields, meadows, and roadsides from Maine to Wisconsin, south to Florida and Texas

Hardiness Range Zones 4 to 8

Ornamental Attributes and Uses The slender stems of this garden-worthy sumac are tipped with a shock of finely textured, glossy pinnate foliage. Pyramidal clusters of greenish-yellow flowers are surrounded by rings of foliage, lending a tropical air. In fall, the foliage glows red and purple, and the reddish fruit clusters droop, unlike those of other sumacs.

Growing Tips Plant in moist or dry, average humusy, loamy, or sandy soil in full sun or light shade. Winged sumac tolerates a wide variety of soils and moisture regimes, as well as airborne salt. Like all sumacs, this species suckers, but its smaller size and finer texture mean that it romps less. Remove wayward suckers with a sharp spade when necessary.

Related Alternative *Rhus glabra*, smooth sumac, is larger, 8 to 15 feet tall, with erect flower and seed heads on stout branches; it grows from Ontario, west to Manitoba, south to Georgia and Texas.

More Native Alternatives For a list of additional native shrubs, visit www.bbg.org/nativealternatives.

Attributes at a Glance
Rhus copallina

Open, sparsely branched shrub

6 to 12 feet tall and wide

Branched, erect flower clusters

Glossy, pinnately divided leaves

Drooping red berry clusters

Brilliant red autumn color

Invasive Shrub
Spiraea japonica • Japanese Spirea
Current Invaded Range: Maine and Michigan, south to Georgia and Tennessee; watch elsewhere in the East and Midwest

Native Alternative
Spiraea betulifolia
Shiny-Leaf Meadowsweet

Native Habitat and Range New Jersey and Pennsylvania, south to Florida and Alabama; Ontario and Minnesota west to British Columbia and Oregon

Hardiness Range Zones 4 to 8

Ornamental Attributes and Uses This low, mounding to vase-shaped multi-stemmed shrub is densely covered with foliage and grows one to three feet tall and three to four feet wide. It is naturally compact and easy to fit into smaller gardens and in tight spaces. Terminal clusters of fuzzy white flowers cover the plants in summer above a dense mound of lustrous, deep green oval leaves that are broadest above the middle. Its fall color varies from burgundy to yellow. Use shiny-leaf meadowsweet as a foundation shrub, in mixed borders, or as a low hedge.

Growing Tips Plant in average to rich, moist but well-drained soil in full sun to partial shade. The shrub is easy to grow and pest free. Prune the crowns by removing old canes to the ground every year or two.

Related Alternative *Spiraea alba*, white spirea, is a larger, rangy shrub to three feet tall and six feet wide with elongated flower clusters and blunt, lance-shaped leaves. It grows in moist meadows and pond margins from Nova Scotia to Manitoba, south to North Carolina and Missouri.

Attributes at a Glance
Spiraea betulifolia

Small, dense, mounding shrub

1 to 3 feet tall and 3 to 4 feet wide

Burnished chestnut to gray zigzag twigs

White, domed flower clusters in early summer

Lustrous, deep green leaves

Yellow to orange and burgundy autumn color

Native Alternative
Spiraea densiflora
Mountain Spirea

Native Habitat and Range Open woods, streamsides, clearings, and rocky slopes from Alberta and British Columbia, south to Wyoming and California

Hardiness Range Zones 3 to 8

Ornamental Attributes and Uses Domed, glowing pink terminal flower clusters float above the broadly oval, rich green foliage of mountain spirea in early summer. The flowers are followed by mahogany-colored seed heads composed of many small dried capsules that remain attractive all winter. Use this shrub as a hedge, screen, or in mixed borders.

Growing Tips Plant in rich, evenly moist soil in full sun or partial shade. The shrub grows best with ample moisture and cool night temperatures. It spreads by suckers to form dense, wide clumps. Remove the suckers for propagation or to control spread. Thin old stems at the ground or prune the shrub to the ground to renew.

Related Alternative *Spiraea douglasii,* rose spirea—Alaska, south to Montana and California.

More Native Alternatives *Ceanothus americanus,* New Jersey tea (page 59)—Quebec and Minnesota, south to Florida and Texas. *Diervilla lonicera,* bush honeysuckle (page 61)—Virginia and Minnesota, and in the mountains to Tennessee. *Fothergilla gardenii,* witch alder (page 58)—North Carolina south to Florida and Alabama. *Itea virginica,* Virginia sweetspire, (page 60)—New Jersey and Missouri, south to Florida and Louisiana. For a list of additional native shrubs, visit www.bbg.org/nativealternatives.

Attributes at a Glance
Spiraea densiflora

Upright to rounded form

2 to 4 feet tall with an equal or greater spread

Bright pink flower clusters in summer

Rounded, rich green foliage

Yellow to orange autumn color

Dense, twiggy winter silhouette

Invasive Shrub
Tamarix ramosissima • Tamarisk

Current Invaded Range: Virginia south to Georgia, west to California; Alberta south to Texas; Pacific Northwest

Native Alternative
Chilopsis linearis
Desert Willow

Native Habitat and Range Desert washes, streamsides, and riverbanks from Colorado to California, south to New Mexico and Mexico

Hardiness Range Zones 6 to 10

Ornamental Attributes and Uses Flamboyant terminal clusters of pink and white tubular flowers cover desert willow in spring and summer. This long-blooming plant will display flowers along with thin, pealike green seedpods that dry to brown. The linear leaves taper at both ends and seem to cluster toward the tips of the branches, especially as the season progresses and the soil dries. Desert willow is a somewhat irregular upright oval to rounded densely branched shrub or small tree. It may be pruned into a single- or multistemmed tree. Use it as a hedge, accent, or in mixed borders. It also makes a beautiful specimen or patio tree if properly pruned.

Growing Tips Plant in average to rich, moist soil in full sun or light shade. Once established desert willow is drought tolerant, but it will defoliate during prolonged dry spells. It is relatively pest free but may be attacked by aphids.

Attributes at a Glance
Chilopsis linearis

Large, upright to rounded shrub or small tree

15 to 25 feet tall and 10 to 15 feet wide

Pink and white tubular flowers in spring and summer

Linear, medium-green foliage

Yellow autumn color

Irregular winter silhouette with ragged gray bark

Native Alternative
Prosopis glandulosa var. *glandulosa*
Honey Mesquite

Native Habitat and Range Intermittent streams, arroyos, and riverbanks from Kansas and Texas, west to New Mexico and Mexico

Attributes at a Glance
Prosopis glandulosa var. *glandulosa*

Broad, oval to vase-shaped crown

20 to 25 feet tall and 25 to 30 feet wide

Fine-textured, compound foliage

Fragrant, catkin-like flower spikes

Irregular, sculptural winter silhouette

Hardiness Range Zones 7 to 10

Ornamental Attributes and Uses This small- to medium-sized weeping tree may be single-stemmed with low branches or a clump with an irregularly branching form. Showy, fragrant cream flowers in dense spikes are borne at the nodes in spring. Tough, beanlike pods form in summer. The lush, bright green, pinnately divided leaves drop as summer heats up. the branches are spiny. Use honey mesquite as a specimen tree, patio tree, or screen.

Growing Tips Plant in average sandy to humus-rich, well-drained neutral to alkaline soil in full sun. This tough desert denizen tolerates extreme drought, heat, and wind, and moderate amounts of salt but can't take heavy or wet soil. It grows faster in rich, moist sites. It is tap-rooted, so transplant when young. It branches to the ground, so it must be pruned into tree form for most gardens.

Native Alternative
Fallugia paradoxa
Apache Plume

Native Habitat and Range Semidesert foothills, canyons, and arroyos in southern California, Arizona, New Mexico, Mexico, and Texas

Hardiness Range Zones 5 to 10

Ornamental Attributes and Uses This upright, twiggy shrub is semievergreen depending on the severity of drought conditions. It ranges from four to eight feet high with a spread of six feet. Showy, pristine white flowers that resemble single roses open in late spring and early summer, followed by feathery plumes that bear and disperse the seeds. The deep green, quilted leaves are carried in clusters up the stems. Use Apache plume as a hedge, in mass plantings, or as a specimen in desert gardens

Growing Tips Plant in full sun to partial shade in average sandy or loamy, near-neutral soil that hasn't been amended. Prune Apache plume hard to control its size and shape and to keep it from becoming too twiggy. The established plant is tough, tolerant of drought, reflected heat, and poor soil. It is intolerant of humidity and wet soils.

Attributes at a Glance
Fallugia paradoxa

Rounded to mounding twiggy shrub

4 to 8 feet tall and 6 feet wide

Small white flowers

Decorative silken plumes

Native Alternative
Spiraea douglasii
Rose Spirea

Native Habitat and Range Open woods, stream edges, clearings, and

rocky slopes from Alaska, south to Montana and California

Hardiness Range Zones 4 to 8

Ornamental Attributes and Uses Rose spirea is a dense, mounding to spreading shrub three to seven feet tall with an equal or greater spread. Elongated, glowing pink terminal flower clusters float above ragged-tipped, lance-shaped, gray-green foliage in early summer. Use rose spirea as a hedge, screen, or in mixed borders.

Growing Tips Plant in rich, evenly moist soil in full sun or partial shade. Rose spirea grows best with consistent moisture. It spreads by suckers to form thickets. Thin old stems at the ground and prune to the ground to rejuvenate the clump. Suckers are easily removed for propagation or to control spread of the clumps.

More Native Alternatives *Holodiscus discolor*, ocean spray (page 182)— Alberta and British Columbia, south to Arizona and California. *Neviusia alabamensis*, Alabama snow-wreath (page 129)—Mississippi, Alabama, Georgia, Tennessee, and Arkansas. For a list of additional native shrubs, visit www.bbg.org/nativealternatives.

Attributes at a Glance
Spiraea douglasii

Upright to rounded shrub

3 to 7 feet tall and wide

Bright pink elongated flower clusters in summer

Lanceolate, rich green foliage

Yellow to orange autumn color

Dense, twiggy winter silhouette

Invasive Shrub
Taxus cuspidata • Japanese Yew

Current Invaded Range: New York and southern New England;
Ohio and Kentucky

Native Alternative
Taxus canadensis
American Yew

Native Habitat and Range Limy soils
and limestone or sandstone outcropping,
usually under large trees or on north-fac-
ing slopes, from Newfoundland and
Manitoba, south to Virginia, Tennessee,
and Iowa

Hardiness Range Zones 2 to 7

Ornamental Attributes and Uses
American yew is a spreading to weakly
upright shrub, usually with horizontal
branches, three to six feet tall and six
to eight feet wide. It is a delicate and
underutilized native species with half-
inch needles tightly packed along the
ascending branches. Fleshy red arils
cover the hard, poisonous seeds. Use it
as a high groundcover or foundation
planting in cool, shady gardens. It is
not suitable for hedging.

Growing Tips Plant in evenly rich,
moist, neutral soil in shade. It does
not tolerate heat or drought and will
winter burn in sunny or windy spots.
Though not as versatile as other
species, American yew excels where
conditions are to its liking. Deer graze
heavily on all yews.

Related Alternative *Taxus brevifolia*,
Pacific yew, forms a graceful, spreading shrub. It grows from Alaska south
to California. *Taxus floridanum*, Florida
yew, found in peninsular Florida, is
larger and a bit coarser, with longer
needles.

SHRUBS

Attributes at a Glance
Taxus canadensis

**Spreading to ascending
horizontal shrub**

**3 to 6 feet tall and 6 to 8 feet
wide**

Deep green dense needles

Native Alternative
Thuja occidentalis
Arborvitae

Native Habitat and Range Swamps, fens, limestone cliffs, and outcroppings from Nova Scotia to Manitoba, south to North Carolina mountains, Tennessee, and Indiana

Hardiness Range Zones 3 to 7

Ornamental Attributes and Uses Arborvitae is an upright, narrow oval to conical tree 20 to 50 feet tall and 6 to 20 feet wide. The dense, evergreen needles are backed in fan-shaped branchlets. Almost a cliché, this durable evergreen makes an excellent trimmed hedge or natural screen.

Growing Tips Plant in evenly moist, humus-rich neutral soil in sun or shade. Though native to limy soils, landscape plants exhibit a wide tolerance of pH and moisture levels. The best growth is achieved on rich, evenly moist soils, but this species is amazingly drought tolerant once established. Deer will graze this plant to the trunk.

Related Alternative *Thuja plicata*, western redcedar, has a more relaxed crown with open, elegant fans of foliage. It grows from Alaska, south along the western slope of the Rockies to California.

More Native Alternatives *Juniperus virginiana*, eastern redcedar (page 28)— eastern and central North America. For a list of additional native shrubs, visit www.bbg.org/nativealternatives.

Attributes at a Glance
Thuja occidentalis

Upright narrow to conical tree

20 to 50 feet tall and 6 to 20 feet wide

Dense, evergreen needles

Small, dry cones

Excellent hedge plant

Invasive Shrubs
Viburnum dilatatum • Linden Viburnum; *V. lentago*
Tea Viburnum; *V. plicatum* • Double-File Viburnum;
V. sieboldii • Siebold Viburnum

Current Invaded Range: New York, south to Virginia

Native Alternative
Aronia arbutifolia
Red Chokeberry

Native Habitat and Range Swamps, woodland clearings, wetland forests, and outcroppings from New England and Florida, west to Missouri and Texas

Hardiness Range Zones 5 to 9

Ornamental Attributes and Uses This upright to spreading, deciduous shrub reaches ten feet tall and six feet wide. White flowers appear in mid-spring as the bright green foliage of red chokeberry unfurls. The glossy red fruit persists into winter long after the crimson-red leaves have fallen. Red chokeberry has great presence in fall and winter and acts as a bird attractor. Use it in mass plantings, informal hedge or hedgerow, upland pond plantings, and to add seasonal interest in the mixed border.

Growing Tips Red chokeberry thrives in full sun or partial shade in acidic soil. It tolerates wet or dry soil conditions but won't perform in soils that are intensely alkaline. Optimum fruiting and fall color occur in full sun. On established plants cut back a third of the old shoots to the ground after flowering to regenerate growth. It has a tendency to sucker, forming dense clumps.

Attributes at a Glance
Aronia arbutifolia

Mounding to rounded medium-sized shrub

10 feet tall and 6 feet wide

Domed clusters of white spring flowers

Glossy, oval foliage

Clusters of red berries

Brilliant red to burgundy autumn color

Native Alternative
Callicarpa americana
American Beautyberry

Native Habitat and Range Meadows, dunes, and open, well-drained woodlands from Virginia and Missouri, south to Florida and Texas (also West Indies)

Hardiness Range Zones 6 to 10

Ornamental Attributes and Uses This shrub grows six to eight feet tall with a slightly vase-shaped, open habit with its branches facing outward. It is somewhat coarse in leaf texture, with toothed green leaves that may reach eight inches in length. Tiny, lavender cymes borne in clusters around the stem produce luscious drupes in show-stopping magenta in autumn. The distinctive fruit lures birds to feed in late autumn and early winter. Use beautyberry in mass plantings for optimal fall effect or at the midpoint or back of a mixed border.

Growing Tips Plant in well-drained fertile soil in full sun to partial shade. Plants growing in full sun yield more fruit. They also bear more fruit if planted in a group. Beautyberry tolerates dry rocky sites, sandy soil, and salt. Once established, it requires little water or pruning and is very pest and disease resistant. Rejuvenate older shrubs by cutting one third of the oldest wood off at the ground. Avoid heading cuts, which produce twiggy, weak growth.

Attributes at a Glance
Callicarpa americana

Broad, rounded shrub

6 to 8 feet tall and wide

Oval leaves

Lavender flowers

Purple berries

Native Alternative
Ilex montana
Mountain Holly

Native Habitat and Range Rich woods and dry, rocky slopes and clearings from Nova Scotia to Minnesota, south to Florida and Arkansas

Hardiness Range Zones 3 to 7

Ornamental Attributes and Uses The vivid scarlet berries of this holly color in August and September, contrasting with the rich green foliage before it turns bright yellow in fall. The leaves and berries cluster on short spurlike branches. The berries last well unless eaten by birds. Use this uncommon shrub as a deciduous screen, or as a specimen or accent at the edges of woods or next to a pond.

Growing Tips Plant in full sun or partial shade in moist, fertile well-drained acidic soil. Once established, it tolerates drought. For good berry set, plant one male close to a group of females. Plants become open-crowned in dense shade.

More Native Alternatives *Aronia melanocarpa*, black chokeberry (page 84)—Newfoundland to Ontario, south to Georgia and Arkansas. *Ilex verticillata*, winterberry holly (page 98)—Nova Scotia to Minnesota, south to Florida and Arkansas. *Neviusia alabamensis*, Alabama snow-wreath (page 129)—Mississippi, Alabama, Georgia, Tennessee and Arkansas. *Viburnum nudum* var. *nudum*, smooth witherod (page 128)—Massachusetts south to Florida, west to Texas. *Viburnum opulus* var. *americanum*, American highbush cranberry (page 126)—Newfoundland and south to British Columbia, Indiana and Washington. For a list of additional native shrubs, visit www.bbg.org/nativealternatives.

Attributes at a Glance
Ilex montana

Medium to large shrub with a broad crown

6 to 12 feet tall and wide

Narrowly oval green foliage

Brilliant red berries

Vase-shaped winter silhouette

Invasive Shrub
Viburnum opulus var. *opulus*
European Cranberry Bush

Current Invaded Range: Nova Scotia and Michigan, south to Virginia and Iowa

---

Native Alternative
Viburnum opulus var. *americanum*
Highbush Cranberry

Native Habitat and Range Swamps, low woods, and stream edges from

Attributes at a Glance
Viburnum opulus var. *americanum*

Upright, large shrub

8 to 12 feet tall and wide

Large, domed lacecap flowers in late spring and early summer

Rich green, maplelike foliage

Brilliant red fleshy fruit

Deep burgundy autumn color

Coarse, open winter silhouette

Newfoundland, south to British Columbia, Indiana, and Washington

Hardiness Range Zones 2 to 8

Ornamental Attributes and Uses This upright, multistemmed large shrub grows to eight feet tall and has a slightly irregular branching pattern, especially when grown in partial shade. Elegant, white lacecaps festoon this magnificent shrub in early summer, accented by deeply lobed foliage that turns rich wine-red in autumn. Edible marble-sized scarlet fruits create a stunning show. They color while the foliage is still green, and the contrast is dazzling. Use highbush cranberry as a screen or hedge, in mass plantings, or in large borders.

Growing Tips Plant in rich, evenly moist soil in full sun or shade. Plants in shade will not flower as heavily as those with more light. Highbush cranberry is easy to grow and carefree, with moderate drought tolerance once established.

Related Alternatives *Viburnum edule*, squashberry, ranges farther north, and its three-lobed, toothed leaves are smaller; the flower heads lack the sterile flowers that make highbush cranberry so showy. The bright red fruit is quite tasty and is widely used by native peoples in the Pacific Northwest. It is found from Newfoundland and Labrador and Alaska, south to Pennsylvania, Iowa, and Washington.

Native Alternative
Sambucus racemosa var. *racemosa* (*pubens*)
Scarlet Elder

Native Habitat and Range Open woods, woodland borders, streambanks, and roadsides from Newfoundland to British Columbia, south to North Carolina, Minnesota, and California

Hardiness Range Zones 3 to 7

Ornamental Attributes and Uses Showy in flower and fruit, this beauty has elongated clusters of creamy-white flowers in early to midspring on zigzag twigs. Flowers quickly give way to scarlet berries in summer, which show off beautifully against the pinnately divided leaves, deep green in summer, yellow in fall. Use this four- to eight-foot (sometimes to ten feet) upright arching shrub in wildlife borders, screens, or in drifts at the edges of woods.

Growing Tips Plant in evenly moist, humus-rich neutral to acidic soil in sun to partial shade. It tolerates moderate drought but may burn in strong afternoon sun where temperatures are high. Prune to maintain an even shape; cut back hard to encourage fresh growth.

Related Alternative *Sambucus canadensis*, elderberry, is larger and more graceful, to 12 feet tall and wide, and grows from Nova Scotia to Manitoba, south to Florida and Mexico.

More Native Alternatives For a list of additional native shrubs, visit www.bbg.org/nativealternatives.

Attributes at a Glance
Sambucus racemosa var. *racemosa* (*pubens*)

Upright arching form

4 to 8 feet tall and wide

Clusters of white flowers

Scarlet berries in summer

Yellow autumn color

Invasive Shrub
Viburnum lantana • Wayfaring Tree
Current Invaded Range: Maine and Michigan, south to Maryland and Illinois

Native Alternative
Viburnum nudum var. *nudum*
Smooth Witherod

Native Habitat and Range Low woods, swamps, edges of marshes, and streamsides from Massachusetts south to Florida, west to Texas

Hardiness Range Zones 4 to 8

Ornamental Attributes and Uses The elegant form of this preeminent shrub is an upright oval to broad mound that can reach 18 feet (but 6 to 9 feet tall and wide is more common). Domed clusters of creamy-white flowers show off against glossy, deep green oval foliage in late spring and are followed by fleshy berries that turn from green to pink and finally waxy blue. The autumn foliage is flaming scarlet to burgundy and persists for nearly a month. Use smooth witherod as a hedge, foundation shrub, in mass plantings, or in mixed borders.

Growing Tips Plant in rich, evenly moist soil in full sun or partial shade. This shrub is sensitive to prolonged drought but tolerates soggy soils and periodic flooding. Remove old stems every two to three years as needed. Birds relish the berries.

Attributes at a Glance
Viburnum nudum var. *nudum*

Broad, rounded form

6 to 9 feet tall and wide

Domed clusters of creamy-white flowers in late spring

Glossy, deep green foliage

Blue berries that attract birds

Native Alternative
Neviusia alabamensis
Alabama Snow-Wreath

Native Habitat and Range Open woods and rocky cliffs in Mississippi, Alabama, Georgia, Tennessee, and Arkansas

Hardiness Range Zones 4 to 8

Ornamental Attributes and Uses This elegant and underutilized shrub offers billowing sprays of snow-white flowers like powder puffs and pointed, toothed oval leaves that are decoratively pleated. The autumn foliage is rich yellow, and the winter twigs are chestnut-colored with exfoliating bark. Use Alabama snow-wreath in a shrub border, as a hedge or screen, or in a mixed border. It is also good for massing on a bank or at the edge of the woods.

Growing Tips Plant in moist, humus-rich soil in full sun or partial shade. Once established, Alabama snow-wreath is drought tolerant; it also takes deep shade but will bloom sparsely. It spreads by runners that are easily removed for propagation or to limit the plant's size. Cut back old canes every two to three years to keep the plant vigorous and graceful. Shape as necessary; prune to the ground if necessary to encourage fresh growth.

More Native Alternatives *Clethra alnifolia*, summersweet (page 63)—Maine south to Florida, and west to Texas. *Itea virginica*, Virginia sweet-spire (page 60)—New Jersey and Missouri, south to Florida and Louisiana. *Lindera benzoin*, spicebush (page 99)—Maine and Ontario, south to Florida and Texas. *Viburnum nudum* var. *cassinoides*, witherod (page 108)—Newfoundland and Michigan, south in the mountains to Georgia. For a list of additional native shrubs, visit www.bbg.org/nativealternatives.

SHRUBS

Attributes at a Glance
Neviusia alabamensis

Upright, vase shaped shrub

4 to 6 feet tall and 6 to 8 feet wide

Foamy white flowers along the stems

Pleated leaves that turn yellow in autumn

Invasive Shrub
Vitex agnus-castus • Chaste Tree
Current Invaded Range: Pennsylvania and Oregon, south to
Florida, Texas, and California

Native Alternative
Aesculus parviflora
Bottle-Brush Buckeye

Native Habitat and Range Open
woods, floodplains, and woodland edges
in central Alabama and adjacent Georgia

Hardiness Range Zones 4 to 9

Attributes at a Glance
Aesculus parviflora

Broad to rounded shrub

8 feet tall and 10 feet wide

Upright spikes of fuzzy white
flowers in summer

Palmately compound leaves

Yellow autumn foliage

Large, leathery fruit

Coarse, eccentric winter silhouette

Ornamental Attributes and Uses
Sweetly fragrant candles of long, fuzzy
white flowers open on erect, one- to
two-foot spikes over several weeks in
high summer. The palmately divided
leaves have five to seven deep green,
oblong leaflets that taper at both ends.
The autumn color is yellow to gold.
Shiny brown nuts are carried inside
pods with leathery husks. Use this shrub
as a specimen, hedge, or in a border.

Growing Tips Plant in rich, evenly
moist soil in full sun or partial shade. It
is tolerant of alkaline conditions. Slow
to reach maturity, it nevertheless
becomes quite large, so plan accordingly.

Related Alternative *Aesculus pavia*, red
buckeye, is larger and coarser, to 25 feet
tall and wide with deep red flowers in
early summer. It grows in North Carolina
to Illinois, south to Florida and Texas.

Native Alternative
Oxydendrum arboreum
Sourwood

Native Habitat and Range Open woods, edges of clearings, rocky outcroppings, and roadsides from Pennsylvania to Indiana, south to Florida and Louisiana

Hardiness Range Zones 5 to 9

Ornamental Attributes and Uses In high summer, sourwood's pendent, branched clusters of scented bell-shaped flowers delight bees and other nectar aficionados. The narrowly oval foliage is lustrous, deep green in summer and turns to flame in autumn. Use sourwood as a dazzling specimen, in borders, as a screen, or at the edge of a woodland for accent.

Growing Tips Plant in moist, humus-rich acidic soil in full sun or light shade. This is a tough, drought-tolerant tree. It is slow to establish and slow growing under ideal conditions. In marginal sites, growth is at a snail's pace. Transplant it balled and burlapped in spring, or try a small, containerized plant with the potting mix mostly removed.

More Native Alternatives *Chionanthus virginicus*, fringe tree (page 43)—New Jersey, Kentucky, and Missouri, south to Florida and Texas. *Clethra alnifolia*, summersweet (page 63)—Maine, south to Florida, and west to Texas. *Fothergilla major*, mountain witch alder (page 58)—North Carolina to Georgia and Alabama *Morella (Myrica) cerifera*,

southern wax myrtle (page 81)—New Jersey, south to Florida, west to the lower Mississippi Valley and Texas. For a list of additional native shrubs, visit www.bbg.org/nativealternatives.

Attributes at a Glance
Oxydendrum arboreum

Upright rounded to columnar tree

15 to 40 feet tall and 6 to 15 feet wide

Pendent clusters of bell-shaped summer flowers

Narrowly oval foliage

Flaming autumn color

Irregular winter silhouette

Invasive Vine
Akebia quinata • Five-Leaf Akebia

Current Invaded Range: Massachusetts to Michigan, south to Georgia and Louisiana

---

Native Alternative
Parthenocissus quinquefolia
Virginia Creeper

Native Habitat and Range Woodland borders, clearings, meadows, and road-

sides from Quebec, Manitoba, and Utah, south to Florida and Texas

Hardiness Range Zones 3 to 9

Ornamental Attributes and Uses Virginia creeper's fiery-red to burgundy foliage sets off its wax-covered indigo berries to perfection. Add the cerise stalks on the berries and a finer autumn display you will seldom see from any vine. Plants color in early autumn and often drop their foliage while the berries are still fresh. The handlike leaves have five oval to lance-shaped, coarsely toothed leaflets in deep, lustrous green. Use the vine as a screen on a fence, over an arbor, or climbing up a tree.

Growing Tips Plant in rich, moist soil in sun or partial shade. The best berry set and autumn color develop in sun. Virginia creeper is drought tolerant but may defoliate early. In deep shade, the vines will scramble over the ground in search of a host upon which to climb from the shadows, making it useful as a groundcover. Virginia creeper can reach 50 feet or more as it scales trees, but it is easily pruned into a well-behaved garden denizen. Holdfasts may damage mortar, so use it on walls with caution.

Attributes at a Glance
Parthenocissus quinquefolia

Climbing vine with holdfasts

Palmate leaves with five leaflets

Smoky-blue berries on red stalks

Flaming autumn color

Native Alternative
Campsis radicans
Trumpet Vine

Native Habitat and Range Woodland borders, clearings, meadows, and roadside fences and trees from Pennsylvania to Missouri, south to Florida and Texas

Hardiness Range Zones 4 to 9

Ornamental Attributes and Uses Brilliant orange trumpets, clustered at the drooping tips of this gorgeous native vine, sound the arrival of summer. The pinnately divided leaves have 9 to 11 leaflets with ragged, toothed edges and quilted surfaces. The autumn color is yellow. Both beloved and despised, trumpet vine ranks among the most beautiful of our vines, but it is fast growing and may be aggressive. Plants form huge trunks as they scale trees and fenceposts, but they are easily controlled in the garden with pruning. Use it as a screen on a fence or let it clamber over an arbor or climb up a tree. This showy vine can reach 40 feet or more as it scales trees.

Growing Tips Plant in rich, moist soil in sun or partial shade. Trumpet vine flowers best in full sun. Prune it heavily as needed to control size and spread.

More Native Alternatives *Lonicera sempervirens*, trumpet honeysuckle (page 141)—Connecticut to Nebraska, south to Florida and Texas For a list of additional native plants, visit www.bbg.org/nativealternatives.

Attributes at a Glance
Campsis radicans
Climbing vine with holdfasts

Brilliant orange flowers

Pinnately divided leaves

VINES

Invasive Vine
Ampelopsis brevipedunculata • Porcelain Berry
Current Invaded Range: New Hampshire to Wisconsin, south to Georgia and Mississippi

Native Alternative
Ampelopsis arborea
Peppervine

Native Habitat and Range Low woods, bottomlands, swamps, and roadsides from Maryland to Missouri, south to Florida, Texas, and New Mexico

Hardiness Range Zones 7 to 9

Ornamental Attributes and Uses The chameleon berries of peppervine change from green to white to red and finally to black. The bipinnate leaves have pointed, deeply toothed, or lobed margins and are deep rich green in summer. They turn orange to red in autumn. This climbing vine grows 15 to 30 feet and can be aggressive in rich, open soils.

Growing Tips Plant in average to rich, sandy or loamy soil in full sun or partial shade. This vine colors and fruits best in sun but will tolerate considerable shade. It also tolerates wet soil and mild drought. Prune as necessary to control shape and limit spread.

More Native Alternatives *Lonicera sempervirens*, trumpet honeysuckle (page 141)—Connecticut to Nebraska, south to Florida and Texas. *Parthenocissus quinquefolia*, Virginia creeper (page 132)—Quebec, Manitoba, and Utah, south to Florida and Texas For a list of additional native plants, visit www.bbg.org/nativealternatives.

Attributes at a Glance
Ampelopsis arborea

Climbing vine with tendrils

Ferny foliage

Black berries

Orange autumn color

Invasive Vine
Celastrus orbiculatus • Oriental Bittersweet

Current Invaded Range: New England to Minnesota, south to Georgia and Texas

Native Alternative
Celastrus scandens
American Bittersweet

Native Habitat and Range Open woods, woodland borders, shrub thickets, and fencerows from New Brunswick to Manitoba, south to Florida and Texas

Hardiness Range Zones 3 to 8

Ornamental Attributes and Uses When compared with Oriental bittersweet, this native American species is the critic's choice. Its red-orange fruits are more than twice the size of the Asian species', and since this is the one asset bittersweet has to offer, it is a wonder *Celastrus orbiculatus* was ever cultivated. The fruits of American bittersweet are carried in dense, terminal racemes rather than small axillary clusters. Its climbing to twining stems are clothed in broad oval leaves with elongated tips, and they turn clear yellow in autumn before dropping, allowing the berries to show to best advantage. This vigorous and robust vine grows 20 feet or considerably more if not pruned.

Growing Tips Plant in average to rich, evenly moist soil in full sun or light shade. The plant tolerates abuse, including heat, drought, and even salt. Only the female of this dioecious plant bears fruit. To assure pollination, plant a male as well. Though not as rampant as its Asian counterpart, American bittersweet is a large vine that benefits from pruning to control its spread. Prune it as needed before new growth begins.

More Native Alternatives
Parthenocissus quinquefolia, Virginia creeper (page 132)—Quebec, Manitoba, and Utah, south to Florida and Texas. For a list of additional native plants, visit www.bbg.org/nativealternatives.

Attributes at a Glance
Celastrus scandens

Climbing vine

Rounded foliage

Large red-orange berries

Yellow autumn color

VINES

Invasive Vine
Hedera helix • English Ivy

Current Invaded Range: New York and Michigan, south to Florida and Texas; Pacific Northwest, south through California

---

Native Alternative
Pachysandra procumbens
Allegheny Spurge

Native Habitat and Range Rich deciduous or mixed coniferous woods and coves in acidic soil from North Carolina

and Kentucky, south to Florida and Louisiana

Hardiness Range Zones 4 to 9

Ornamental Attributes and Uses This sublime native groundcover has whorls of broad, satiny evergreen oval leaves with blunt terminal lobes at the tips of the decumbent stems. Unlike the familiar Japanese spurge, the flowers bloom in the center of the leafy clumps in early spring. The new foliage emerges bright sea-green mottled with pale blotches. In autumn, the frost brings out deep purple-blue shades in the background with silvery mottling. Use Allegheny spurge as a groundcover under shrubs and flowering trees or in rock gardens. The multistemmed clumps rise only up to about a foot high but form carpets three to six feet wide.

Growing Tips Plant in moist, humus-rich acidic soil in light to full shade. The plant tolerates dense shade but must have consistent moisture for best growth. You can remove old growth after flowering, but the fresh foliage neatly obscures the old, so cleanup is not necessary. The plants spread slowly at first, but within a few years they form broad, rounded clumps. Divide the clumps in spring before new growth emerges.

Attributes at a Glance
Pachysandra procumbens

Dense, slow-spreading groundcover

Paddle-shaped evergreen leaves

Fuzzy spring flowers

Rich winter foliage color

Native Alternative
Xanthorhiza simplicissima
Shrub Yellowroot

Native Habitat and Range Rich woods and stream edges, mostly in the Appalachians from New York, south to Florida and Louisiana

Hardiness Range Zones 3 to 9

Ornamental Attributes and Uses This stoloniferous shrub forms extensive colonies four to eight feet wide with upright, sparsely branched stems one to three feet tall. Chains of tiny yellow or brownish-purple stars dangle from the tips of the naked stems in early spring. As the flowers fade, the finely divided leaves with ragged, lobed leaflets emerge in whorls at the tips of the stems. Green seed capsules add summer interest. The fall foliage is yellow to bronze. Use it as an understory shrub in woodland plantings.

Growing Tips Plant in consistently moist, humus-rich acidic soil in light to full shade. Shrub yellowroot is easy to grow and remarkably cold hardy. In northern zones, snow cover helps the stems withstand bitter cold. In some winters, the stems may be killed to the snow line or ground level. Remove any dead stems down to live growth in spring. Stray stems are easy to remove to control spread or for propagation.

Attributes at a Glance
Xanthorhiza simplicissima

Small deciduous colonizing shrub

Subtle chains of small starlike flowers

Lacy, divided foliage

Yellow to bronze autumn color

Native Alternative
Gaultheria shallon
Salal

Native Habitat and Range

Woodlands, clearings, and rocky slopes from Alaska and British Columbia, south to northern California

Hardiness Range Zones 6 to 9

Ornamental Attributes and Uses

Beloved in the garden and in flower arrangements, the lustrous evergreen, heart-shaped leaves of salal are an icon of the Northwest. This ubiquitous, versatile shrub forms a dense mound of arching stems tipped with drooping racemes of white or pink-stained bells carried on bright red stalks. The flowers give way to blueberry-sized fruit eaten by birds. Clumps increase by creeping stems and can form dense, broad tangles one to five feet tall and three to eight feet wide. Use salal in mass plantings, as a groundcover, or in pots.

Growing Tips Plant in evenly moist, humus-rich acidic soil in light to full shade. Salal tolerates full sun, but its foliage is easily bleached or burned. It is ideally suited for moist shade, where it grows enthusiastically, often to the point of aggressiveness. Plant it only in areas that can accommodate its spread, or place it in a deep, bottomless container for control. The trailing stems are easily removed to keep the clump in check when it spreads beyond its allotted space. Renew entire clumps by shearing all the stems to the ground.

Attributes at a Glance
Gaultheria shallon

Low-mounding or groundcover shrub

Racemes of drooping bell-shaped flowers

Leathery evergreen leaves

Blue-black berries

Native Alternative
Mahonia nervosa
Longleaf Mahonia

Native Habitat and Range Open, often dry, rocky slopes and forests from southern British Columbia, south to California and northern Idaho

Hardiness Range Zones 5 to 8

Ornamental Attributes and Uses This spreading to upright, suckering, evergreen groundcover shrub has pinnate leaves that resemble holly leaves. It grows one foot tall (rarely, two) and two to four feet wide. The spring foliage is tinged with bronze-red before darkening to emerald and assumes hints of reddish purple in fall and winter. Electric yellow flowers in erect racemes in late winter or early spring are followed by abundant edible purple-blue fruit in fall. Use this shrub underneath shade and flowering trees and for groundcover, mass plantings in naturalized areas, and hedgerows.

Growing Tips Grow in moist, well-drained soil rich in acidic humus in light to full shade. This versatile plant tolerates dry soil, dense shade, root competition, and airborne salt. Provide supplemental water until the plant is established. Prune to remove suckers if desired. Mahonias require pollination by the same or a compatible species to set fruit. Renew entire clumps by shearing all stems to the ground.

Related Alternative *Mahonia repens*, creeping mahonia, is more compact. It grows to one foot tall and forms tight

patches two to four feet wide. It is found from North Dakota to British Columbia, south to New Mexico and California.

More Native Alternatives *Arctostaphylos uva-ursi*, bearberry (page 87)—Labrador and British Columbia, south to Virginia, New Mexico, and California. For a list of additional native plants, visit www.bbg.org/nativealternatives.

Attributes at a Glance
Mahonia nervosa

Evergreen groundcover shrub

Reddish-purple fall color

Bright yellow flowers

Purple-blue berries

Invasive Vine
Jasminum dichotomum, J. fluminense • Jasmine
Current Invaded Range: Florida

Native Alternative
Gelsemium sempervirens
Carolina Jessamine

Native Habitat and Range Low, open woods, savannas, pond margins, and hedgerows from Virginia and Arkansas, south to Florida, Texas, and Louisiana

Hardiness Range Zones 7 to 10

Ornamental Attributes and Uses The fragrant yellow bells of Carolina jessamine are a sure sign of spring in the South. It produces a profusion of flowers for several months, and the glossy, pointed oval leaves remain attractive all year, taking on a bronzy patina in fall. Unpruned, the vine climbs to 15 feet or more. Use it on fences, to cascade over bowers, or to frame doorways.

Growing Tips Plant in rich, evenly moist soil in sun or light shade. Lush growth and best flower production depend on even moisture and fertile soil. The vine varies in hardiness. In the northern reaches of its range, buy stock from local sources.

Related Alternative *Gelsemium rankinii*, swamp jessamine, lacks the fragrance of Carolina jessamine and has smaller flowers. It blooms in fall and sporadically into spring, nicely extending the bloom season when the two are combined. It is native from North Carolina south to Florida and Louisiana.

More Native Alternatives For a list of additional native plants, visit www.bbg.org/nativealternatives.

Attributes at a Glance
Gelsemium sempervirens

Climbing evergreen vine

Fragrant, long-lasting yellow flowers

Pointed, glossy leaves

Invasive Vine
Lonicera japonica • Japanese Honeysuckle
Current Invaded Range: New England, Wisconsin, and California, south to Florida, Texas, and Arizona

Native Alternative
Lonicera sempervirens
Scarlet Honeysuckle

Native Habitat and Range Low open woods, woodland margins, and roadsides from Connecticut to Nebraska, south to Florida and Texas

Hardiness Range Zones 4 to 8

Ornamental Attributes and Uses A twining vine 10 to 12 feet long, with succulent young stems that age to brown with exfoliating bark, this is an aristocrat among native vines, valued for its prolific flowers and decorative sea-green foliage. The leaves are opposite at the nodes, but below the flower clusters they form a shield-shaped ring around the stem. Small red berries add a color note in summer and autumn.

Growing Tips Plant in evenly moist, sandy or loamy soil in full sun or partial shade. The plant blooms freely all season given ample light. It may be rangy but seldom grows vigorously enough to become a nuisance. Trim scarlet honeysuckle as needed to control its size and promote continued flowering. Powdery mildew may cover the foliage in hot, dry weather, but it has little effect on the plant's health. Spray it with baking soda mixed with water for control.

Related Alternatives *Lonicera ciliosa* (orange honeysuckle), found in cooler regions from British Columbia, south to Montana and California, is a similar vining species with red-orange to cerise flowers. It does not tolerate excessive

heat. *Lonicera dioica*, limber honeysuckle, is a similar shrubby to vining species with yellow to orange flowers. It is found from Nova Scotia to Saskatchewan, south to North Carolina and Oklahoma.

Attributes at a Glance
Lonicera sempervirens

Well-behaved deciduous vine

Scarlet flowers

Small red berries

Gray-green leaves

Exfoliating winter bark

VINES

Native Alternative
Clematis columbiana
Rock Clematis

Native Habitat and Range Mountain slopes and rock outcroppings from Manitoba to British Columbia, south to Texas and Oregon

Hardiness Range Zones 4 to 7

Ornamental Attributes and Uses Pendent flowers with four petallike

Attributes at a Glance
Clematis columbiana

Climbing vine

Nodding blue-purple flowers

Plumed seed heads

Yellow autumn color

sepals in rich blue-purple grace the rambling to climbing stems of this showy vine in summer. The ternately compound leaves with pointed, narrowly oval leaflets turn yellow in autumn. The flowers give way to powder puffs of seeds with long plumes. A mature vine may reach six to eight feet. Use it as a groundcover or train it on a fence or lattice.

Growing Tips Plant in moist but well-drained, neutral, humus-rich soil in full sun to light shade. This clematis scrambles over rocks and shrubs but can be trained up suitable supports. Prune after flowering, as this species flowers on year-old wood.

Related Alternatives *Clematis texensis*, scarlet clematis, is a Texas endemic with nodding, tubular red flowers with flared tips to the sepals. *Clematis viorna*, leatherflower, is a wide-ranging vine with quilted, trifoliate leaves and tubular purple flowers throughout the summer. It is found from Pennsylvania to Missouri, south to Georgia and Arkansas.

More Native Alternatives *Campsis radicans*, trumpet vine (page 133)— Pennsylvania to Missouri, south to Florida and Texas. *Gelsemium sempervirens*, Carolina jessamine (page 140)— Virginia and Arkansas, south to Florida, Texas, and Louisiana. *Parthenocissus quinquefolia*, Virginia creeper (page 132)—Quebec, Manitoba, and Utah, south to Florida and Texas. For a list of additional native plants, visit www.bbg.org/nativealternatives.

Invasive Vine
Lygodium japonicum • Japanese Climbing Fern
Current Invaded Range: North Carolina and Oklahoma, south to Florida and Texas (also Hawaii and Puerto Rico)

Native Alternative
Lygodium palmatum
American Climbing Fern

Native Habitat and Range Low open woods, sandy clearings, streambanks, and bog margins from Maine to Ohio, south to Georgia and Mississippi

Hardiness Range Zones 4 to 8

Ornamental Attributes and Uses The delicate wiry stems of American climbing fern twine through shrubs and up other forms of support, displaying unique, hand-shaped fronds with five to seven fingerlike lobes. The small fertile fronds are borne at the stem tips. Use this vine in naturalized gardens or in bog gardens. It may reach 5 to 15 feet.

Growing Tips Plant in moist, acidic sand or humus in full sun or partial shade—this plant tends to die out in too much shade. This species is difficult to establish and difficult to keep thriving, though when happy it grows vigorously and is quite attractive.

More Native Alternatives *Gelsemium sempervirens*, Carolina jessamine (page 140)—Virginia and Arkansas, south to Florida, Texas, and Louisiana. For a list of additional native plants, visit www.bbg.org/nativealternatives.

Attributes at a Glance
Lygodium palmatum
Twining vine

Hand-shaped evergreen leaves

Invasive Vine
Merremia tuberosa • Wood Rose
Current Invaded Range: Florida (also Hawaii)

Native Alternative
Ipomoea pes-caprae
Railroad Vine

Native Habitat and Range Dunes and sandy flats from South Carolina to Florida and Texas (also Hawaii and Puerto Rico)

Hardiness Range Zones 9 to 10

Ornamental Attributes and Uses This huge trailing herbaceous vine can scramble 100 feet or more, rooting as it snakes over dunes and beach debris just above the high-tide mark. Its large, paddlelike glossy leaves are folded along the midrib and have a depressed tip, so they look a little like hoofs. Up-facing, tubular lavender flowers open with the sun and wither by noon. The seedpods split to release rounded seeds. This vine is excellent for dune stabilization and erosion control, as well as in ornamental settings large enough to support it visually. The leaves and roots are edible but may be toxic in large quantities.

Growing Tips Plant in sandy or loamy, well-drained soil in full sun. Railroad vine tolerates drought, heat, and salt. Prune it as needed to control the spread.

More Native Alternatives For a list of additional native plants, visit www.bbg.org/nativealternatives.

Attributes at a Glance
Ipomoea pes-caprae

Trailing herbaceous perennial vine

Large spatula-shaped leaves

Lavender flowers

Invasive Vine
Wisteria floribunda • Japanese Wisteria;
W. sinensis • Chinese Wisteria

Current Invaded Range: New Jersey and Indiana, south to Florida and Louisiana

Native Alternative
Wisteria frutescens (macrostachya)
American Wisteria

Native Habitat and Range
Bottomlands, streambanks, swamps, and woodland borders in Virginia and Missouri, south to Florida and Texas

Hardiness Range Zones 4 to 9

Ornamental Attributes and Uses
Wisteria is a southern garden icon, grown for its gorgeous, fragrant chains of richly colored flowers. Though not as dramatic (or as rampant) as its Asian cousins, the wild native wisteria is a sweetly scented, climbing vine with smooth, gray-brown stems clothed in pinnately divided leaves bearing 7 to 11 pointed oval leaflets. Erect to pendent racemes of purple-blue flowers open in late spring and early summer. It also flowers erratically later in the season. After the flowers fade, inflated, knobby beanlike pods develop and ripen in autumn. The foliage turns clear yellow to golden in autumn.

Growing Tips
Plant in moist, humus-rich soil in full sun to partial shade. This vine will grow in full shade but does not flower as heavily. Unlike the Asian species, which can be shy to bloom when young, American wisteria begins blooming when the vine is only a few feet long.

Related Alternative
Wisteria macrostachya, Kentucky wisteria, is sometimes sold as a separate species.

Attributes at a Glance
Wisteria frutescens

Climbing vine

Purple-blue to white flowers

Pinnately divided leaves

Yellow autumn foliage

VINES

Invasive Plant
Aegopodium podagraria • Bishop's Weed
Current Invaded Range: Eastern and central North America; Pacific Northwest

Native Alternative
Asarum canadense
Canada Wild Ginger

Native Habitat and Range Deciduous or, rarely, mixed coniferous forests, bottomlands, and slopes from New Brunswick to Ontario, south to North Carolina, Alabama, and Arkansas

Hardiness Range Zones 3 to 9

Attributes at a Glance
Asarum canadense

Perennial herbaceous groundcover

Heart-shaped, satiny leaves

Brick-red flowers in spring

Ornamental Attributes and Uses

Canada wild ginger is a fast-spreading groundcover with satiny, broadly heart-shaped deciduous leaves up to eight inches wide. The reddish-brown flowers with long-pointed lobes open just as the leaves are expanding but are quickly obscured by the foliage. The hidden flowers are pollinated by fungus gnats. All parts of the plant have a pungent, gingerlike fragrance. Use as a groundcover under trees and shrubs or in woodland gardens. Plants stand up to a foot tall and spread to form mats two to three feet wide.

Growing Tips Wild gingers are carefree garden dwellers. Plant them in consistently moist, neutral, humus-rich soil in partial to full shade. Canada wild ginger is the only species that tolerates limy soils. It spreads rapidly to form a dense, neat groundcover of exceptional beauty. Divide overgrown clumps in early spring as the leaves are emerging or as they go dormant in fall. Start fresh seed inside, or sow outside when ripe in midsummer. Seedlings germinate quickly, but the plants develop slowly. They will freely self-sow in the garden.

Related Alternative *Asarum caudatum*, long-tailed ginger, is the western North American counterpart of this species, found from the western slope of the Montana Rockies, west to the coastal forests from British Columbia to California. It has slightly smaller, quilted leaves and flowers with long, twisted tails on each petal.

Native Alternative
Aralia nudicaulis
Wild Sarsaparilla

Native Habitat and Range Deciduous or mixed coniferous woods; also dry open woods and savannas from Newfoundland to British Columbia, south to Virginia, in the mountains to Georgia, and Colorado

Hardiness Range Zones 3 to 8

Ornamental Attributes and Uses Sarsaparilla forms open colonies from fleshy, creeping rhizomes noted for their pungent aroma. Sarsaparilla beer was once made from these rhizomes but now comes from artificial flavorings. The leaves emerge with a whorl of three pinnately compound segments atop a slender stalk 1 to 1½ feet tall. The leaves are shiny and tinged with red as they emerge but fade to green as they expand. The flower structures are also arranged in a triad. The small green flowers, produced in late spring or early summer, are aggregated into spherical clusters about the size of a golf ball. Use sarsaparilla as an open groundcover under shrubs and trees or in naturalized settings.

Growing Tips Plant sarsaparilla in average to rich, moist soil in light to full shade. Established plants tolerate dry soil with ease.

More Native Alternatives For a list of additional native herbaceous plants, visit www.bbg.org/nativealternatives.

Attributes at a Glance
Aralia nudicaulis

Rhizomatous perennial groundcover

Deep green, divided foliage

Yellow autumn color

HERBACEOUS PLANTS

Invasive Plant
Carpobrotus edulis • Ice Plant
Current Invaded Range: Florida and California

Native Alternative
Glandularia (Verbena) canadensis
Rose Verbena

Native Habitat and Range Open woods, clearings, waste places, and roadsides from Pennsylvania and Illinois, south to Florida and Texas

Hardiness Range Zones 5 to 10

Ornamental Attributes and Uses Rose verbena has 8- to 18-inch trailing wiry stems with sharply toothed and lobed oval leaves. The flat terminal flower clusters elongate into short spikes as the showy purple, rose, or white flowers

open. Use rose verbena in borders, mass plantings, or for erosion control.

Growing Tips Plant in well-drained sandy or loamy soil in full sun to light shade. Rose verbena is a tough heat- and drought-tolerant perennial that blooms tirelessly during the summer. It spreads quickly to form a showy groundcover. When blooming wanes, shear plants back to encourage fresh growth and flowers.

Related Alternatives *Glandularia bipinnatifida*, Dakota mock vervain, has finely cut foliage and flattened clusters of lavender-purple to rose flowers and is found on prairies and in open plains, rocky hillsides, and canyons from Wisconsin to California, south to Georgia and Mexico. *Verbena neomexicana*, hillside verbena, is an upright species with purple flowers in spring and autumn. It grows in open areas, plains, deserts, and canyons from Texas to California.

Attributes at a Glance
Glandularia canadensis

Trailing perennial from a fibrous-rooted crown

Showy purple, rose, or white flowers

Deeply lobed opposite leaves

Native Alternative
Zauschneria californica
California Fuchsia, Hummingbird Trumpet

Native Habitat and Range Scrub and lightly shaded stream edges from California to Baja

Hardiness Range Zones 7 (with protection) to 10

Ornamental Attributes and Uses The brilliant scarlet tubular flowers of wild fuchsias have flat faces with four notched petals and protruding stamens. An inflated four-lobed sheath covers the tube, giving the impression of eight petals. Flowering begins in high summer and continues until hard frost. The semievergreen, lance-shaped to narrowly oval foliage is softly hairy to woolly and clothes the upright to sprawling stems, which radiate from a dense, suckering crown and may grow to three feet tall. The plants form large, dense colonies to three feet wide under favorable conditions. Use them atop walls, in rock gardens, xeriscapes, and gravel beds to add months of carefree color as well as erosion control.

Growing Tips Plant in average to rich, well-drained soil in full sun or light shade. California fuchsia is extremely drought tolerant once established, though it blooms more reliably and fully with even moisture. After frost, cut the stems back and reshape the plant, leaving several buds per stem on the woody crown. New growth begins when the weather warms. This plant spreads from runners and may need to be checked, especially when used in small gardens.

More Native Alternatives For a list of additional native herbaceous plants, visit www.bbg.org/nativealternatives.

Attributes at a Glance
Zauschneria californica

Low, spreading shrub

Flaming red-orange flowers attractive to hummingbirds

Softly hairy foliage

Invasive Plant
Centaurea cyanus • Bachelor's Button
Current Invaded Range: Northwest; watch elsewhere

Native Alternative
Erigeron speciosus
Showy Fleabane

Native Habitat and Range Open woods, meadows, and roadsides from Alberta and British Columbia, south to the Black Hills, New Mexico, and Oregon

Hardiness Range Zones 4 to 7

Ornamental Attributes and Uses Showy fleabane is a wide-ranging and variable species growing from 6 to 20 inches tall and one to two feet wide, depending on geographical origin and fertility of the soil. A blooming machine with two-inch blue, purple, or white daisies in early and midsummer, later at higher elevations, it forms a basal rosette and multiple flowering stems from a thick taproot. Use it at the front of beds, as a groundcover, or in meadow plantings with clumping rather than turf-forming grasses.

Growing Tips Plant in average to rich, evenly moist soil in full sun or light shade. Plants self-seed freely in open ground. Avoid crowding it in with taller plants, as it resents competition.

Related Alternatives *Erigeron compositus*, cut-leafed daisy, is a montane to alpine species with white, pink, or blue flowers on compact stems to a foot tall over deeply dissected foliage. It is found from Alaska, south through the Rockies, and west to California. *Erigeron peregrinus*, subalpine fleabane, grows from the Rockies to the Coast Range and has blue flowers on one- to two-foot stems.

Attributes at a Glance
Erigeron speciosus

Low, clumping perennial

Flat blue flowers

Long bloom season

Native Alternative
Polemonium pulcherrimum
Jacob's Ladder

Native Habitat and Range Open woods, meadows, and roadsides from Alaska, south throughout the Rockies, west to the Cascades

Hardiness Range Zones 2 to 7

Ornamental Attributes and Uses Jacob's ladder is noted for its distinctive, pinnately divided leaves and sky-blue to blue-violet flowers carried in loose clusters atop succulent stems. It has five overlapping petals that form a cup or shallow saucer, depending on the species. The plant grows from a crown of fibrous roots. Use it for informal and formal gardens alike and in masses under shrubs or airy flowering trees.

Growing Tips Plant in evenly moist, humus-rich soil in full sun or partial shade. In warm regions, partial shade is a must to keep the plant from burning—it does not tolerate the heat of Zones 8 or warmer. After flowering, cut the bloom stalks to the ground; the foliage will remain attractive all season. This plant seldom needs division.

More Native Alternatives *Symphyotrichum* (*Aster*) *cordifolium,* common wood aster (page 152)— Nova Scotia to Ontario, south to Georgia and Kansas. For a list of additional native herbaceous plants, visit www.bbg.org/nativealternatives.

Attributes at a Glance
Polemonium pulcherrimum

Clumping, multistemmed perennial

Terminal clusters of blue flowers

Fernlike basal foliage

Invasive Plant
Cichorium intybus • Chicory
Current Invaded Range: Most of North America

Native Alternative
Symphyotrichum (Aster) cordifolium
Common Wood Aster

Native Habitat and Range Open woods, meadows, clearings, and roadsides from Nova Scotia to Ontario, south to Georgia and Kansas

Hardiness Range Zones 3 to 8

Ornamental Attributes and Uses In late summer and early autumn, the multistemmed clumps of this woodland aster erupt into domes of sky-blue to white, ¾-inch flowers. The branched stems from three to five feet tall have five-inch, lance-shaped, toothed leaves with broad heart-shaped bases. This species is best used in drifts with ferns and shrubs, or in the middle or rear of perennial borders.

Growing Tips Plant in moist, humus-rich soil in light to partial shade. Established plants tolerate dry soil. They spread to form attractive groundcovers and self-sow freely. Divide overgrown clumps as necessary in early spring or after flowering.

Related Alternatives *Symphyotrichum grandiflorum*, large-flowered aster, is an open, sparsely branched plant to three feet tall with two-inch, dark purple flowers borne singly at the ends of the coarse branches. It grows in clumps increased by runners and is found in pine savannas, open mixed pine and hardwood forests, and on roadsides in acidic soils in the piedmont and coastal plain of Virginia and North Carolina. *Symphyotrichum laeve*, smooth aster, has pale lavender-blue flowers with smooth blue-green foliage on stems two to five feet tall and one to two feet wide. The basal leaves are narrowly heart-shaped; the stem leaves are greatly reduced. It grows from Maine to Saskatchewan, south to Alabama and Colorado.

Attributes at a Glance
Symphyotrichum cordifolium

Clumping, multistemmed perennial

Terminal panicle of blue flowers

Heart-shaped foliage

Yellow to red autumn color

Native Alternative
Linum lewisii
Prairie Flax

Native Habitat and Range Prairies, plains, and flats from Michigan to Alaska, south to Louisiana, California, and Texas

Hardiness Range Zones 3 to 7

Ornamental Attributes and Uses The deep electric-blue, saucer-shaped flowers of flax are held in open, branching clusters that droop at their tips. The blue-green foliage is small and needlelike. The wiry, fibrous stems form vase-shaped clumps one to three feet tall and one to two feet wide. Flax has a long history of cultivation for fiber, oil, and ornament. High-quality flax fiber is used to make linen cloth and rope. The seed produces linseed oil, an important ingredient in paints. Its unique and coveted flower color adds beauty to borders, rock gardens, and dry meadows.

Growing Tips Plant in average, sandy or loamy, well-drained soil in full sun or light shade. Once established it needs little care and seldom requires division. Flax is a tough, long-lived perennial but will die out if crowded or overfed. The clumps increase to an impressive mound of soft foliage and bright flowers. The plant self-sows freely in open ground.

More Native Alternatives *Polemonium pulcherrimum*, Jacob's ladder (page 151)—Alaska to New Mexico,

California, and Texas. For a list of additional native plants, visit www.bbg.org/nativealternatives.

Attributes at a Glance
Linum lewisii

Perennial with a stout, woody rootstock

Intense blue flowers

Wiry stems with needlelike leaves

Invasive Plant
Coronilla varia • Crown Vetch
Current Invaded Range: Eastern and central North America

Attributes at a Glance
Asclepias verticillata

Running, deep-rooted perennial

Clusters of creamy flowers

Needlelike leaves

Golden autumn color

Native Alternative
Asclepias verticillata
Whorled Milkweed

Native Habitat and Range Prairies, meadows, open woods, and roadsides from Massachusetts and Saskatchewan, south to Florida and Arizona

Hardiness Range Zones 3 to 9

Ornamental Attributes and Uses This slender, airy plant has stems clothed in tight whorls of two- to four-inch needlelike leaves. The small, creamy-white flowers are held in tight, spherical clusters near the top of the stem in mid- to late summer. The plant spreads by creeping rhizomes to form large, dense colonies up to a foot tall and two to four feet wide that hold soil against wind and water, especially in concert with other deep-rooted perennials or bunch grasses. Use whorled milkweed in borders, in meadow and prairie plantings, and for erosion control on slopes.

Growing Tips Plant in rich, evenly moist soil in full sun or light shade. Established plants tolerate dry soils. Since this plant spreads by underground runners and may be aggressive in small gardens, plant it in a bottomless container to control its spread, or remove unwanted shoots as they appear.

Native Alternative
Apocynum androsaemifolium
Spreading Dogbane

Native Habitat and Range Prairies, meadows, open woods, and roadsides from Massachusetts and Saskatchewan, south to Florida and Arizona

Hardiness Range Zones 3 to 9

Ornamental Attributes and Uses
Spreading dogbane is an undiscovered jewel with nodding open pink or white bells set off by deep green, waxy oval leaves. The sweet-scented flowers open for months in late spring through summer, followed by pencil-thin pods that split to release seeds carried on silken parachutes. The autumn foliage turns yellow, orange, or rose. The rounded, shrubby crowns are to four feet tall and wide and die back to the ground in winter. This tough native grows throughout much of North America and varies in stature and bloom time accordingly. Use it in a formal bed or informal meadow, in wildlife plantings, and for erosion control.

Growing Tips Plant in average to rich, neutral to acidic, well-drained soil in sun or light shade. This species spreads by underground stems to form open mats with dense, soil-holding roots and is good for erosion control when combined with other deep-rooted perennials and grasses. Plant it in a bottomless container to control its spread, or remove unwanted shoots as they appear.

More Native Alternatives *Arctostaphylos uva-ursi*, bearberry (page 87)— Labrador and British Columbia, south to Virginia, New Mexico, and California. *Parthenocissus quinquefolia*, Virginia creeper (page 132)—Quebec, Manitoba, and Utah, south to Florida and Texas. For a list of additional native herbaceous plants, visit www.bbg.org/nativealternatives.

Attributes at a Glance
Apocynum androsaemifolium

Shrubby perennial with a rounded crown

Open clusters of fragrant nodding flowers

Leathery oval leaves

Yellow to mauve autumn color

Invasive Plant
Daucus carota • Queen-Anne's Lace
Current Invaded Range: Throughout North America

Native Alternative
Angelica venenosa
Hairy Angelica

Native Habitat and Range Open woods, clearings, meadows, glades, and roadsides from Massachusetts to Minnesota, south to Florida, Mississippi and Arkansas

Hardiness Range Zones 4 to 8

Attributes at a Glance
Angelica venenosa

Clump-forming perennial from a deep taproot

Compound umbels of snowy-white flowers in summer

Deep green, intricately divided foliage

Burgundy autumn color

Ornamental Attributes and Uses
Angelica's domed umbels of white flowers closely resemble Queen-Anne's lace but are more compact. The summer-blooming flowers are attractive to a wide range of insects. This upright, single-stemmed to clump-forming perennial grows one to four feet tall and wide and has lacy, glossy, deep green leaves that are divided into small, toothed leaflets. In fall, the foliage colors to yellow and rich burgundy before the plant goes dormant. Use it in meadows, wildflower gardens, and formal beds.

Growing Tips Plant in average to rich, moist but well-drained soil in full sun to shade. This long-lived and trouble-free plant grows from a deep, branched taproot and develops into a multi-stemmed clump in sun.

Related Alternatives *Angelica arguta*, Lyall's angelica, is similar in flowering period and overall aspect. It grows in meadows, along streams, and in montane zones from Alaska, south to Wyoming and California.

More Native Alternatives *Parthenium integrifolium*, wild quinine (page 156)—Quebec to Ontario, south to Georgia and Texas. *Pycnanthemum* species, mountain mint—Nova Scotia to Manitoba, south to Florida and Texas. *Valeriana* species, valerian—throughout North America. For a list of additional native herbaceous plants, visit www.bbg.org/nativealternatives.

Invasive Plant
Digitalis purpurea • Foxglove
Current Invaded Range: Pacific Northwest; watch elsewhere

Native Alternative
Iliamna rivularis
Mountain Hollyhock

Native Habitat and Range Prairies, subalpine meadows, and roadsides from Alberta and British Columbia, south to Colorado, Nevada, and Oregon

Hardiness Range Zones 4 to 8

Ornamental Attributes and Uses Mountain hollyhock produces dense spikes of pink flowers two inches across atop stout stems clothed in large, five- to seven-lobed maplelike leaves. Established plants grow five feet tall and wide or larger under ideal conditions. *Iliamna* is a more delicate relative of hollyhocks but far less susceptible to rust and other problems. Use it in beds and borders, as well as in meadows and other informal settings.

Growing Tips Plant in average humus-rich, evenly moist neutral soil in full sun or light shade. This plant wilts easily in dry situations and declines rapidly during prolonged droughts. Clumps are stoloniferous and spread slowly outward. Remove stray stems for propagation or to control spread.

Related Alternative *Iliamna latibracteata*, California wild hollyhock, is a leafier species of *Iliamna*. It is found along roadsides, woodland borders, and in meadows in Oregon and California.

More Native Alternatives *Chamerion* (*Epilobium*) *angustifolium*, fireweed (page 173)—most of North America.

Verbena hastata, blue vervain—Nova Scotia and British Columbia, south to Florida and Arizona. For a list of additional native herbaceous plants, visit www.bbg.org/nativealternatives.

Attributes at a Glance
Iliamna rivularis

Shrubby perennial from a deep taproot

Tall spikes of showy pink flowers

Maplelike leaves

Yellow autumn color

Buttonlike seed heads

HERBACEOUS PLANTS

Invasive Plant
Eichhornia crassipes • Water Hyacinth

Current Invaded Range: North Carolina and Missouri, south to Florida and Texas; Arizona and California

Native Alternative
Pontederia cordata
Pickerel Weed

Native Habitat and Range Pond margins, marshes, and slow-moving streams from Nova Scotia to Minnesota, south to Florida and Texas

Hardiness Range Zones 3 to 10

Ornamental Attributes and Uses The lush, tropical-looking elongated foliage of pickerel weed is accented by copious spikes of purple flowers borne throughout the summer. This upright emergent aquatic perennial reaches one to three feet tall and forms wide clumps of exceptional beauty. Use it in containers in water gardens and formal pools or in earthen ponds and along the margins of streams.

Growing Tips Plant in heavy, rich soil or sand in the ground or in containers in rich clay soil. Containerized plants need regular feeding with pelletized fertilizer for aquatic plants. As they go dormant, trim the plants back so that the dying growth will not foul the water.

More Native Alternatives For a list of additional native herbaceous plants, visit www.bbg.org/nativealternatives.

Attributes at a Glance
Pontederia cordata

Emergent aquatic perennial

Showy spikes of blue-purple flowers

Lush, glossy foliage

Invasive Plant
Foeniculum vulgare • Fennel

Current Invaded Range: Maine, Michigan, and Oregon, south to Florida, Texas, and California

Native Alternative
Zizia aurea
Golden Alexanders

Native Habitat and Range Open woods, floodplains, meadows, and prairies from Quebec and Saskatchewan, south to Florida and Texas

Hardiness Range Zones 3 to 9

Ornamental Attributes and Uses The flattened heads of yellow flowers provide a bright accent in the spring garden, when yellow is a welcome color. The lush, dissected foliage is attractive all summer and turns shades of wine in autumn. Golden Alexanders grow from fibrous-rooted crowns with many leafy stems one to three feet tall and wide. This parsley relative is a larval food plant for many butterflies, including swallowtails. Use it in meadow plantings and borders.

Growing Tips Plant in humus-rich, moist soil in full sun to moderate shade.

The plants are drought tolerant when established. They form full clumps in a few years time but seldom need division.

Related Alternative *Zizia aptera* (heartleaf Alexanders), found from New York to British Columbia, south to Georgia and Nevada, has basal rosettes of deep green, shiny heart-shaped four- to six-inch leaves. The one- to two-foot plants exhibit an open form. The stem leaves have three to five toothed, oval leaflets. The flower clusters are up to 1½ inches across.

Attributes at a Glance
Zizia aurea

Multistemmed herbaceous perennial

Yellow spring flowers

Ferny, deep green foliage

Yellow to red autumn foliage

Invasive Plant
Gypsophila paniculata • Baby's Breath
Current Invaded Range: New Brunswick to British Columbia, south to Pennsylvania, Oklahoma, and California

Native Alternative
Euphorbia corollata
Flowering Spurge

Native Habitat and Range Prairies, clearings, open woods, and roadsides from Quebec to Ontario, south to Georgia and Texas

Hardiness Range Zones 3 to 8

Ornamental Attributes and Uses The broad, domed inflorescences of this plant, sometimes called prairie baby's breath, bear small yellow flowers surrounded by pairs of showy, pristine white bracts. Young plants bear single stems clothed in elongated elliptical sea-green leaves with smooth, waxy surfaces. Mature clumps, one to three feet tall and wide, are multistemmed and floriferous. Though tough, flowering spurge doesn't compete in crowded borders, so place it to the front, surrounded by low plants. Use it in meadows and prairies with clumping grasses or in rock gardens.

Growing Tips Plant flowering spurge in average to rich, well-drained soil in full sun or light shade. It is extremely drought tolerant and long lived once established. The plants spread slowly by runners to form open colonies; self-sown seedlings may also appear on open ground.

Attributes at a Glance
Euphorbia corollata

Broad, domed clusters of white flower heads

Smooth, elliptical sea-green foliage

Yellow to orange autumn color

Native Alternative
Krascheninnikovia (Ceratoides) lanata
Winterfat

Native Habitat and Range Dry plains, open sand flats, and mesas from Saskatchewan to Washington, south to Texas and California, into Mexico

Hardiness Range Zones 6 (with protection) to 9

Ornamental Attributes and Uses This curious subshrub forms an airy vase of flexible stems clothed in small, woolly blue-green linear leaves that mingle with the inconspicuous flowers in dense spikes. In late summer, females of this dioecious species display silken hairs that seem to glow in the sun. Use winterfat as a garden ornamental, or for erosion control and revegetation of difficult soils. The plant grows to two feet tall and wide.

Growing Tips Plant in sandy to loamy, neutral to alkaline soil in full sun. Winterfat prefers cooler desert areas and needs some shade where daytime temperatures are extreme. It grows from a woody base and adds new stems each year. Remove old stems in spring after the showy heads have lost their luster, and the fresh growth will form a new, floriferous crown.

More Native Alternatives For a list of additional native herbaceous plants, visit www.bbg.org/nativealternatives.

Attributes at a Glance
Krascheninnikovia lanata

Clumping subshrub with a vaselike form

Cottony white flower spikes

Woolly, linear foliage

Invasive Plant
Hesperis matronalis • Dame's Rocket

Current Invaded Range: Most of northern North America, south to North Carolina, Arkansas, and California

Native Alternative
Phlox carolina
Carolina Phlox

Native Habitat and Range Open woods, meadows, and roadsides from North Carolina and Kentucky, south to Florida and Mississippi.

Hardiness Range Zones 4 to 8

Ornamental Attributes and Uses Carolina phlox has brilliant, elongated clusters of fragrant pink flowers crown stems sparsely clothed in pairs of glossy, pointed leaves. It forms erect, multi-stemmed clumps one to three feet tall and wide, with evergreen basal rosettes of oval foliage. Carolina phlox shows to best advantage planted in clumps or drifts; it's great for beds and borders as well as meadows and other naturalistic plantings. Several cultivars are available in a variety of colors.

Growing Tips Plant in rich, evenly moist soil in full sun or partial shade. The plants slowly spread to form dense, multistemmed clumps or open drifts. Remove spent flower heads if you don't want seedlings. Divide clumps every three to four years in spring. To avoid mildew problems, give the plants abundant moisture, good air circulation, and thin dense clumps. If mildew occurs, spray with wettable sulfur one to two times per week. Rabbits and deer love to eat phlox.

Related Alternatives *Phlox paniculata*, border phlox, has large trusses of fragrant flowers that come in a range of purples, blues, pinks, reds and white atop two- to five-foot stems in summer. The flowers are tubular at the base and flair at the end to form flat five-petaled faces. It is native from Pennsylvania and Illinois, south to Florida and Louisiana. *Phlox glaberrima*, smooth phlox, is found from Maryland to Wisconsin, west to Florida and Oklahoma and has reddish-purple to pink and sometimes white flowers.

Attributes at a Glance
Phlox carolina

Multistemmed perennial from fibrous-rooted crown

Terminal cluster of bright pink or white flowers

Glossy, narrow pointed foliage

Native Alternative
Sidalcea malviflora
Checkerbloom

Native Habitat and Range Prairies, subalpine meadows, and roadsides from Alberta and British Columbia, south to Colorado, Nevada, and Oregon

Hardiness Range Zones 3 to 7

Ornamental Attributes and Uses Checkerbloom resembles a small delicate hollyhock. It has stout stems with deeply cut, palmately lobed leaves. The two-inch pink or rose-mallowlike flowers are intermingled with the leaves in open spikes on the upper third of the stems. Plants vary in size regionally, averaging two to four feet tall and two to three feet wide. Checkerbloom is a good plant for the middle or rear of the border or for meadow gardens. Many cultivars are available in a range of colors on compact two-foot plants.

Growing Tips Plant in average to rich, moist but well-drained soil in full sun or light shade. The plants increase to form large clumps from a woody rootstock with fibrous roots. Cut them to the ground after flowering to promote fresh foliage. If the plants overgrow their space or die out in the middle, lift the clumps in fall and discard the old portions. Replant vigorous divisions into amended soil.

More Native Alternatives *Chamerion* (*Epilobium*) *angustifolium*, fireweed (page 173)—most of North America.

For a list of additional native herbaceous plants, visit www.bbg.org/nativealternatives.

Attributes at a Glance
Sidalcea malviflora

Multistemmed perennial from a stout taproot

Tall spikes of pink flowers

Rounded, quilted leaves

Yellow autumn color

HERBACEOUS PLANTS

Invasive Plant
Iris pseudacorus • Yellow Flag Iris
Current Invaded Range: Most of North America

Native Alternative
Iris versicolor
Blue Flag Iris

Native Habitat and Range Freshwater wetlands from Newfoundland to Manitoba, south to Virginia and Minnesota

Hardiness Range Zones 2 to 8

Ornamental Attributes and Uses The blue-purple flowers of this iris open in succession on sparse, elongated two- to three-foot scapes in late spring and early summer. Attractive, straplike foliage borne in tight fans overtops the scapes after flowering and remains attractive all season. Plant blue flag in drifts along pond margins and stream edges, or plunge containerized plants in ornamental ponds.

Growing Tips Plant in rich, heavy, moist to wet soils, placing the rhizomes at or just below the soil surface. It thrives in garden beds with constant moisture or at watersides submerged in up to six inches of water. Blue flag spreads steadily by striated cordlike rhizomes to become broad, dense clumps in just a few seasons. Containerized plants need dividing and replanting every two to three years. Cut old foliage down to the rhizome as it fades each autumn to avoid pest and disease problems.

Related Alternatives *Iris brevicaulis*, lamance iris, found from Ohio and Kansas south to Alabama and Texas, is similar to blue flag, but the deep blue, four-inch flowers are carried on lax, one-foot stalks below the two-foot leaves. *Iris virginica*, southern blue flag, native to the coastal plain from Virginia to Florida and west to Texas, carries its flowers even with the two- to three-foot leaves. The tips of the leaves droop downward, giving the clumps a unique appearance. *Iris fulva*, copper iris, is found in Illinois and Missouri, south to Georgia and Texas. *Iris missouriensis*, Missouri iris or western blue flag, is found in South Dakota and British Columbia, south to Mexico and California.

Attributes at a Glance
Iris versicolor
Blue flowers

Elongated, straplike foliage

Invasive Plant
Lespedeza cuneata • Chinese Lespedeza
Current Invaded Range: New England, Michigan, and Nebraska, south to Florida and Texas

Native Alternative
Lespedeza capitata
Roundheaded Bushclover

Native Habitat and Range Prairies, meadows, glades, and roadsides from New Brunswick and South Dakota, south to Florida and Texas

Hardiness Range Zones 3 to 9

Ornamental Attributes and Uses The stems of these dense, attractive sub-shrubs stand upright in open colonies to great effect. The three-lobed leaves alternate up the wiry stems. The upper axils and tip of the stems bear dense, globular flower clusters with small pale pink flowers surrounded by narrow bracts. The one- to three-foot stems die back to the woody crown each winter. Use roundheaded bushclover in naturalized settings such as prairie gardens or for erosion control and soil building.

Growing Tips Plant in average to rich, moist but well-drained soil in sun or light shade. This plant is slow to settle in but is ultimately deep rooted, and once established, it endures heat and prolonged drought with aplomb. Like all legumes, the roots fix atmospheric nitrogen and enrich the soil. It emerges late in the season.

More Native Alternatives *Astragalus canadensis*, Canada milkvetch—most of North America. For a list of additional native herbaceous plants, visit www.bbg.org/nativealternatives.

Attributes at a Glance
Lespedeza capitata

Nitrogen-fixing legume

Dense flower heads on leafy stalks

Yellow to russet autumn color

Persistent winter seed heads

HERBACEOUS PLANTS

Invasive Plant
Leucanthemum vulgare (*Chrysanthemum leucanthemum*) • Ox-Eye Daisy
Current Invaded Range: Throughout North America

Native Alternative
Pycnanthemum virginianum, Virginia Mountain Mint

Native Habitat and Range Open woods, meadows, and prairies from Maine and North Dakota, south to Georgia and Oklahoma

Hardiness Range Zones 3 to 8

Ornamental Attributes and Uses Virginia mountain mint produces frothy mounds of small white flowers spotted with purple in broad, flattened inflorescences. The attractive two-inch, linear leaves smell like minty oregano. The two- to three-foot plants turn bright yellow in autumn, with showy gray seed heads that persist through the winter. Use Virginia mountain mint in meadow and prairie plantings or in roomy beds where it can spread.

Growing Tips Plant in moist, humus-rich soil in full sun. This plant spreads rapidly and needs division every two years to keep it from swamping other plants. Lift clumps in early spring or autumn and replant the vigorous portions.

Related Alternatives *Pycnanthemum. muticum,* short-toothed mountain mint, is a stunning plant with broad clusters of dense heads with small quarter-inch white flowers accented by broad, white-frosted bracts. The pointed oval leaves are peppermint scented. Plants grow to three feet tall and wide and are found growing from New York and Michigan, south to Florida and Louisiana. *Pycnanthemum tenuifolium,* narrow-leaf mountain mint, is similar to Virginia mountain mint, but the needlelike leaves are smaller and more narrow, and the 1- to 1½-foot plant has a more delicate appearance. It is found from Maine and Wisconsin, south to South Carolina and Texas. *Pycnanthemum torreyi,* Torrey's mountain mint, has a more open appearance and slightly toothed leaves. It is found from Connecticut and Illinois, south to Georgia and Kansas.

Attributes at a Glance
Pycnanthemum virginianum

Perennial with creeping, fibrous-rooted stems

Dainty, flattened flower heads

Aromatic mint- or oregano-scented leaves

Charcoal-gray seed heads

Native Alternative
Parthenium integrifolium
Wild Quinine

Native Habitat and Range Moist prairies, low meadows, and open woods from Massachusetts and Minnesota, south to Georgia and Arkansas

Hardiness Range Zones 4 to 8

Ornamental Attributes and Uses Wild quinine offers lustrous foliage and long-lasting white flowers throughout the season. Plants bloom beautifully in spite of searing heat and months of drought. Established clumps have toothed, egg-shaped to broadly lanceolate basal leaves to one foot long and a dozen or more leafy stems to four feet tall crowned with flat clusters of small knobby white flowers in mid- to late summer. Use wild quinine as a specimen or as filler in the middle of the border with bold-textured plants. In meadow and prairie gardens, combine it with grasses. The charcoal-gray seed heads are attractive in the garden throughout the winter and can be used indoors in dried arrangements.

Growing Tips Plant wild quinine in moist, deep rich soil in full sun or light shade. The fleshy taproot imparts drought tolerance.

Attributes at a Glance
Parthenium integrifolium

Multistemmed, taprooted perennial

Flat clusters of white flowers

Deep green, toothed oval foliage

Charcoal-colored seed heads

Drought tolerant

Native Alternative
Melampodium leucanthum
Blackfoot Daisy

Hardiness Range Zones 7 to 9

Native Habitat and Range Dry, gravely limestone soils on prairies, plains, and slopes from Kansas and Colorado, south to Texas and Arizona

Ornamental Attributes and Uses

Blackfoot daisy forms rounded clumps of lance-shaped, soft gray foliage on one-foot stems, covered with one-inch, yellow-centered white daisies in summer. In warmer zones it may bloom sporadically throughout the winter as well as during the growing season. When out of bloom, the lance-shaped, silvery-gray foliage is soft and effective as a foil for other plants. Blackfoot daisy blooms as much as some annuals. Use it in beds and borders, informal gardens, or in containers. It is perfect for rock gardens and in the crevices of rock walls.

Growing Tips Plant in average to lean, neutral to slightly acid, well-drained soils in full sun. This plant is tough and adaptable, but good drainage is essential or it will rot. Set out young plants, as established clumps resent disturbance. This plant may be short lived, but self-sown seedlings will appear.

Related Alternative *Melampodium cinereum*, hoary blackfoot, is very similar to *M. leucanthum*, and the two species are sometimes placed together. This species is found only in Texas.

Attributes at a Glance
Melampodium leucanthum

Ever-blooming perennial with white daisies

Dense, attractive mounds from tough, branched taproots

Felted silver-green foliage

Native Alternative
Erigeron pulchellus
Robin's Plantain

Native Habitat and Range Meadows, prairies, and roadsides from Nova Scotia and Ontario, south to Florida and Texas.

Hardiness Range Zones 3 to 8

Ornamental Attributes and Uses This showy, floriferous groundcover species blooms for weeks in late spring and early summer. It forms broad clumps over one foot tall and two to three feet wide from short, creeping rhizomes. Stiff stems each bear a single one-inch lilac to pale blue, occasionally white flower. The basal rosettes of fuzzy oval leaves are semievergreen. Plant Robin's plantain at the front of borders and beds, in rock gardens, on slopes, or in meadows and other informal places. The dense broad clumps are often buried in mounds of flowers.

Growing Tips Plant in moist but well drained rich soil in full sun or light shade. Good drainage is a must for Robin's plantain. It may be short lived but self-sows freely.

More Native Alternatives For a list of additional native herbaceous plants, visit www.bbg.org/nativealternatives.

Attributes at a Glance
Erigeron pulchellus

Groundcover perennial with fibrous roots

Buttonlike white or lilac daisies in late spring or early summer

Basal rosettes of oval leaves

HERBACEOUS PLANTS

Invasive Plant
Lotus corniculatus • Bird's Foot Trefoil
Current Invaded Range: Most of North America

Native Alternative
Baptisia bracteata
Long-Bracted Wild Indigo

Native Habitat and Range Sandy prairies, savannas, roadsides, and dry open woods from Michigan and Minnesota, south to Kentucky and Texas

Hardiness Range Zones 3 to 9

Ornamental Attributes and Uses The tightly packed, drooping clusters of wild indigo's creamy-yellow flowers are borne at the tips of stiff leaf stems. The one- to two-inch, three-lobed leaves are softly hairy. This species blooms in early spring

Attributes at a Glance
Baptisia bracteata

Tap-rooted long-lived perennial

Creamy-yellow flowers in drooping terminal spikes

Inflated dark gray seedpods

before other baptisias. The low, compact one- to two-foot spreading plant goes dormant in mid- to late summer. Use it in borders or naturalized meadow plantings.

Growing Tips Plant in average to rich, sandy or loamy soil in full sun or light shade. It is extremely drought tolerant once established. Slow growing at first, it eventually spreads to form huge clumps. Transplant it when young to avoid damaging the taproot. Space the plants at least three feet apart.

Related Alternatives *Baptisia sphaerocarpa,* yellow wild indigo, found from Missouri south to Alabama and Texas, is taller, to three feet, and bears upright spikes of deep yellow flowers and fabulous seedpods. *Baptisia tinctoria,* horsefly weed, has a rounded, open crown with small leaves and terminal clusters of small flowers in July. It is found from Maine to Minnesota, south to Georgia and Iowa.

Native Alternative
Lotus rigidus
Deer Vetch

Native Habitat and Range Roadsides, dry rocky plains, and prairies from Utah and California, south to Mexico and Baja California

Hardiness Range Zones 7 to 10

Ornamental Attributes and Uses The yellow to orange-stained flowers of deer vetch open on wiry stems in late winter and spring. Its small compound leaves have three to five oval leaflets that are shed in times of drought. This plant is a subshrub that generally dies back partially or completely to its thick, water-seeking rootstock in winter. Use deer vetch for erosion control, soil improvement, and in garden settings. The plants have an upright to mounded, open crown with wiry stems from one to three feet tall and wide.

Growing Tips Plant deer vetch in average to rich, sandy or loamy soil in full sun or light shade; however it tolerates poor soils because it can fix atmospheric nitrogen. It is also extremely drought and cold tolerant once established, but provide supplemental water in summer if possible. Prune deer vetch to reshape the crown or to remove winter-killed growth as necessary.

More Native Alternatives *Asclepias verticillata,* whorled milkweed (page 154)—Massachusetts and

Saskatchewan, south to Florida and Arizona. For a list of additional native herbaceous plants, visit www.bbg.org/nativealternatives.

Attributes at a Glance
Lotus rigidus

Perennial subshrub with rounded, open crown

Nitrogen-fixing legume

Bright yellow flowers in terminal clusters

Invasive Plant
Lysimachia nummularia • Moneywort

Current Invaded Range: Nova Scotia and Manitoba, south to Georgia, Louisiana, and Colorado; also British Columbia to California

Native Alternative
Mitchella repens
Partridgeberry, Wintergreen

Native Habitat and Range Mixed woods, pinelands, clearings, and rocky slopes from Nova Scotia and Minnesota, south to Florida and Texas

Hardiness Range Zones 3 to 9

Ornamental Attributes and Uses Partridgeberry is a sweet trailing plant with shiny rounded or oval evergreen leaves, each with a distinctive white stripe down the midvein. The paired, snow-white flowers have four fringed petals that form half-inch stars in summer. The ruby-red berries persist through the following summer after they are formed. This perennial grows to four inches tall and forms dense mats in time. The trailing stems form fibrous roots at the nodes as it grows. Choose partridgeberry as a groundcover under shrubs or for weaving through other wildflowers, sedges, and ferns.

Growing Tips Plant in humus-rich, moist, acidic soil in light to full shade. Divide the plants in spring or take stem cuttings in early summer.

More Native Alternatives For a list of additional native herbaceous plants, visit www.bbg.org/nativealternatives.

Attributes at a Glance
Mitchella repens

Low, semievergreen groundcover

Fragrant starry white flowers

Wintergreen-scented red berries

Invasive Plant
Lythrum salicaria, L. virgatum • Purple Loosestrife
Current Invaded Range: Most of North America, south to North Carolina, Oklahoma, and California

Native Alternative
Chamerion (Epilobium) angustifolium
Fireweed

Native Habitat and Range Open woods, meadows, and roadsides as well as burned areas throughout most of North America

Hardiness Range Zones 2 to 8

Ornamental Attributes and Uses Showy rose-pink flowers open for months in terminal spires above erect to slightly drooping, leafy stems. Plants spread by runners to form dense clumps and may form huge colonies in rich soils. Their aggressive nature causes many to shy away from using them in gardens, but the long flowering season is hard to duplicate.

Growing Tips Fireweed thrives in average to rich, evenly moist soils in full sun or light shade. Established plants have moderate drought tolerance. In the wild, this plant colonizes disturbed sites, and it luxuriates in well-prepared garden beds. Plant it in deep, bottomless containers to slow the spread, or choose a site with challenging soil. Remove the silky seed heads to prevent enthusiastic self-sowing.

Attributes at a Glance
Chamerion angustifolium

Elongated spires of bright rose-pink flowers

Erect stems clothed in narrowly oval foliage

Yellow autumn color

HERBACEOUS PLANTS

Native Alternative
Liatris pycnostachya
Prairie Blazing Star, Kansas Gayfeather

Native Habitat and Range Wet prairies and low meadows from Indiana to North Dakota, south to Texas and Mississippi

Attributes at a Glance
Liatris pycnostachya

Tall perennial from a thick corm

Erect spikes of tiny purple flowers in midsummer

Grasslike basal leaves and bottlebrush stems

Hardiness Range Zones 3 to 9

Ornamental Attributes and Uses Prairie blazing star is a giant of its genus, with three- to five-foot spikes of densely packed, red-violet to mauve flower heads on stiff, leafy stems. The deep green basal leaves are up to a foot long, but the leaves get smaller as they blend into the flowers. Plants bloom in midsummer and are extremely showy when grown in clumps. Plant in meadow and prairie gardens in the company of their native companions or use them in beds and borders.

Growing Tips Plant prairie blazing star in rich, evenly moist soil in full sun. It often needs staking to keep it erect. Give it plenty of room without competition from other plants to keep it vigorous. Clumps seldom need division for cultural reasons but can be propagated by dividing of the corms in early fall. Mice and voles love to eat the corms.

Related Alternative *Liatris spicata*, spike gayfeather—found from New York and Wisconsin, south to Florida and Louisiana—is one of the most popular species. The compact, two- to four-foot stems bear terminal spikes of deep red-violet flowers in narrow, tightly packed heads. The leafy stems are stiff and seldom need support. Excellent cultivars are available in a variety of colors and sizes.

Native Alternative
Filipendula rubra
Queen-of-the-Prairie

Native Habitat and Range Low meadows and prairies, wetlands, bottomlands, and ditches from New York and Wisconsin, south to North Carolina and Kentucky; naturalized elsewhere

Hardiness Range Zones 3 to 9

Ornamental Attributes and Uses Elegant, frothy heads of tiny five-petaled flowers with protruding stamens open in summer atop tall, stately stems to six feet tall. The fluffy, cotton-candy heads of hot pink or rose flowers may reach nine inches across. The intensity of the flower color is quite variable. The seed heads are attractive in fall and winter. The bloom stalks are sparsely clothed with bold, foot-long deep green, pinnately divided leaves with maplelike terminal leaflets. Use queen-of-the-prairie in formal borders, with shrubs, or in meadow and pond-side plantings.

Growing Tips Plant queen-of-the-prairie in evenly moist, humus-rich soil in full sun or light shade. It luxuriates in highly moist soils, even growing alongside creeks or ponds. If leaves become tattered or crispy, cut them back to the ground and fresh foliage will emerge. Clumps spread rapidly by creeping stems and need frequent division to keep them from overrunning their neighbors. Old clumps can be quite tough and may require a knife or shears to separate them. Powdery mildew and spider mites are occasional problems on plants grown in hot, dry places.

Attributes at a Glance
Filipendula rubra

Clumping to running perennial

Cotton-candy plumes

Bold, maplelike foliage

Native Alternative
Asclepias incarnata
Swamp Milkweed

Native Habitat and Range Low meadows and prairies, wet ditches, and marshes from Nova Scotia to Saskatchewan, south to Florida and New Mexico

Hardiness Range Zones 3 to 8

Ornamental Attributes and Uses This stately milkweed has flat, terminal clusters of pale rose to deep rose-purple flowers in early summer, followed by erect, cylindrical pods that split to release seeds on silken parachutes. Tall stems to five feet are clothed in opposite, four- to six-inch, lance-shaped leaves. The plant grows in loose clumps. Use swamp milkweed in a bog or water garden or place containerized plants in shallow pools and garden ponds.

Growing Tips Plant in rich, evenly moist to wet soil in full sun or light shade. Though water loving, established plants will tolerate dry soils too. Swamp milkweed spreads by underground runners and may be invasive in small gardens. Plant it in a bottomless container to control its spread or remove unwanted shoots as they appear. The seedpods may become infested with red aphids, which seem to do no permanent harm.

Related Alternative *Asclepias speciosa*, showy milkweed—found from Manitoba to British Columbia, south to Iowa and Oklahoma—is a compact plant to three feet with opposite, four- to eight-inch pale green leaves and axillary clusters of starry rose-purple flowers. The flowers are especially showy because the petals are not fully reflexed and they surround the central "horns" to form a half-inch starry corolla.

Attributes at a Glance
Asclepias incarnata

Multistemmed perennial from a stout crown

Flat clusters of rose-red flowers

Lance-shaped foliage turns yellow to rose in autumn

Monarch butterflies feed on foliage

Native Alternative
Verbena hastata
Blue Vervain

Native Habitat and Range Wet meadows and prairies, wetland margins, marshes, and ditches from Nova Scotia and British Columbia, south to Florida and Arizona

Hardiness Range Zones 3 to 8

Ornamental Attributes and Uses Blue vervain blooms throughout the summer and into autumn, longer than most other perennials. This graceful erect species has long, narrow, toothed leaves and branched, candelabra-like spikes of blue, occasionally white, tubular flowers with flat five-petaled faces. This plant grows three to five feet tall and forms a multi-stemmed clump. Plant it beside a pond or in a bog garden.

Growing Tips Plant in rich, evenly moist to wet soil in full sun or light shade. This adaptable wetland species stands flooding and moderate drought.

More Native Alternatives *Iliamna rivularis*, wild hollyhock (page 157)—Alberta and British Columbia, south to Colorado, Nevada, and Oregon. *Sidalcea malviflora*, checkerbloom (page 163)—Alberta and British Columbia, south to Colorado, Nevada, and Oregon. For a list of additional native herbaceous plants, visit www.bbg.org/nativealternatives.

Attributes at a Glance
Verbena hastata

Moisture-loving clumping perennial

Stiff spikelike clusters of blue (occasionally white) flowers

Coarsely toothed, lance-shaped foliage

HERBACEOUS PLANTS

Invasive Plant
Melilotus albus, M. officinalis • Sweet Clover

Current Invaded Range: Most of North America (also Hawaii and Puerto Rico)

Native Alternative
Veronicastrum virginicum
Culver's Root

Native Habitat and Range Open woods, meadows, prairies, floodplains, and outcroppings from Ontario and Manitoba, south to Georgia and Louisiana

Hardiness Range Zones 3 to 9

Ornamental Attributes and Uses Upright, branched terminal candelabra-shaped spikes of white flowers are carried at the tips of leafy stems that bear pointed, lance-shaped foliage in whorls of four. The tightly packed flowers have protruding stamens that give the spikes a fuzzy look. The multistemmed, erect clumps reach three to five feet tall and one to three feet wide. Culver's root adds lift and excitement to beds and borders as well as prairie gardens and other naturalized settings.

Growing Tips Plant in rich, moist soil in full sun or light shade. Culver's root thrives with consistent moisture; though it tolerates intermittently dry soils, it wilts with prolonged drought. The plants form multistemmed clumps that are easily divided in early spring or autumn.

Attributes at a Glance
Veronicastrum virginicum

Multistemmed herbaceous perennial

Erect creamy-white flower spikes

Toothed, lance-shaped leaf whorls

Native Alternative
Thermopsis montana
Mountain Goldenbanner

Native Habitat and Range Roadsides, rocky slopes, prairies, and open woods from Alberta to British Columbia, south to New Mexico, Arizona, and Mexico

Hardiness Range Zones 3 to 8

Ornamental Attributes and Uses The narrow, upright stems of mountain goldenbanner are crowned with dense spikes of lemon-yellow flowers in spring. Alternate sea-green leaves—each consisting of three oval leaflets joined to a short stalk—sparsely clothe the succulent stems. The plant forms multistemmed clumps one to three feet tall and wide from woody, fibrous-rooted crowns. Use it in borders or naturalized settings.

Growing Tips Plant in average to rich, moist but well-drained soil in full sun or light shade. In warm zones, partial shade and consistent water are recommended. The plants form tight, erect clumps that increase in breadth each year. Established clumps dislike disturbance, and division is seldom necessary. If the foliage declines after flowering, cut the plant back to the ground.

Related Alternatives *Thermopsis rhombifolia*, golden banner, is a short, colonizing species to one foot tall found in dry semidesert habitats, canyons, and meadows from Saskatchewan south to New Mexico. *Thermopsis villosa,* Carolina bush pea, found in open woods from North Carolina to Georgia, is a stately species with stiff stalks crowned by 8- to 12-inch dense, spiky clusters of lemon-yellow flowers. The plants reach five feet tall and two to three feet wide.

More Native Alternatives For a list of additional native herbaceous plants, visit www.bbg.org/nativealternatives.

Attributes at a Glance
Thermopsis montana

Upright, multistemmed perennial

Yellow flowers in erect terminal spikes

Trifoliate leaves

Narrow brown seedpods

HERBACEOUS PLANTS

Invasive Plant
Pinellia ternata • Pinellia
Current Invaded Range: Southern New England and Mid-Atlantic states; California

---

Attributes at a Glance
Arisaema dracontium

Herbaceous perennial from a corm

Deeply divided foliage of 7 to 9 leaflets

Unusual green-hooded flower

Native Alternative
Arisaema dracontium
Green Dragon

Native Habitat and Range Deciduous woods, stream edges, and wetland borders from Quebec to Minnesota, south to Florida and Texas

Hardiness Range Zones 4 to 9

Ornamental Attributes and Uses A single deeply divided leaf, 1 to 1½ feet wide with seven to nine leaflets, sits above a green spathe with a long, tonguelike spadix for which the plant is named. The curious foliage of green dragon makes a wonderful accent in front of shrubs or in a mixed foundation planting. This unique wildflower grows 1 to 2½ feet tall.

Growing Tips Plant in moist to wet, acidic to neutral soil in full sun to light shade. Green dragon tolerates poorly drained soils; in drier sites, it will go dormant when water is scarce. Self-sown seedlings may be plentiful.

Related Alternative *Arisaema triphyllum*, Jack-in-the-pulpit, has three-lobed, 8- to 12-inch-long leaves that frame a showy green and purple spathe, which droops at the tip to hide the short spadix. It grows one to three feet tall and is found from Nova Scotia to Manitoba, south to Florida and Louisiana.

More Native Alternatives For a list of additional native herbaceous plants, visit www.bbg.org/nativealternatives.

Invasive Plant
Polygonum cuspidatum (*Fallopia japonica*)
Giant Knotweed

Current Invaded Range: Most of North America

Native Alternative
Aruncus dioicus
Goatsbeard

Native Habitat and Range Open woods, rocky slopes, and roadsides from Ontario to Alaska, south in the east to Georgia and Oklahoma, and in the west to California

Hardiness Range Zones 3 to 8

Ornamental Attributes and Uses Terminal plumes of frothy white flowers cap the erect, leafy stems of this shrub-sized perennial. Both the male and female plants of this dioecious species are attractive in bloom, and the female flowers are followed by dense clusters of small brown seed capsules. This upright oval to mounding perennial grows two to five feet tall and wide, and with age, the plant forms a multistemmed clump of exceptional beauty and commanding presence in beds, borders, and wild-flower gardens; multiple plantings also make an attractive seasonal hedge or screen.

Growing Tips Plant goatsbeard in rich, evenly moist soil in full sun to shade—the more light the plants receive, the taller and fuller they grow and the better they bloom. Mature clumps have large crowns with thick, fibrous roots that are difficult to transplant.

Attributes at a Glance
Aruncus dioicus

Terminal plumes of creamy-white flowers

Lush, divided foliage with quilted leaflets

Yellow autumn color

Dried seed heads

Native Alternative
Holodiscus discolor
Ocean Spray

Native Habitat and Range Dry woodlands, rock outcroppings, scree slopes, and forest edges from Alberta and British Columbia, to Arizona and California

Hardiness Range Zones 6 to 9

Ornamental Attributes and Uses Ocean spray forms an upright, medium to large shrub with arching branches that spread to 12 feet tall and wide. Foamy sprays of creamy-white flowers flow from the tips of erect branches in midsummer. The scalloped, oval leaves turn yellow in autumn. The dried seed heads are decorative in autumn and winter. This beautiful shrub is adaptable to garden situations, particularly xeriscape gardens, adding unique beauty and zest to mixed borders, naturalistic plantings, and hedges.

Growing Tips Plant in moist, well-drained soil enriched with humus in sun or partial shade. Plants are heat and drought tolerant when established. They do not thrive in regions where humidity and nighttime temperatures are high.

More Native Alternatives For a list of additional native herbaceous plants, visit www.bbg.org/nativealternatives.

Attributes at a Glance
Holodiscus discolor

Upright to mounding form

Cascading terminal sprays of creamy-white flowers

Oval to rhomboid, quilted leaves

Yellow autumn color

Irregular winter silhouette

Invasive Plant
Potentilla recta • Potentilla
Current Invaded Range: Most of North America

Native Alternative
Potentilla arguta
Prairie Cinquefoil

Native Habitat and Range Prairies, clearings, open woods, and roadsides from Quebec and Manitoba, south to Virginia and Arizona

Hardiness Range Zones 3 to 8

Ornamental Attributes and Uses Prairie cinquefoil is a showy, underappreciated wildflower with open, terminal clusters of one-inch, creamy-yellow flowers and hairy stems bearing sparse foliage above a rosette of palmate leaves with five-toothed leaflets. It forms upright, multistemmed clumps 1 to 2½ feet tall and 1 foot wide. Place it at the front of borders with lower plants that offer little competition or in meadows and other informal situations.

Growing Tips Plant prairie cinquefoil in average, sandy to loamy, well-drained soil in full sun or light shade. It is drought tolerant once established and may be short lived in rich, heavy soils. It self-sows freely if its seed heads are not removed.

More Native Alternatives For a list of additional native herbaceous plants, visit www.bbg.org/nativealternatives.

Attributes at a Glance
Potentilla arguta

Multistemmed clumping perennial

Terminal clusters of creamy-yellow flowers

Basal rosettes of palmate leaves

HERBACEOUS PLANTS

Invasive Plant
Ranunculus ficaria • Lesser Celandine

Current Invaded Range: New Hampshire to Michigan, south to Virginia and Missouri; British Columbia to Oregon

Native Alternative
Chrysogonum virginianum
Green-and-Gold

Native Habitat and Range Open woods, clearings, and roadsides from Quebec, south to Florida and Louisiana

Hardiness Range Zones 4 to 8

Ornamental Attributes and Uses This low, spreading groundcover, four to eight inches tall and two to three feet wide, forms a star-studded mat of velvety foliage that is as attractive at the front of a formal border as it is in a naturalistic sitting. Each flower is composed of a button of small disc flowers surrounded by five to seven bright yellow rays. It blooms from spring through midsummer, expanding in height and spread as the season progresses. The felted foliage may be evergreen to semideciduous, depending on the botanical variety. This plant is rare over much of its natural range.

Growing Tips Plant green-and-gold in average to rich, sandy, or loamy soils in full sun to partial shade. It spreads steadily to form broad, virtually weed-free mats. Where summers are hot and humid, the plant is susceptible to crown or root rot. Avoid mulches and crowding to minimize these problems. There are a number of selections available, many of which are superior to the species in form and adaptability.

More Native Alternatives *Zizia aptera*, heart-leaf Alexanders—New York to British Columbia, south to Georgia and Nevada. For a list of additional native herbaceous plants, visit www.bbg.org/nativealternatives.

Attributes at a Glance
Chrysogonum virginianum

Starry yellow flowers in spring and summer

Velvety deep-green foliage

Invasive Plant
Trifolium T. arvense, T. aureum, T. campestre, T. dubium, T. fragiferum, T. hybridum, T. incarnatum, T. pratense, T. repens, T. resupinatum • Clovers

Current Invaded Range: Throughout North America

Native Alternative
Dalea (Petalostemum) purpurea
Purple Prairie Clover

Native Habitat and Range Dry or moist prairies, savannas, and open woods from Indiana and Alberta, south to Alabama and New Mexico

Hardiness Range Zones 3 to 9

Ornamental Attributes and Uses Purple prairie clover has 1- to 2½-inch button- to cigar-shaped heads of bright violet flowers in sparsely branched clusters in June and July. It forms flashy, fountainlike clumps two to three feet high that are heavily weighted with blooms attractive to bees and butterflies. The dried seed heads are handsome in winter. Use in gardens, prairies and restorations, and for wildlife forage.

Growing Tips Plant in rich, moist soil in full sun or light shade. The plant thrives with consistent moisture but is tough and adaptable and tolerates intermittently dry soils. The clumps have deep taproots and seldom need division. Like true clovers, prairie clover fixes atmospheric nitrogen and adds it to the soil.

Related Alternatives *Dalea candida*, white prairie clover, is taller, has white flowers that bloom later, and grows in wetter sites than *D. purpurea*. It is found from Indiana and Saskatchewan, south to Alabama and Arizona. *Dalea multiflora*, many-flowered prairie clover, found from Iowa and Kansas, south to Arkansas and Texas, is a more squat, bushy plant to two feet tall with dense clusters of white,

buttonlike heads. *Dalea villosa* has pale purple to white flowers carried on one- to two-foot stems in summer. It is found from Wisconsin to Saskatchewan, south to Texas and Colorado.

More Native Alternatives For a list of additional native herbaceous plants, visit www.bbg.org/nativealternatives.

Attributes at a Glance
Dalea purpurea

Clump-forming perennial

Buttonlike flower heads

Tidy, trifoliate leaves

Yellow autumn color

Invasive Plant
Tripleurospermum maritimum subsp. *inodorum*
(*Matricaria perforata*) • Scentless Chamomile

Current Invaded Range: New Brunswick to British Columbia, south to Virginia and Oregon

Native Alternative
Erigeron philadelphicus
Philadelphia Fleabane

Native Habitat and Range Meadows, prairies, plains, and waste places throughout most of North America

Hardiness Range Zones 3 to 8

Ornamental Attributes and Uses Philadelphia fleabane, a widespread and somewhat weedy species from one to two feet tall and wide, is a profuse bloomer with one-inch white to lavender daisies in early summer. The plant forms a basal rosette and multiple flowering stems from a fibrous-rooted crown. Use it at the front of beds, as a groundcover, or in a meadow.

Growing Tips Plant in average to rich, evenly moist soil in full sun or partial shade. The plants self-seed freely in open ground. Avoid crowding Philadelphia fleabane with taller plants, as it resents competition. After seed dispersal occurs, in midsummer, cut it to the ground. Grow it as a biennial or short-lived perennial.

More Native Alternatives For a list of additional native herbaceous plants, visit www.bbg.org/nativealternatives.

Attributes at a Glance
Erigeron philadelphicus

Tall biennial or short-lived perennial

White, pink, or lavender flowers in early summer

Invasive Plant
Vinca minor, V. major • Periwinkle
Current Invaded Range: Maine to Ontario, south to Georgia and Texas; Utah, Arizona, and Washington

Native Alternative
Waldsteinia fragarioides
Barren Strawberry

Native Habitat and Range Open woods and borders of clearings from Maine and Quebec, west to Minnesota, south to Georgia and Indiana

Hardiness Range Zones 4 to 8

Ornamental Attributes and Uses This tough groundcover bears trifoliate evergreen leaves in dense, broad clumps and is studded with butter-yellow flowers in spring. Use it as an attractive, weed-free carpet or for erosion control. This perennial groundcover spreads by runners to form tidy patches two to six inches tall and one to three feet wide.

Growing Tips Plant in average to rich well-drained soil in full sun or light shade. Barren strawberry is drought tolerant and thrives in poor sandy or clay soils. The plants spread slowly and are not aggressive.

Attributes at a Glance
Waldsteinia fragarioides

Low, dense groundcover

Yellow flowers in spring

Glossy, three-lobed evergreen leaves

HERBACEOUS PLANTS

Native Alternative
Paxistima myrsinites
Oregon Box

Native Habitat and Range Coniferous woodlands, stream edges, and rocky slopes from Alberta and British Columbia, south to Texas and California

Hardiness Range Zones 4 to 8

Ornamental Attributes and Uses A common sight in northwestern forests, this tidy and useful shrub has small, toothed evergreen leaves paired on stiff stems. Small red flowers cluster in the leaf axils in spring. The plant forms a mounding shrub two to three feet tall and three to five feet wide. Use it as a foundation shrub, low hedge, in mass plantings, and in naturalized settings.

Growing Tips Plant in average to rich, moist, neutral to acidic soil in light to full shade. Plants may get leggy in dark evergreen shade, but they grow well. In cool, northern zones oregon box will tolerate full sun. Prune it as needed to reshape the crown.

Related Alternative *Paxistima canbyi*, cliffgreen, is a smaller, low-growing, fine-textured species found growing from Pennsylvania and Ohio, south to North Carolina and Tennessee.

More Native Alternatives *Arctostaphylos uva-ursi*, bearberry (page 87)—Labrador and British Columbia, south to Virginia, New Mexico, and California. *Pachysandra procumbens*, allegheny spurge (page 136)—North Carolina and Kentucky, south to Florida and Louisiana. For a list of additional native herbaceous plants, visit www.bbg.org/nativealternatives.

Attributes at a Glance
Paxistima myrsinites

Low, spreading evergreen shrub

Small, oval leaves

Red axillary flowers

Invasive Grass
Agropyron cristatum • Crested Wheatgrass
Current Invaded Range: Central North America and the Southwest

Native Alternative
Pascopyrum (Agropyron) smithii
Western Wheatgrass

Native Habitat and Range Plains and washes, rocky slopes, and prairies from Ontario to British Columbia, south to Tennessee, Texas, and California

Hardiness Range Zones 3 to 8

Ornamental Attributes and Uses This attractive and durable creeping grass has tufts of narrow, blue-green foliage and one- to two-foot stems of crescent-shaped spikelets. A cool-season species, it greens up early in the season and flowers in early summer; it is semidormant during the hot, dry summer months. The plants are deep rooted and are good for permanent, durable forage and erosion control. They withstand continual grazing, making them invaluable for range and right of-way plantings.

Growing Tips Plant in average to rich, sandy or loamy, alkaline to slightly acidic soil in full sun. This species is drought tolerant but prefers deeper, moist sites and self-sows in open ground. The plant is deep rooted and long lived.

More Native Alternatives *Schizachyrium scoparium*, little bluestem—Maine and Quebec to Alberta, south to Florida and Arizona. For a list of additional native plants, visit www.bbg.org/nativealternatives.

Attributes at a Glance
Pascopyrum smithii

Tufted, creeping cool-season grass

Dense, narrow plumes

Russet autumn color

Invasive Grass
Arundo donax • Giant Reed
Current Invaded Range: Maryland, Kansas, and California, south to Florida and Arizona (also Hawaii and Puerto Rico)

Native Alternative
Arundinaria gigantea
Giant Cane

Native Habitat and Range Low woods, bottomlands, swamps, pine barrens, mountain ravines, and stream edges from New Jersey and Kansas, south to Florida and Texas

Hardiness Range Zones 6 to 10

Ornamental Attributes and Uses Giant cane is an upright, spreading grass two to five feet tall and four to six feet wide with bamboolike canes with leaves tufted at the nodes. Throughout winter, many of the blades drop but are replaced by fresh tufted growth in spring, along with new canes. This is an attractive grass where its size and rambunctious nature are appropriate.

Growing Tips Plant in moist to wet, loamy or sandy soils in sun or shade. A bit of a romper, this beautiful native cane is seldom cultivated. In rich soils, it spreads aggressively but is controlled by competition or planting in a deep, bottomless container to arrest its spread. Trim old, sparsely leafed canes to the ground to make room for fresh growth.

Attributes at a Glance
Arundinaria gigantea

Dense, thicket-forming cane grass

Tall, dense tawny plumes

Short, stiff blades

Native Alternative
Nolina bigelovii
Bigelow's Bear Grass

Native Habitat and Range Desert canyons and rocky slopes and plateaus in California, Nevada, and Arizona, south into Mexico

Hardiness Range Zones 8 to 10

Ornamental Attributes and Uses This massive, clumping species has erect, thin blue-green evergreen blades that resemble a delicate yucca. Tall trunks support the globes of foliage from which rise five-foot stalks bearing huge, branched plumes of small greenish-white flowers. The overall effect is imposing, to say the least. Mature clumps have many trunks of varying heights and may stand eight feet tall and stretch six feet across. Use this plant as a bold accent, screen, or mass planting, or in xeriscape plantings. Backlit clumps are stunning.

Growing Tips Plant in well-drained, sandy or loamy soil in full sun or light shade. Bigelow's bear grass is extremely drought and heat tolerant but quickly succumbs to waterlogging. It is not easily moved, so choose its site carefully.

Related Alternative *Nolina parryi*, Parry's nolina, is similar, with longer green blades and a more upright form. It is found in desert canyons and arroyos in California and Arizona.

More Native Alternatives *Saccharum* (*Erianthus*) *giganteum*, sugarcane

plumegrass—Long Island, New York, south to Florida, west to central Mississippi Valley and Texas. For a list of additional native plants, visit www.bbg.org/nativealternatives.

Attributes at a Glance
Nolina bigelovii

Clumping, trunked yuccalike plant

Round tufts of stiff blades

Tall stalks of small greenish-white flowers in spring

Persistent dry flower stalks

GRASSES

Invasive Grass
Bromus inermis • Smooth Brome
Current Invaded Range: Eastern and central North America

Native Alternative
Schizachyrium scoparium
Little Bluestem

Native Habitat and Range Meadows, prairies, roadsides, dunes, and fields from Maine and Quebec to Alberta, south to Florida and Arizona

Hardiness Range Zones 3 to 8

Ornamental Attributes and Uses Little bluestem turns acres of prairie

glistening silver in autumn. This adaptable bunchgrass adds fine texture and perpetual motion to meadow gardens, mass plantings, prairie and meadow restorations, and borders. Plants begin growth in summer, and the silvery seeds are prominently displayed late in the season on burgundy or golden stalks. Deep, fine-textured roots make this an excellent choice for erosion control. Clumps of this upright grass grow one to three feet tall and to two feet wide.

Growing Tips Plant in average sandy or loamy, well-drained soil in full sun or light shade. Established plants have deep water-seeking roots that hold the soil and impart excellent drought tolerance. Plugs are inexpensive and establish quickly if planted before mid-autumn. Trim the plants back to just above the ground in spring to make way for new growth.

More Native Alternatives *Tridens flavus*, purpletop—New Hampshire to Nebraska, south to Florida and New Mexico. For a list of additional native plants, visit www.bbg.org/nativealternatives.

Attributes at a Glance
Schizachyrium scoparium

Thin, graceful, colorful stalks

Silvery, arched plumes in autumn

Invasive Grass
Cenchrus ciliaris (Pennisetum ciliare) • Bufflegrass
Current Invaded Range: Desert Southwest (also Hawaii)

Native Alternative
Pleuraphis (Hilaria) rigida
Big Galleta

Native Habitat and Range Dunes, desert washes, and open canyons from California and Utah, south to Baja and northern Mexico

Hardiness Range Zones 7 (with protection) to 10

Ornamental Attributes and Uses This handsome, tough bunchgrass has tufts of broad, blue-green foliage and two- to three-foot stems with dense, narrow spikes. A cool-season species, it greens up early in the season and flowers in early summer; the plants are semidormant during the hot, dry summer months. The winter foliage is gray. Big galleta is deep rooted and works well for permanent, durable erosion control; it's also ideal in naturalized xeriscape gardens.

Growing Tips Plant in average sandy or loamy, well-drained soil in full sun or light shade. The deep roots of established plants lend them exceptional drought tolerance. Cut away old foliage every year or two in winter to make room for fresh growth.

More Native Alternatives *Pascopyrum (Agropyron) smithii*, western wheatgrass—Ontario to British Columbia, south to Tennessee, Texas, and California. For a list of additional native plants, visit www.bbg.org/nativealternatives.

Attributes at a Glance
Pleuraphis rigida
Tall, coarse bunchgrass

Blue-green leaf blades

Stiff, upright inflorescence

Invasive Grass
Cortaderia selloana, C. jubata • Pampas Grass

Current Invaded Range: Virginia and Tennessee, south to Georgia, Louisiana, and Texas; Oregon, Utah, and California

---

Native Alternative
Saccharum (*Erianthus*) *giganteum*
Sugarcane Plumegrass

Native Habitat and Range Meadows, open woods, and roadsides from Long Island, New York, south to Florida, west to central Mississippi Valley and Texas

Hardiness Range Zones 5 to 8

Ornamental Attributes and Uses This gorgeous clumping grass forms a spreading vase of wide blades that droop at the tips and tall culms (stems) to ten feet tall bearing billowing plumes that open red and dry to silver. Mature clumps bear multiple culms and form massive clumps up to five feet wide. Use sugarcane plumegrass as an accent, screen, deciduous hedge, or in mixed borders. Place clumps of it where they are backlit to accentuate their beauty.

Growing Tips Plant in moist, loamy or sandy soils in full sun or light shade. In rich soils, the grass grows vigorously, becoming large but maintaining its upright stature. Lean soil keeps clumps a bit smaller. Sugarcane plumegrass is drought tolerant and moderately tolerant of waterlogging.

Related Alternatives *Saccharum alopecuroidium,* silver plumegrass, is found on drier sites from New Jersey to Arkansas, south to Florida and Texas. It is similar to sugarcane plumegrass, but the basal foliage is more compact, with few leaves on the flowering scapes, and smaller plumes. *Saccharum brevibarbe* var. *contortum,* shortbeard plumegrass, grows on wetter sites. The awns (thin, rigid extensions) in the flower spikes are twisted, creating a dense plume. This plant thrives in wet or moist soils from Virginia to Oklahoma, south to Florida and Texas.

Attributes at a Glance
Saccharum giganteum

Large grass with tall autumn plumes

Tufts of arching blades

Russet to burgundy autumn color

Native Alternative
Muhlenbergia lindheimeri
Lindheimer's Muly Grass

Native Habitat and Range Desert canyons and rocky slopes and plateaus in Texas and Mexico

Hardiness Range Zones 7 to 9

Ornamental Attributes and Uses This beautiful clumping species has erect to spreading thin, semievergreen blades that droop at the tips, forming a fine-textured vase. Tall culms to five feet bear silky, featherlike plumes that mature from purple-brown to tan. Mature clumps form a dense, rounded crown that measures five feet wide. Use this grass as an accent, screen, or mass planting, or in mixed borders.

Growing Tips Plant in well-drained, loamy or sandy soils in full sun or light shade. It is drought tolerant but quickly succumbs to waterlogging. This grass is adaptable to cultivation beyond its native range, even in the humid East.

Related Alternative *Muhlenbergia rigens*, deer grass, has a similar form and size, with narrow inflorescences borne in profusion above a dense, wiry vase of foliage. It is found at higher elevations from New Mexico to California, into Mexico.

More Native Alternatives *Nolina bigelovii*, Bigelow's bear grass (page 191)—California, Nevada, and Arizona, south into Mexico. For a list of additional native plants, visit www.bbg.org/nativealternatives.

Attributes at a Glance
Muhlenbergia lindheimeri

Clumping grass with a broad, rounded crown

Low tufts of arching blades

Featherlike plumes

Yellow to tawny autumn color

Invasive Grass
Cynodon dactylon • Bermudagrass
Current Invaded Range: Southern states from Mid-Atlantic to California (also Hawaii and Puerto Rico)

Native Alternative
Festuca rubra
Red Fescue

Native Habitat and Range Meadows, hillsides, boggy sites, and roadsides from central Canada south to Georgia, Colorado, and California

Hardiness Range Zones 3 to 8

Ornamental Attributes and Uses Red fescue, a northern grass that works well in many parts of the upper to middle South, is attractive and tough with tufts of narrow, deep green blades and one- to two-foot spikes. A cool-season species, it greens up early in the season and flowers in early summer.

Attributes at a Glance
Festuca rubra

Fine-textured cool-season turf grass

Thin, deep green blades

This grass is deep rooted and makes a durable lawn.

Growing Tips Plant in rich, moist soil in sun or light shade. The plants show moderate drought tolerance but may go semidormant in hot, dry weather. Let the grass blades grow long and mow infrequently, especially when the weather is hot.

Related Alternative *Festuca californica*, California fescue, is native from British Columbia south to Montana and California. It is a robust and shade-tolerant species.

More Native Alternatives *Tridens flavus*, purpletop—New Hampshire to Nebraska, south to Florida and New Mexico. For a list of additional native plants, visit www.bbg.org/nativealternatives.

Invasive Grass
Eragrostis curvula • Weeping Lovegrass
Current Invaded Range: New England, Illinois, and Utah, south to Florida and California; Pacific Northwest

Native Alternative
Sporobolus heterolepis
Prairie Dropseed

Native Habitat and Range Prairies, meadows, barrens, and roadsides from Quebec and Saskatchewan, south to Delaware, Texas, and Colorado

Hardiness Range Zones 3 to 8

Ornamental Attributes and Uses Prairie dropseed is a good-looking, resilient bunchgrass with tufts of long, narrow, bright green foliage and one- to three-foot plumes of fragrant flowers. The fragrance originates from a sticky substance that coats the inflorescence and has a scent that has been likened to peaches or buttered popcorn. A warm-season species, it greens up in early summer and flowers in midsummer. The foliage turns yellow to pumpkin orange in late summer and early autumn. The winter rosettes are russet. An ornamental grass suitable for formal gardens, meadows, prairies, and containers, its deep roots make it also a good species for permanent, durable erosion-control plantings.

Growing Tips Plant in rich, moist, neutral or acidic soil in sun or light shade. Prairie dropseed shows good drought tolerance but is stunted by prolonged hot, dry weather. It survives burning or hard mowing while dormant.

Attributes at a Glance
Sporobolus heterolepis
Clumping warm-season grass

Fine-textured blades

Vase-shaped inflorescences

Yellow to orange autumn color

GRASSES

Native Alternative
Carex pansa
California Meadow Sedge

Native Habitat and Range Dunes and open areas from British Columbia to California

Hardiness Range Zones 6 to 8

Ornamental Attributes and Uses This is an attractive and tough, turf-forming sedge with tufts of long, narrow, bright green leaves and short flower spikes. The foliage remains evergreen in all but the coldest weather. Meadow sedge greens up in early spring and flowers in midsummer. Use this versatile sedge as a lawn substitute, in meadows, or to stabilize slopes. It is deep rooted and makes permanent, durable erosion-control plantings.

Growing Tips Plant in rich, moist, neutral soil in sun or light shade. This sedge shows good drought tolerance and stands up to periodic mowing.

Related Alternative *Carex texensis,* Catlin sedge, is an adaptable species for sun or shade that handles light foot traffic. It is found from Quebec south to Georgia and Texas.

More Native Alternatives *Tridens flavus,* purpletop—New Hampshire to Nebraska, south to Florida and New Mexico. For a list of additional native plants, visit www.bbg.org/nativealternatives.

Attributes at a Glance
Carex pansa

Durable creeping sedge

Medium-textured evergreen blades

Forms a tight turf

Invasive Grass
Festuca arundinacea • Tall Fescue
Current Invaded Range: North America

Native Alternative
Tridens flavus
Purpletop

Native Habitat and Range Meadows, disturbed ground, pastures, and roadsides from New Hampshire to Nebraska, south to Florida and New Mexico

Hardiness Range Zones 5 to 9

Ornamental Attributes and Uses The alternate common name grease grass refers to the slick feel of this grass's violet midsummer inflorescences. The drooping, branched inflorescence stands three to five feet above a basal clump of medium-wide, bright green blades that form a skirt a foot or less above the ground. Purpletop clumps green up early in the season and flower in early to midsummer. They are deep rooted and make permanent and durable erosion-control plantings. Try them in meadow and prairie plantings for a spot of color.

Growing Tips Plant in average to rich, loamy or sandy soil in full sun or light shade. The best growth occurs on moist, rich loam. Mow purpletop after its seeds shatter or in spring before new growth starts.

More Native Alternatives *Schizachyrium scoparium*, little bluestem—Maine and Quebec to Alberta, south to Florida and Arizona. For a list of additional native plants, visit www.bbg.org/nativealternatives.

Attributes at a Glance
Tridens flavus

Early warm-season, clumping grass

Broad bright green blades

Tall, naked stem with open plume of purple flowers

GRASSES

Invasive Grass
Imperata cylindrica • Cogon Grass
Current Invaded Range: South Carolina to Arkansas, south to
Florida and Louisiana; Pacific Northwest

Native Alternative
Andropogon glomeratus
Bushy Beardgrass

Native Habitat and Range Low
woods, margins of ponds and marshes,
wet pine savannas, and roadsides from
New York to Illinois, south to Florida
and Texas, west to California.

Hardiness Range Zones 5 to 9

Ornamental Attributes and Uses The
ragged, club-shaped heads of bushy
beardgrass stand on stiff, leafy stalks
above basal tufts of thin, arching blades.
The curious heads are composed of
rigid, tightly packed bracts as well as silvery plumes that look like a feather
duster. Use this grass as a dramatic
accent or to add lift to beds, or plant it
in informal settings such as at the edge
of a pond. The plant grows two to four
feet tall and one to two feet wide.

Growing Tips Plant in average to rich,
moist soil in full sun. Bushy beardgrass
is widely adaptable to drought and wet
soil. Established plants form dense,
multistemmed clumps that slowly creep
outward. It is a unique grass for wet
spots where few other plants thrive.

More Native Alternatives For a list of
additional native plants, visit
www.bbg.org/nativealternatives.

Attributes at a Glance
Andropogon glomeratus

Clumping perennial grass

Bulbous, leafy seed heads

Tawny autumn color

Invasive Grass
Miscanthus sacchariflorus • Maiden Grass
Current Invaded Range: New Brunswick to Manitoba, south to
Pennsylvania, Missouri, and Nebraska

Native Alternative
Spartina pectinata
Prairie Cordgrass

Native Habitat and Range Low meadows and prairies, freshwater marshes, and ditches from Newfoundland to Alberta, south to Florida, Texas, and Washington

Hardiness Range Zones 3 to 8

Ornamental Attributes and Uses This elegant large running grass forms a spreading vase of wide drooping blades and erect culms (stems) six to eight feet tall with plumes of stiff branchlets held like rungs on a ladder. Mature clumps bear multiple culms and can form massive colonies up to 15 feet wide in the wild. Use prairie cordgrass as an accent, screen, or in a mixed border (where is must be restrained); it is also good for erosion control and habitat restoration.

Growing Tips Plant in average to rich, moist soil in full sun. Prairie cordgrass thrives in wet soil and can take frequent inundation, yet it is also surprisingly drought tolerant. Established plants form dense, wiry clumps that slowly creep ever outward unless controlled by being planted in a bottomless container.

More Native Alternatives For a list of additional native plants, visit www.bbg.org/nativealternatives.

Attributes at a Glance
Spartina pectinata

Tall, running perennial grass

Erect, stiff plumes

Wide, arching blades

Yellow to russet autumn color

GRASSES

Invasive Grass
Miscanthus sinensis • Japanese Silver Grass

Current Invaded Range: New England to Wisconsin, south to Florida and Louisiana; Colorado and California

Native Alternative
Sorghastrum nutans
Indiangrass

Native Habitat and Range Meadows, prairies, glades, and roadsides from

Attributes at a Glance
Sorghastrum nutans

Clumping grass with ascending, tufted foliage

Silky golden plumes

Red to russet autumn color

Maine to Manitoba, south to Florida, Arizona, and Mexico

Hardiness Range Zones 3 to 9

Ornamental Attributes and Uses This gorgeous bunchgrass has erect to spreading blades that droop at the tips and tall culms (stems) to six feet tall that bear silky one-sided plumes of sun-kissed gold. Mature clumps bear many culms and may measure three feet wide. Use Indiangrass as a screen or deciduous hedge, as an accent, or in mixed borders. Place clumps of it where they are backlit to accentuate their beauty.

Growing Tips Plant in loamy or sandy soils in full sun or light shade. In rich soils, the plant grows weak stems that may flop in the wind or rain. Lean soil is best for upright growth. Indiangrass is drought tolerant; its blades curl inward when water is scarce.

More Native Alternatives *Saccharum* (*Erianthus*) *giganteum,* sugarcane plumegrass (page 194)—Long Island, New York, south to Florida, west to the central Mississippi Valley and Texas. *Panicum virgatum,* switchgrass (page 205)—throughout most of North America. For a list of additional native plants, visit www.bbg.org/nativealternatives.

Invasive Grass
Paspalum notatum var. *saurae*, *P. notatum* var. *latifolium* • Bahia Grass

Current Invaded Range: Virginia and Tennessee, south to Florida, west to Texas; also California

Native Alternative
Paspalum notatum var. *notatum*
American Bahia Grass

Native Habitat and Range Meadows and open areas from Virginia to Illinois, south to Florida, west to Texas

Hardiness Range Zones 6 to 9

Ornamental Attributes and Uses This is a native variety of an otherwise invasive grass from South America. It is an attractive and durable turf grass with tufts of narrow, blue-green foliage and one- to two-foot spikes, each bearing a pair of long, stiff spikelets. A cool-season species, it greens up early in the season and flowers in early summer; the grass is semidormant during the hot, dry summer months. American bahia grass forms a dense sod suitable for turf and erosion-control plantings.

Growing Tips Plant in average, sandy or loamy, well-drained soil in full sun or light shade. Established plants are drought tolerant.

More Native Alternatives *Carex pansa*, California meadow sedge (page 198)—British Columbia to California. *Tridens flavus*, purpletop (page 199)—New Hampshire to Nebraska, south to Florida and New Mexico. For a list of additional native plants, visit www.bbg.org/nativealternatives.

Attributes at a Glance
Paspalum notatum var. *notatum*

Cool-season turf grass

Fine-textured blades

Invasive Grass
Pennisetum setaceum • Fountain Grass
Current Invaded Range: Florida to California; possibly farther north

---

Native Alternative
Muhlenbergia capillaris
Hairawn Muhly

Native Habitat and Range Found in dry, open woods, pine barrens, and on rocky slopes from Massachusetts to Indiana, south to Florida and Texas

Hardiness Range Zones 7 to 9

Ornamental Attributes and Uses This spectacular species has erect to spreading, thin blades that droop at the tips to form a fine-textured skirt for the airy, rosy-red plumes displayed in a spherical crown over them. Mature clumps form a dense crown that measures three feet tall and wide. Use hairawn muhly as an accent, screen, or in mass planting; in mixed borders, place toward the front where there is minimal competition.

Growing Tips Plant in well-drained, loamy or sandy soils in full sun or light shade. This grass is drought tolerant but cannot take waterlogging.

More Native Alternatives For a list of additional native plants, visit www.bbg.org/nativealternatives.

Attributes at a Glance
Muhlenbergia capillaris

Clumping grass with a rounded crown

Low tufts of arching blades

Airy red plumes

Russet to tawny autumn color

Invasive Grass
Phalaris arundinacea • Reed Canary Grass, Gardener's Garters

Current Invaded Range: Most of North America north of the Gulf Coast states

---

Native Alternative
Panicum virgatum
Switchgrass

Native Habitat and Range Prairies, dunes, meadows, open pine woods, and along wet ditches and edges of freshwater marshes throughout most of North America

Hardiness Range Zones 3 to 9

Ornamental Attributes and Uses The airy, beaded inflorescences of switchgrass are held above the gracefully arching foliage on thin but stiff, leafy stalks. The spring foliage may be red tinged, and in autumn plants turn rich russet to burgundy. Clumps vary in stature from three to eight feet tall and four to five feet wide. Use switchgrass as a specimen in the garden, in containers, in mass plantings, or naturalized in prairie plantings.

Growing Tips Plant in average to rich, moist soil in full sun. Switchgrass is widely adaptable to drought and wet soil. Established plants form dense, wiry clumps that slowly creep outward. When, in time, the center dies out, dig the clump, discard the dead center, and replant in fresh soil.

More Native Alternatives For a list of additional native plants, visit www.bbg.org/nativealternatives.

Attributes at a Glance
Panicum virgatum

Clump-forming perennial grass

Airy plumes of small seeds

Russet to red autumn color

GRASSES

For More Information

BOOKS ABOUT NATIVE PLANTS

Florida's Best Native Landscape Plants,
by Gil Nelson, 2003
University Press of Florida, 2003

*Gardening With Native Plants of the Pacific
Northwest,* by Arthur Kruckeberg
University of Washington Press, 1997

Gardening With Native Plants of the South,
by Sally Wasowski with Andy Wasowski
Taylor Publishing Company, 1994

*Gardening With the Native Plants of
Tennessee,* by Margie Hunter
University of Tennessee Press, 2002

*Gardening With Wildflowers and Native
Plants,* edited by Claire Sawyers
Brooklyn Botanic Garden, 1989

*Going Native: Biodiversity in Our Own
Backyards,* edited by Janet Marinelli
Brooklyn Botanic Garden, 1996

*Landscaping With Native Plants in the
Middle Atlantic Region,* by Elizabeth
DuPont
The Brandywine Conservancy, 1978

*Landscaping With Native Plants of Texas and
the Southwest,* by George O. Miller
Voyageur Press, 1991

*Landscaping With Wildflowers and Native
Plants,* by William H.W. Miller
Chevron Chemical Company, 1984

Native Perennials: North American Beauties,
edited by Nancy Beaubaire
Brooklyn Botanic Garden, 1998

Native Plants in the Coastal Garden, by
April Pettinger and Brenda Costanzo
Timber Press, 1996

*Native Plants of the Northeast: A Guide to
Gardening and Conservation,* by Donald
Leopold
Timber Press, 2005

*Native Treasures: Gardening With the Plants
of California,* by Nevin Smith
University of Washington Press, 1997

*Natural Landscaping: Designing With Native
Plant Communities,* by John Diekelmann
and Robert Schuster
University of Wisconsin Press, 2002

*The New England Wild Flower Society Guide
to Growing and Propagating Wildflowers of
the United States and Canada,* by William
Cullina
Houghton Mifflin, 2000

Roadside Use of Native Plants, by Bonnie
Harper-Lore and Maggie Wilson
Island Press, 2000

*Wildflower Gardens: 60 Spectacular Plants
and How to Grow Them in Your Garden,*
edited by C. Colston Burrell
Brooklyn Botanic Garden, 1999

WEBSITES ABOUT NATIVE PLANTS

www.natareas.org
Natural Areas Association: international
nonprofit with mission to advance the
preservation of natural diversity; land management information

www.natureserve.org
Nature Serve Explorer: online encyclopedia
of 50,000 plants and ecological communities of the U.S. and Canada

www.centerforplantconservation.org
Center for Plant Conservation: information

for homeowners and land managers offering a directory of state contacts

www.nps.gov/plants
Plant Conservation Alliance: federal interagency organization sharing information and resources on behalf of native plants

www.wildflower.org
Lady Bird Johnson Wildflower Center: botanical garden with mission to educate about environmental necessity, economic value, and natural beauty of wildflowers and native plants

BOOKS ABOUT INVASIVE PLANTS

Exotic Pests of Eastern Forests, edited by Kerry O. Britton
USDA Forest Service and the Tennessee Exotic Pest Plant Council, 1997

Invasive Exotic Species in the Sonoran Region, edited by Barbara Tellman
Arizona-Sonora Desert Museum Press, 2002

Invasive Plants: Changing the Landscape of America, by R. Westbrooks
Federal Interagency Committee for the Management of Noxious and Exotic Weeds, 1998

Invasive Plants of California's Wildlands, by Carla Bossard, John M. Randall, and Marc C. Hosbovsky
University of California Press, 2003

Invasive Plants of the Upper Midwest, by Elizabeth J. Czarapata
University of Wisconsin Press, 2005

Invasive Plants: Weeds of the Global Garden, edited by John M. Randall and Janet Marinelli
Brooklyn Botanic Garden, 1996

Northwest Weeds, the Ugly and Beautiful Villains of Fields, Gardens, and Roadsides, by Ronald Taylor
Mountain Press Publishing, 1990

Weed Control Methods Handbook, by Mandy Tu, Callie Hurd, and John M. Randall
The Nature Conservancy, 2001
http://tncweeds.ucdavis.edu/handbook

Weeds of the Northeast, by Richard H. Uva, Joseph C. Neal, and Joseph M. DiTomaso, Cornell University Press, 1997

Weeds of the West, edited by Tom D. Whitson Western Society of Weed Science, 1999

WEBSITES ABOUT INVASIVE PLANTS

www.aquat1.ifas.ufl.edu
Center for Aquatic and Invasive Plants: images and information about Florida species

www.fhwa.dot.gov/environment/vegmgt/
Federal Highway Administration: roadside vegetation management

www.invader.dbs.umt.edu
Invaders Database System: University of Montana: noxious weed lists for Northwest as well as other U.S. states and Canadian provinces

www.newfs.org
New England Wild Flower Society: plants of New England

www.nps.gov/plants/alien
Weeds Gone Wild: Plant Conservation Alliance

www.plants.usda.gov
National Plant Database Project

tncweeds.ucdavis.edu/
The Nature Conservancy: Global Invasive Species Initiative

www.uni.edu/irvm
University of Northern Iowa Roadside Vegetation Center: Integrated Roadside Vegetation Management

www.usgs.nau.edu/swepic/swemp
Southwest Exotic Plant Information Clearinghouse: practical information serving the Southwest

www.weedcenter.org
Center for Invasive Plant Management: information about western weeds

Contributors

C. Colston Burrell is a garden designer, photographer, naturalist, and award-winning author. He gardens on ten wild acres in the Blue Ridge Mountains near Charlottesville, Virginia, where he grows natives and the best plants of the global garden. He is principal of Native Landscape Design and Restoration, which specializes in blending nature and culture through artistic design. Cole has written many books on gardening and plants, and he is a contributing editor for *Horticulture* and writes regularly for *Fine Gardening, Landscape Architecture,* and *American Gardener.* He has edited or contributed to more than a dozen Brooklyn Botanic Garden handbooks, including most recently *Intimate Gardens* (2005), *Spring-Blooming Bulbs* (2002), and *The Sunny Border* (2002). In addition to writing, Cole lectures in the College of Architecture and Landscape Architecture at the University of Virginia as well as internationally on topics of design, plants, and ecology, drawing from a lifetime of studying native plants in the wild and in gardens as well as from his experience as a curator at the U.S. National Arboretum and the Minnesota Landscape Arboretum.

Bonnie Harper-Lore's professional training has focused on the design, restoration, and management of native plant communities. A restoration ecologist for the Federal Highway Administration, for the past 13 years she has managed a national native wildflower program, which has evolved into the Roadside Vegetation Management Program. She serves as a founding member of two federal interagency committees: the Federal Interagency Committee for the Management of Noxious and Exotic Weeds (FICMNEW) and the Plant Conservation Alliance (PCA), both formed in 1994. Bonnie is also on the World Conservation Union (IUCN) list of North American plant experts.

Janet Marinelli is the former director of publishing at Brooklyn Botanic Garden. She has written extensively about biological invasion and other conservation issues. She edited BBG's pioneering first handbook on invasive plants, *Invasive Plants: Weeds of the Global Garden* (1996). She was a founding board member of the New York State Invasive Plant Council. She serves on the steering committee of the Center for Urban Restoration Ecology and the plant conservation committee of the American Public Garden Association. Her latest book, *Plant* (Dorling Kindersley, 2005), showcases 2,000 species worldwide that are threatened in the wild but alive and well in gardens.

BBG thanks Jil Swearingen and the Plant Conservation Alliance's Alien Plant Working Group for providing a list of invasive garden plants drawn from the federal list of plants known to infest natural areas around the United States (page 211).

Map

Jeff Wilkinson page 9

Photos

Photos that appear in the encyclopedia section of this book are either marked "i" for invasive plant or "n" for native plant.

David Cavagnaro cover, pages 5 right, 31i, 31n, 33n, 36n, 38n, 39n, 42n, 46n, 51i, 52i, 72i, 74n, 90n, 97n, 111n, 118n, 123n, 135n, 145i, 163n, 164n, 165n, 166, 174 (and back cover)n, 175n, 191n, 192n, 197n, 201i, 205n

Jerry Pavia pages 2, 5 left, 7, 10 bottom, 12n, 13i, 14n, 15n, 16n, 17n, 18n, 19n, 20n, 22n, 23n, 25n, 26n, 32n, 34i, 36i, 42i, 43n, 47n, 48n, 49n, 50i, 51n, 53i, 58i, 58n, 59n, 60n, 62i, 62n, 63n, 65n, 68n, 72n, 73n, 78n, 81i, 82, 84n, 85n, 87n, 90i, 91i, 93i, 93n, 95n, 98n, 100n, 101n, 102i, 103i, 109i, 109n, 110n, 111i, 115i, 116n, 120n, 121i, 122n, 123i, 124n, 126n, 128i, 128n, 129n, 130i, 130n, 132i, 132n, 133n, 136n, 140n, 141n, 142n, 144i, 145n, 146n, 147n, 148n, 150i, 153n, 155n, 157i, 157n, 158i, 158n, 159i, 159n, 160i, 162n, 167n, 168n, 173 (and back cover)n, 176n, 177n, 178n, 181n, 182n, 184n, 185i, 185n, 186n, 187i, 187n, 194i, 200i, 201n, 202n, 204n, 205i

Cece Fabbro page 6

Bernd Blossey, www.invasive.org pages 10 top, 173i

Roger Hammer pages 12i, 30n, 56n, 92n, 112n, 113n, 140i

Susan Glascock pages 13n, 21n, 34n, 35n, 37n, 53n, 55n, 68n, 81n, 83n, 86n, 88n, 94n, 99n, 104n, 105n, 108n, 114n, 117n, 134n, 137n, 138n, 139n, 169n, 190n

Paul Wray, www.invasive.org or www.forestryimages.org pages 17i, 24i, 27n, 40i, 40n, 47i, 50n, 77i

Chuck Bargeron, www.invasive.org pages 20i, 27i, 46i, 136i, 141i

Ted Bodner, www.invasive.org or www.forestimages.org pages 23i, 107n, 203i

Louis-M. Landry page 24

Forest & Kim Starr (USGS) pages 26i, 28i, 30i, 143i, 193i, 197i

Joseph G. Strauch Jr. pages 28n, 41n, 54i, 106n, 121n, 131n, 143n, 154i, 179n, 181i

Walter S. Judd pages 29n, 57n, 203n

James H. Miller, www.invasive.org pages 37i, 39i, 84i, 87i, 165i, 190i, 199i, 202i

C. Colston Burrell pages 44n, 64n, 103n, 154n, 172n, 194n, 199n

Derek Fell pages 45, 198

Jessie M. Harris pages 52n, 91n, 115n, 125n, 144n, 150n, 171n, 180i, 183n

Billy B. Boothe pages 54n, 180n

John M. Randall, The Nature Conservancy pages 56i, 146i, 148i

Betsy Strauch pages 61n, 135i,

Michael Shephard, www.invasive.org page 65i

Charles Mann pages 66n, 67n, 70n, 71n, 75n, 76n, 79n, 119n, 149n, 195n, 204i

Stephen Ingram pages 69n, 102n, 196n

Eric Coombs, www.invasive.org pages 73i, 173 (and back cover)i

George Chamuris page 77n

Kent Brothers page 80n

J.S. Peterson, USDA-NRCS Plants Database page 89n

USDA APHIS Archives, www.invasive.org page 92

Brother Alfred Brousseau, Saint Mary's College of California page 96n

Chris Evans, www.invasive.org pages 98i, 105i, 156i, 170i

Leslie J. Mehrhoff, IPANE pages 107i, 134i, 172i, 184i

Mandy Tu, The Nature Conservancy page 112i

Stephen D. Hight, www.invasive.org page 113i

Steve Dewey, www.invasive.org page 117i

Amadej Trnkoczy pages 126i, 127n

Dave Powell, www.invasive.org or www.forestryimages.org pages 151n, 189i, 192i

Mary Ellen Harte, www.invasive.org or forestryimages.org pages 152i, 166i, 188n

Thomas G. Barnes pages 152n, 156n, 160n, 170n

Gary A. Monroe page 161

Tom Heutte, www.invasive.org page 162i

Stacey Leicht, IPANE page 164i

University of Alaska, www.invasive.org page 178i

USDA ARS Archives, www.invasive.org page 183i

Elizabeth Bella, www.invasive.org page 186i

USDA-NRCS Plants Database page 189n

Hartmut Wisch page 193n

Charles T. Bryson, www.invasvie.org page 196i

Trent M. Draper page 200n

List of Invasive Garden Plants

Drawn from the WeedUS: Database of Plants Invading Natural Areas in the United States (http://www.nps.gov/plants/alien/list/WeedUS.xls) and printed with the permission of the Plant Conservation Alliance (PCA).

SCIENTIFIC NAME	COMMON NAME(S)	STATE(S) WHERE INVASIVE
Abrus precatorius	rosary pea; crab's eyes	FL
Abutilon theophrasti	velvetleaf; Indian mallow: butterprint; pie-maker	MI, OR, VA, WA
Acacia auriculiformis	earleaf acacia	FL
Acacia longifolia	Sydney golden wattle	CA, FL
Acacia melanoxylon	Australian blackwood; blackwood acacia	CA, HI
Acacia retinodes	water wattle; wirilda	CA, FL
Acer campestre	hedge maple; field maple	OH
Acer ginnala	Amur maple	CT, IL, MA, MO, NY, VT, WI
Acer palmatum	Japanese maple	VA, DC
Acer platanoides	Norway maple	CT, DC, DE, IL, IN, MA, MD, ME, MI, NH, NJ, NY, OR, PA, TN, VA, VT, WI, WV
Acer pseudoplatanus	Sycamore maple; mock plane	CT, PA
Acroptilon repens	hardheads	AZ, CO, ID, NV, OR, SD, UT, WA, WI, WY
Adenanthera pavonina	red sandal wood, coralwood	FL
Aegilops cylindrica	jointed goatgrass	AZ, OK, OR, WA
Aegopodium podagraria	goutweed, bishop's weed, ground elder	CT, MI, NJ, PA, VT, WI
Aesculus hippocastanum	horse chestnut	GA, ME, OR, PA, WI
Agropyron cristatum	crested wheatgrass	NV, UT
Agrostis capillaris	colonial beatgrass	OR, TN, VA, WA
Agrostis gigantea	redtop	NY, OR, TN, VA
Agrostis stolonifera	creeping bentgrass	AZ, CA, HI, NV, OR, TX, UT, WA
Ailanthus altissima	tree-of-heaven; stinking shumac; copal tree; varnish tree	AZ, CA, CT, DC, DE, FL, HI, IN, KY, LA, MA, MD, MI, MO, NC, NH, NJ, NM, NY, OH, OK, OR, PA, RI, SC, TN, VA, WA, WI, WV
Aira caryophyllea	silver hairgrass	CT, HI
Ajuga reptans	creeping bugleweed; carpet bugleweed	MD, TN, VA
Akebia quinata	five-leaf akebia; chocolate vine	DC, MD, NJ, KY, PA, VA
Albizia julibrissin	silk tree; mimosa	DC, FL, GA, KY, LA, MA, NC, NJ, SC, TN, VA, WV
Albizia lebbeck	woman's tongue tree; lebbeck tree	FL
Alcea rosea	hollyhock	CA
Alhagi maurorum	camel thorn	AZ, CO, OR, UT, WA
Allamanda cathartica	golden-trumpet; common allamanda	FL
Alliaria petiolata	garlic mustard	AK, CT, DC, DE, GA, IA, IL, IN,

SCIENTIFIC NAME	COMMON NAME(S)	STATE(S) WHERE INVASIVE
Alliaria petiolata (cont.)		KY, MA, MD, ME, MI, MO, NC, NH, NJ, NY, OH, OR, PA, TN, VA, VT, WI, WV
Allium vineale	field garlic, crow garlic, wild garlic	CT, MD, NC, NJ, PA, TN, VA, WV
Alnus glutinosa	black alder; European alder	IL, IN, MI, NY, PA, WI
Alopecurus arundinaceus	creeping foxtail; reed foxtail	NE
Alopecurus myosuroides	slender meadow foxtail	OR, WA
Alternanthera philoxeroides	alligatorweed	GA, KY, IL, NC, SC, TN, TX, VA
Amaranthus spinosus	spiny amaranth	HI, TN
Ammophila arenaria	European beach grass	CA, OR, WA
Ampelopsis brevipedunculata	Amur peppervine; porcelainberry	CT, DC, DE, MA, MD, NJ, NY, PA, RI, VA, WI, WV
Anagallis arvensis	scarlet pimpernel; poor-man's weatherglass; shepherd's dock	AZ, CA, HI, NV
Anchusa azurea	Italian bugloss	OR
Anthemis cotula	mayweed; stinking camomile; common dog fennel	CO, HI, TN
Anthoxanthum odoratum	sweet vernal grass	DC, HI, MD, OR, WA
Anthriscus sylvestris	wild chervil	OR, WA
Apera interrupta	dense silkybent	OR, WA
Apium graveolens	celery	CA, UT
Aralia elata	Japanese angelica	PA
Araujia sericifera	white bladder-flower	CA
Arctium lappa	burdock; beggar's buttons, clotbur	SD
Arctium minus	common burdock	CO, ID, IL, KY, MD, MI, OH, OR, PA, SC, TN, VA, WA, WI, WV, WY
Ardisia crenata	coral ardisia; hen's eyes; coralberry	FL, TX
Ardisia elliptica	shoebutton ardisia	FL, HI
Arrhenatherum elatius	tall oatgrass	CA, OR, TN, VA, WA
Artemisia absinthium	absinthe; oldman; common wormwood; absinth sagewort	OR, ND, WA
Artemisia stelleriana	oldwoman	NJ
Artemisia vulgaris	mugwort; common wormwood; felon herb	MD, NJ, NY, PA, TN, VA
Arthraxon hispidus	small carpgrass	CT, KY, MD, PA, TN, VA, WV
Arum italicum	Italian arum; Italian lords and ladies	OR
Arundo donax	giant reed; wild cane; cana brava; carrizo	AZ, CA, GA, MD, NM, NV, TX, VA
Asparagus densiflorus	asparagus fern; Sprenger's asparagus fern	FL
Asparagus officinalis	common asparagus; garden asparagus	AZ, SD, TN
Atriplex rosea	tumbling orach, tumbling saltweed	UT
Atriplex semibaccata	Australian saltbush	CA
Avena fatua	wild oats; Tartarian oats	AZ
Bambusa vulgaris	common bamboo; clumping bamboo; feathery bamboo	DC
Barbarea vulgaris	yellowrocket; wintercress	MI
Bassia hyssopifolia	five-hook bassia, fivehorn smotherweed	CA, NV, OR, UT, WA
Bassia scoparia	kochia; summer cypress	AZ, CA, CO, CT, ID, OR, SD, TX, WA
Bauhinia variegata	orchid tree	FL
Berberis thunbergii	Japanese barberry	CT, DC, DE, IN, KY, MA, MD, ME, MO, NC, NH, NJ, NY, OH,

SCIENTIFIC NAME	COMMON NAME(S)	STATE(S) WHERE INVASIVE
Berberis thunbergii (cont.)		PA, RI, TN, VA, VT, WI, WV
Berberis vulgaris	common barberry; jaundice-berry; European barberry	CA, CT, IL, IN, IA, PA, MA, ME, MT, NH, NJ, NM, NY, OH, RI, TN, VT, WI
Berteroa incana	hoary false madwort; hoary alyssum	CO, WY
Betula pendula	European white birch	KY, MD, WA, WI
Bischofia javanica	bishopweed; bischofia; Javawood; toog	FL
Bothriochloa ischaemum var. songarica	yellow bluestem; Turkestan bluestem	TX
Bougainvillea glabra	bougainvillea; paper flower	CA, FL
Brachypodium sylvaticum	slender false-brome	OR, WA
Brassica juncea	Chinese mustard; brown mustard; mustard greens	NV
Brassica nigra	black mustard	CA, SD
Brassica rapa	wild mustard	MD, TN, TX, VA
Brassica tournefortii	African mustard; Asian mustard; Mediterranean turnip; wild turnip	AZ, CA, NV
Breynia disticha	snowbush; foliage flower	FL
Bromus briziformis	rattlegrass; rattlesnake chess	OR, WA
Bromus catharticus	rescue grass	AZ, HI, TX, UT
Bromus commutatus	meadow brome	TN, WV
Bromus diandrus	ripgut brome	AZ, UT
Bromus inermis	smooth brome grass; awnless brome; Hungarian brome;	AZ, CO, IA, ID, IN, MI, MN, MO, NE, OH, OR, SD, TN, WA, WI, WY
Bromus japonicus	Japanese chess	AZ, CO, NE, OK, OR, SD, TN, TX, UT, WA, WY
Bromus rubens	red brome; foxtail brome; foxtail chess	AZ, CA, NV, UT
Bromus secalinus	rye brome	TN, TX
Bromus sterilis	poverty brome	MD, MO, OR, WA
Bromus tectorum	cheatgrass	AZ, CA, CO, CT, HI, ID, NE, NJ, NV, OR, PA, SD, TN, UT, WA, WV, WY
Broussonetia papyrifera	paper mulberry; tapa cloth tree	DC, FL, GA, LA, MD, NC, OK, PA, SC, TN, VA
Bryonia alba	white bryonia	OR, WA
Buddleja davidii	orange-eye butterfly bush; summer lilac	CA, KY, NC, NJ, OR, PA, WA, WV
Buddleja lindleyana	Lindley's butterfly bush	FL, GA, NC, TX
Butomus umbellatus	flowering rush; grassy rush; water gladiolus	CT, NH, VT, WI
Caesalpinia gilliesii	bird-of-paradise shrub	AZ, NM, NV, TX
Cajanus cajan	pigeon-pea	FL
Callicarpa dichotoma	Chinese beauty-berry	NC
Callitriche stagnalis	pond water-starwort	CT, NJ
Calluna vulgaris	heather, Scotch heather, ling	MA, NC, RI
Calophyllum antillanum	beautyleaf; Santa Maria	FL
Calophyllum inophyllum	Indian laurel	FL
Camelina microcarpa	littlepod false flax	SD
Campanula rapunculoides	creeping bell flower; rover bellflower	WI
Cannabis sativa	marijuana; Mary Jane; gallow grass	UT
Capsella bursa-pastoris	shepherd's purse	AZ, CA, HI, MD, NV, UT, VA

SCIENTIFIC NAME	COMMON NAME(S)	STATE(S) WHERE INVASIVE
Caragana arborescens	pea-tree; Siberian pea shrub	WI
Cardamine impatiens	narrow-leaf bittercress	CT, NJ
Cardaria draba	whitetop	AZ, CA, CO, ID, OR, MT, WA, WY
Cardiospermum halicacabum	balloon-vine; heart pea; winter cherry	VA
Carduus acanthoides	spiny plumeless thistle	IA, MN, NJ, OR, SD, VA, WA, WI, WY
Carduus crispus	curly plumeless thistle	NJ
Carduus nutans	nodding plumeless thistle	CO, GA, IA, ID, IL, KS, KY, MD, MN, MO, NC, NE, NJ, OR, PA, SD, TN, VA, WA, WI, WY
Carduus pycnocephalus	Italian plumeless thistle	CA, HI, OR, WA
Carduus tenuiflorus	shore thistle; slender thistle; winged thistle	OR, WA
Carex kobomugi	Asiatic sand sedge; Japanese sedge	MD, NJ, VA
Carica papaya	papaya	FL, HI
Carissa macrocarpa	Amatungula	FL
Carlina vulgaris	Carline thistle	NJ
Carpobrotus edulis	Hottentot-fig; iceplant; sea fig	CA
Casuarina equisetifolia	Australian pine; beach she-oak; beefwood; horsetail tree; South Sea ironweed; mile tree	FL, HI
Casuarina glauca	swamp oak; swamp she-oak;	FL, HI
Catalpa bignonioides	Southern catalpa	CA
Catalpa ovata	Chinese catalpa	CT, MA, MD, PA
Catalpa speciosa	northern catalpa; western catalpa	FL, MD, NJ, TN, VA
Catharanthus roseus	Madagascar periwinkle; rose periwinkle	FL, HI
Caulerpa taxifolia	killer alag	CA
Celastrus orbiculatus	Asian bittersweet; Asiatic bittersweet; Oriental bittersweet	CT, DC, DE, IL, IN, KY, MA, MD, ME, MI, MO, NC, NH, NJ, NY, PA, RI, TN, VA, VT, WI, WV
Cenchrus ciliaris (*Pennisetum ciliare*)	buffel grass	AZ, TX
Cenchrus longispinus	longspine sandbur	OR, WA
Cenchrus spinifex	coastal sandbur	AZ
Centaurea biebersteinii	spotted knapweed	AZ, CA, CO, CT, DE, KY, ID, IL, MA, MD, MI, MN, MT, NC, NJ, NY, OR, PA, SD, TN, UT, VA, WA, WI, WV, WY
Centaurea calcitrapa	red star-thistle	CA, UT
Centaurea cyanus	cornflower; batchellor's button; blue bottle	MD, TN
Centaurea debeauxii ssp. *thuillieri*	meadow knapweed	OR, WA
Centaurea diffusa	diffuse knapweed; white knapweed	AZ, CO, ID, NE, OR, UT, WA, WY
Centaurea jacea	brown knapweed; brown-ray knapweed	NC, OR, VA, WA
Centaurea macrocephala	bighead knapweed	OR, WA
Centaurea melitensis	Maltese star thistle; tocalote	AZ, CA, HI
Centaurea nigra	black knapweed; hard heads	OR, WA
Centaurea nigrescens	Tyrol knapweed	NY
Centaurea solstitialis	yellow star-thistle	CA, ID, OR, NJ, UT, WA
Centaurea transalpina	Alpine knapweed	VA

SCIENTIFIC NAME	COMMON NAME(S)	STATE(S) WHERE INVASIVE
Centaurea triumfettii	squarrose knapweed	OR, WA
Centranthus ruber	red valerian	CA, OR, WA
Cerastium biebersteinii	Boreal mouse-ear chickweed	NJ
Cerastium fontanum	common mouse-ear chickweed; hehine-hauli	MD, VA
Cerastium fontanum ssp. *vulgare*	common mouse-ear chickweed; hehine-hauli	HI, TN
Ceratocephala testiculata	bur buttercup	SD
Cestrum diurnum	day jessamine	FL
Cestrum nocturnum	night-flowering jassamine	FL, GA, HI
Chamaesyce maculata	spotted sandmat	CA, ND, NY
Chelidonium majus	celandine	CT, MD, VT, WI
Chenopodium ambrosioides	Mexican tea; Spanish tea; American wormwood	HI, MD, NJ, TN
Chenopodium berlandieri	pit-seed goosefoot	NV
Chenopodium murale	garden goosefoot; nettle-leaf goosefoot	CA, TN
Chenopodium simplex	giant-seed goosefoot	TX
Chondrilla juncea	rush skeletonweed	AZ, OR, WA
Chorispora tenella	blue mustard; chorispora	CA, ID, OR, WA, WY
Cichorium intybus	common chicory; blue sailors; succory	AZ, CA, ID, MD, MI, OH, PA, TN, UT, VA, WI, WV
Cinnamomum camphora	camphortree	AL, FL, GA, MS, TX
Cirsium arvense	Canada thistle	AK, AZ, CO, CT, DE, IA, ID, IN, MD, MI, MN, MO, MT, ND, NJ, OH, OR, PA, RI, SD, TN, VA, WA, WI, WV, WY
Cirsium vulgare	bull thistle	AK, AZ, CA, CO, HI, ID, MA, MD, MI, MN, MO, NC, NJ, OH, OR, PA, SD, TN, UT, VA, WA, WI, WV, WY
Cistus incanus	hairy rock-rose	CA
Citrullus colocynthis	colocynth; citron; bitter apple; vine of Sodom	CA
Citrus aurantifolia	lime	FL
Citrus aurantium	bigarade; sour orange; Seville orange	FL, GA
Citrus limon	lemon	FL
Citrus sinensis	sweet orange	FL
Clematis orientalis	Oriental virgin's bower	CO, NV
Clematis terniflora	leatherleaf clematis; yam-leaved clematis; sweet autumn virgin's bower	DC, DE, IL, MD, NJ, TN, VA
Clematis vitalba	Traveler's joy	OR, WA
Clerodendrum bungei	rose glory-bower	FL, GA
Clerodendrum chinense	stickbush	FL
Clerodendrum indicum	Turk's turban; tubeflower	FL, GA, SC
Clerodendrum speciosissimum	Javanese glory-bower	FL
Coincya monensis	coincya	CA
Colocasia esculenta	wild taro; dasheen; kalo; eddo	FL
Colubrina asiatica	Asiatic colubrina; latherleaf	FL
Colutea arborescens	bladder senna	CA, CO
Commelina benghalensis	dayflower	GA
Commelina communis	Asiatic dayflower; common dayflower	MD, PA, TN, VA
Conicosia pugioniformis	narrow-leaved iceplant	CA

SCIENTIFIC NAME	COMMON NAME(S)	STATE(S) WHERE INVASIVE
Conium maculatum	poison hemlock, spotted hemlock	AZ, CA, KY, MD, NE, OH, OR, PA, TN, VA, WA, WI, WV
Convallaria majalis	lily of the valley	WI
Convolvulus arvensis	field bindweed	AZ, CA, CO, CT, DE, ID, MI, MO, NE, NV, OH, OR, PA, SD, UT, VA, WA, WI, WY
Conyza bonariensis	South American conyza	CA, HI
Corispermum americanum rydbergii	American bugseed	CA
Corispermum nitidum	shiny bugseed	AZ
Coronilla varia	crown vetch	CT, IN, KY, MD, MI, MO, NC, NJ, OR, TN, VA, WI,
Cortaderia jubata	Andean pampas grass; purple pampas grass	AZ, CA, HI
Cortaderia selloana	pampas grass	AZ, CA, CO, UT
Corylus avellana	common filbert; European hazel	OR
Cotoneaster franchetii	orange cotoneaster	CA
Cotoneaster lacteus	milk-flower cotoneaster	CA
Cotoneaster pannosus	silver-leaf cotoneaster	CA
Crataegus monogyna	singleseed hawthorn; English hawthorn	CA, MA, NY, OR, WA
Crepis tectorum	hawksbeard	AK
Cruciata laevipes	smooth bedstraw	VA
Crupina vulgaris	common crupina	ID, OR, WA
Cryptostegia grandiflora	Palay rubbervine; rubbervine; purple allamandra	FL
Cupaniopsis anacardioides	carrotwood	FL
Cuscuta approximata	clustered dodder	OR, WA
Cuscuta epithymum	clover dodder	OR, WA
Cynanchum louiseae	black swallow-wort; Louis's swallowwort; dog-strangling vine	CT, NH, NY, WI
Cynanchum rossicum	pale swallow-wort; European swallow-wort	NH, NY, WI
Cynara cardunculus	artichoke thistle; cardoon	CA
Cynodon dactylon	Bermuda grass	AZ, CA, FL, GA, HI, NV, OK, TN, TX, UT, VA
Cynoglossum officinale	houndstoungue	AZ, CO, ID, NE, OR, UT, WA, WY
Cynosurus echinatus	bristly dogstail grass	OR
Cyperus amuricus	Asian flat sedge	NJ
Cyperus esculentus	yellow nutsedge; nutgrass	OR, WA
Cyperus iria	ricefield flat sedge	NJ
Cyperus rotundus	nut grass; kili`p`opu; purple flat sedge	HI, NJ
Cytisus scoparius	Scotch broom	CA, DE, GA, MA, NC, NY, OR, SC, TN, VA, WA
Cytisus striatus	Striped broom	CA
Dactylis glomerata	orchard grass; cock'sfoot	AZ, CO, HI, MD, MI, OR, SD, TN, UT, VA, WA, WY
Dactyloctenium aegyptium	Egyptian grass	FL
Dalbergia sissoo	Indiana dalbergia; sissoo	FL
Daphne laureola	spurge laurel	OR, WA
Daphne mezereum	February daphne, mezereum	MA
Datura stramonium	jimsonweed; common thorn apple; Jamestown weed	CT, HI, MD, PA, TN, WV
Daucus carota	Queen Anne's lace; wild carrot	CT, GA, HI, KY, MD, MI, MO,

SCIENTIFIC NAME	COMMON NAME(S)	STATE(S) WHERE INVASIVE
Daucus carota (cont.)		NJ, OR, TN, VA, WA, WI, WV
Delairea odorata	German-ivy, parlor-ivy	CA, HI
Descurainia sophia	flixweed; herb-sophia	CA, HI, ID, NV, OR, SD, UT, WA
Deutzia scabra	deutzia	AR, DC, KY, MD, NC, NJ, PA, TN, VA
Dianthus armeria	deptford pink	MD
Digitalis lanata	Grecian foxglove	WI
Digitalis purpurea	common foxglove	CA, OR, WA
Digitaria sanguinalis	hairy crabgrass	AZ, TN, TX
Dioscorea alata	water yam; white yam	FL
Dioscorea bulbifera	air potato	FL
Dioscorea oppositifolia	cinnamon vine	DC, KY, MD, MO, SC, TN, VA, WV
Dipsacus fullonum	Fuller's teasel	CA, CO, ID, IL, KY, MI, MO, NJ, OH, OR, TN, VA, WA, WI
Dipsacus laciniatus	cut-leaved teasel	IL, MD, MI, MO, NJ, TN, WI
Draba verna	spring draba	UT
Duchesnea indica	Indian strawberry	MI, MD, NJ, PA
Echinochloa colona	corn panicgrass; junglerice	AZ, HI, TN
Echinochloa crus-galli	barnyard grass	AZ, CA, CO, HI, SD, TN, TX
Echium vulgare	viper's bugloss	MD, OR, WA
Egeria densa	giant waterweed, Brazilian water weed	CA, CT, DE, NH, TN, VA, VT
Ehrharta calycina	veldt grass	CA
Eichhornia crassipes	water hyacinth	CA, DE, FL, GA, LA, TX
Elaeagnus angustifolia	Russian-olive; oleaster	AZ, CA, CO, CT, DE, IA, ID, IL, IN, KS, MD, MI, MN, MT, NC, NE, NJ, NM, NV, NY, OK, OR, PA, SD, TN, TX, UT, VA, VT, WA, WI
Elaeagnus multiflora	cherry elaeagnus, gumi, cherry silverberry	KY, NC
Elaeagnus pungens	thorny-olive; thorny elaeagnus	TN, VA
Elaeagnus umbellata	autumn-olive; oleaster	CT, DC, DE, FL, GA, IL, IN, KY, MD, MI, MO, NC, NH, NJ, NY, OH, PA, RI, TN, VA, VT, WI
Eleusine indica	goosegrass; manienie-ali'I	HI, KY
Elsholtzia ciliata	elscholtzia	CT
Elymus repens	quackgrass, couch grass, creeping wild rye	AZ, CO, ID, MD, MI, OH, OR, SD, VA, WA, WI, WY
Epilobium hirsutum	hairy willowherb	WI
Epipactis helleborine	helleborine	WI
Eragrostis cilianensis	stink grass	CA, SD, TX
Eragrostis curvula	weeping lovegrass	AZ, MD, NC, NJ, TN, TX, UT, VA
Eragrostis lehmanniana	Lehmann's love grass	AZ, NM
Erechtites minima	coastal burnweed	OR, WA
Erica cinerea	Scotch heath; twisted heath, ball heather	MA
Erica lusitanica	Spanish heath	CA
Erica tetralix	cross-leaved heath, bog heather	MA, NC
Eriochloa fatmensis	tropical cup grass	CA
Erodium cicutarium	redstem filaree; storksbill	AZ, CA, HI, NV, OR, TN, UT, WA
Eucalyptus camaldulensis	Longbeak eucalyptus; river redgum, Murray redgum	CA
Eucalyptus globulus	Tasmanian blue gum, blue gum	CA, HI

SCIENTIFIC NAME	COMMON NAME(S)	STATE(S) WHERE INVASIVE
Eucalyptus polyanthemos	redbox gum, silver dollar gum	CA
Eucalyptus tereticornis	forest redgum	CA
Eugenia uniflora	Surinam cherry, Brazil cherry, Barbados cherry, pitanga, cayenne cherry	FL
Euonymus alata	winged burning bush; wahoo; winged euonymus; winged spindle-tree	CT, DE, IN, KY, MA, MD, MO, NH, NJ, OH, PA, RI, TN, VA, WI, WV
Euonymus europaea	European spindle tree	IL, KY, MA, MI, NJ, VA, WI
Euonymus fortunei	climbing euonymus	AL, CT, DC, GA, IN, KY, MD, MO, OH, TN, VA, WI
Euphorbia cyparissias	cypress spurge	CT, MA, NJ, NY, RI, WI
Euphorbia esula	leafy spurge, wolf's milk	CA, CO, CT, IA, ID, MI, MN, MT, NC, ND, NE, NJ, OR, SD, UT, VA, WA, WI, WY
Euryops multifidus	sweet resin bush	AZ
Exochorda racemosa	pearlbush	NC, SC
Fatoua villosa	hairy crabweed	TN
Festuca ovina	sheep fescue	NY
Festuca rubra	red fescue	HI, NY
Ficus altissima	false banyan, council tree	FL
Ficus carica	edible fig, common fig, fig tree	CA, FL, IN, NC, PA
Ficus elastica	Assam rubber, Indian rubbertree	FL
Ficus thonningii	Chinese banyan	FL, HI
Filipendula ulmaria	queen-of-the meadow	WI
Firmiana simplex	Chinese parasol tree, Chinese bottle tree, Japanese varnish tree	GA, LA
Flacourtia indica	governor's plum, Madagascar palm	FL
Foeniculum vulgare	fennel	CA, HI, OR, VA, WA
Fragaria vesca ssp. vesca	woodland straw- berry, sowteat strawberry	NJ
Froelichia gracilis	cottonweed; slender snake cotton	CT, NJ
Galega officinalis	goat's rue	PA
Galinsoga parviflora	smooth galinsoga; gallant soldier	HI, MD
Galinsoga quadriradiata	hairy galinsoga; shaggy soldier	MD, TN
Galium mollugo	false baby's breath; wild madder; white bedstraw	NJ, VA
Galium verum	yellow bedstraw, our lady's bedstraw	NJ
Gaura mollis	lizardtail, velvetweed	NV
Genista linifolia	Mediterranean broom	CA
Genista monspessulana	Canary broom; Cape broom; French broom	CA, OR, WA
Genista tinctoria	dyer's greenweed, wood waxen, dyer's broom	DC, MA, ME, MI, MS, NH, WI
Geranium columbinum	cranesbill	MD, TN
Geranium lucidum	shining cranesbill	OR
Geranium robertianum	herb Robert, red robin	OR, WA
Geranium thunbergii	Nepalese cranes-bill; dewdrop cranes-bill	CT
Glechoma hederacea	Gill-over-the-ground; ground ivy	CT, DC, IN, KY, MD, MI, NC, NJ, OR, PA, TN, VA, WI, WV
Grevillea robusta	silkoak	FL, HI
Gypsophila paniculata	baby's breath	CO, MI, OR, WA, WI
Halogeton glomeratus	common halogeton	OR, SD, WA
Hedera helix	English ivy	AZ, CA, DC, DE, GA, KY, LA, MD, NC, NJ, OR, PA, RI, SC,

SCIENTIFIC NAME	COMMON NAME(S)	STATE(S) WHERE INVASIVE
Hedera helix (cont.)		TN, VA, WA, WI, WV
Helianthus ciliaris	Texas blue weed	OR, WA
Helianthus petiolaris	prairie sunflower	NJ
Hemerocallis fulva	fulvous daylily; orange daylily	DC, DE, IL, IN, MD, MI, PA, VA, WI, WV
Hemerocallis lilioasphodelus	lemon day-lily, yellow day-lily	DC, MD, TN, VA
Heracleum mantegazzianum	giant hogweed	OR, PA, WA
Hesperis matronalis	dame's rocket	CO, CT, IN, MD, MI, NJ, PA, TN, VA, WI, WV
Hibiscus syriacus	rose-of-Sharon, althaea	KY, PA, TN, VA
Hibiscus tiliaceus	sea hibiscus, mahoe	FL
Hibiscus trionum	flower-of-an-hour, Venice mallow	OR, WA
Hieracium aurantiacum	orange hawkweed; devils' paintbrush, king devil	AK, CO, ID, MT, OR, TN, WA, WI, WY
Hieracium caespitosum	meadow hawkweed	OR, WA
Hieracium canadense	yellow hawkweed	WI
Hieracium pilosella	mouse-ear hawkweed	NJ, OR, WA
Hieracium piloselloides	kingdevil	CT
Hirschfeldia incana	mustard	CA
Holcus lanatus	common velvet grass	CA, CT, HI, OR, TN, VA, WA
Holcus mollis	creeping velvet grass	OR, WA
Hordeum murinum	wall barley	AZ
Hordeum murinum ssp. *glaucum*	blue-gray barley	CA
Hordeum murinum ssp. *leporinum*	leporinum barley	AZ, CA
Hordeum vulgare	common barley, Nepal barley	ID
Humulus japonicus	Japanese hops	CT, DC, DE, IN, MD, PA, VA
Hydrangea paniculata	panicled hydrangea	MA
Hydrilla verticillata	hydrilla	CT, DC, DE, FL, GA, MD, NC, NH, OR, TN, TX, VA, VT, WA
Hydrocharis morsus-ranae	European frogs-bit	NH, VT
Hygrophila polysperma	green hygro; Indian swampweed	FL
Hymenachne amplexicaulis	West Indian marsh grass	FL
Hyoscyamus niger	black henbane, stinking nightshade	ID
Hypericum perforatum	common St. John's-wort	ID, MI, MO, MT, NY, OR, WA, WI, WY
Hypochaeris radicata	spotted cat's ear	HI, OR, VA, WA
Ilex aquifolium	English holly	CA, MD, OR, WA
Ilex crenata	Japanese holly; box-leaved holly	VA, DC
Impatiens glandulifera	policeman's helmet	OR
Imperata cylindrica	cogongrass	FL, GA, VA
Inula helenium	elecampane	OR
Ipomoea aquatica	water-spinach	FL, TX
Ipomoea hederacea	ivy-leaved morning-glory	KY, TN, VA
Ipomoea lacunosa	whitestar	MD
Ipomoea purpurea	common morning-glory	AZ, KY, TN, VA
Iris pseudacorus	European yellow iris, yellow flag, water flag	CT, DE, MD, NC, NH, OR, TN, VA, VT, WA, WI, WV
Isatis tinctoria	Dyer's woad	OR, UT, VA, WA
Jasminum dichotomum	Gold Coast jasmine	FL
Jasminum fluminense	Brazilian jasmine	FL, HI

SCIENTIFIC NAME	COMMON NAME(S)	STATE(S) WHERE INVASIVE
Jasminum multiflorum	star jasmine	FL
Jasminum sambac	Arabian jasmine	FL
Juniperus virginiana	eastern redcedar	HI, OR
Kerria japonica	Japanese-rose	SC, VA, WA
Koelreuteria paniculata	golden rain-tree	IL
Kummerowia stipulacea	Korean clover, K. lespedeza	KY, TN
Kummerowia striata	Japanese clover, common lespedeza	TN
Kyllinga gracillima	pasture spike sedge	NJ
Lactuca canadensis	Canada lettuce	UT
Lactuca sativa	garden lettuce	CA
Lactuca serriola	prickly lettuce	AZ, CA, ID, NV, OR, SD, TN, UT, WA
Lactuca tatarica	blue lettuce	UT
Laegerstroemia indica	crape myrtle	AL, FL, GA, LA, NC, SC, VA
Lamiastrum galeobdolon	yellow archangel	OR
Lamium amplexicaule	henbit	AZ, MD, TN, TX, WV
Lamium maculatum	spotted dead nettle	MD
Lamium purpureum	purple dead nettle	CT, MD, TN
Lantana camara	lantana; shrub verbena	AZ, FL, HI, SC, TX
Lantana montevidensis	creeping lantana, purple lantana; weeping lantana	AL, FL, GA, LA, NC, SC, VA
Lapsana communis	common nipplewort	HI, VA, WI
Lathyrus latifolius	everlasting pea	MI, OR, WI
Leontodon hirtus	rough hawkbit	OR
Leonurus cardiaca	common motherwort	MI, MN
Lepidium latifolium	perennial pepperweed; broad leaf pepperwort	CA, CO, CT, OR, UT, WA
Lepidium perfoliatum	clasping pepperweed	AZ, CA, ID, SD
Lepyrodiclis holosteoides	False jagged-chickweed	OR, WA
Lespedeza bicolor	bicolor lespedeza, shrubby bush-clover	GA, IN, KY, TN, VA
Lespedeza cuneata	Chinese bush-clover; Chinese lespedeza; sericea lespedeza	AR, DC, GA, IN, KY, MD, MO, NC, NJ, NY, TN, VA, WI, WV
Lespedeza thunbergii	Thunberg's bush-clover	NJ
Leucaena leucocephala	white lead tree; koa haole	FL, HI, TX
Leucanthemum vulgare	ox-eye daisy, margarite	AK, AZ, CA, CO, CT, KY, MD, MI, MO, MT, NJ, NY, OR, TN, WA, WI, WY
Ligustrum amurense	Amur privet	VA
Ligustrum japonicum	Japanese privet, wax-leaf privet	AR, FL, GA, KY, LA, SC, TN, TX
Ligustrum lucidum	glossy privet	FL, NC, TX
Ligustrum obtusifolium	border privet; blunt-leaved privet	CT, DC, IL, MI, NH, NJ, PA, VA
Ligustrum ovalifolium	California privet	CT, FL, NC, PA, VA
Ligustrum quihoui	waxy-leaf privet	NC
Ligustrum sinense	Chinese privet	AL, AR, FL, GA, KY, LA, MD, MS, NC, OH, OK, SC, TN, TX, VA
Ligustrum vulgare	common privet; European privet	CT, DC, DE, IN, KY, LA, MD, MI, MS, NJ, OH, OR, PA, SC, TN, VA, VT, WA, WI, WV
Linaria dalmatica	Dalmatian toadflax	AZ, ID, UT, WA
Linaria dalmatica ssp. *dalmatica*	Dalmatian toadflax	CO, OR, WA, WY

SCIENTIFIC NAME	COMMON NAME(S)	STATE(S) WHERE INVASIVE
Linaria vulgaris	common toadflax; butter-and-eggs; yellow toadflax, wild snap-dragon	AK, CO, CT, MI, MT, NJ, OR, VA, WA, WI, WV, WY
Liriope spicatum	creeping lilyturf	MD, TN
Lobelia chinensis	Chinese lobelia	NJ
Lolium arundinaceum	tall fescue; tall rye grass	AR, GA, ID, MO, NJ, OK, OR, TN, WA, WI
Lolium perenne	perennial ryegrass, English ryegrass	AZ, CA, OR, TN, TX, WA
Lolium pratense	meadow rye grass; tall fescue	DC, IN, KY, MD, MI, MO, OH, OR, SD, TN, UT, VA, WA, WI
Lonicera caprifolium	Italian woodbine	NC
Lonicera etrusca	Etruscan honeysuckle	OR
Lonicera fragrantissima	sweet breath of spring, January jasmine	TN, VA
Lonicera japonica	Japanese honeysuckle	CT, DC, DE, FL, GA, HI, IL, IN, KS, KY, MA, MD, MI, MO, NC, NH, NJ, NY, OH, OK, PA, RI, SC, TN, TX, VA, VT, WI, WV
Lonicera maackii	Amur honeysuckle	CT, DC, DE, GA, IN, KY, MD, MI, MO, NJ, OH, PA, TN, VA, VT, WI
Lonicera morrowii	Morrow's honeysuckle	CT, DC, DE, IN, KY, MA, MD, ME, MI, MO, NC, NH, NJ, NY, OH, PA, RI, TN, VA, VT, WI, WV
Lonicera periclymenum	European honeysuckle; woodbine	ME, NC
Lonicera standishii	Standish's honeysuckle	PA, VA
Lonicera tatarica	Tatarian honeysuckle; Tartarian honeysuckle	AR, CT, DE, IL, IN, IA, KY, MA, MD, MI, NC, NH, NJ, NY, OH, PA, RI, TN, VA, VT, WI
Lonicera ¥ bella	Bell's honeysuckle; pretty honeysuckle; showy bush honeysuckle	CT, IL, MD, ME, MI, NC, NH, NY, PA, RI, TN, VA, VT, WI
Lonicera xylosteum	European fly honeysuckle	CT, MA, MI, MO, NC, NJ, NY, VT
Lotus corniculatus	birds-foot trefoil	CA, IL, MN, MO, OR, TN, VA, WA, WI
Lunaria annua	silver dollar	OR
Luzula luzuloides	oak-forest wood-rush	ME
Lychnis flos-cuculi	ragged robin, cuckoo flower	CT, NJ
Lygodium japonicum	Japanese climbing fern	FL, GA
Lygodium microphyllum	Old World climbing fern	FL
Lysimachia nummularia	moneywort; creeping Jennie	CT, DC, IN, MD, MI, MO, NJ, OR, PA, TN, VA, WI, WV
Lysimachia vulgaris	garden loosestrife	CT
Lythrum salicaria	purple loosestrife	CT, DC, DE, ID, IN, KY, MA, MD, ME, MI, MN, MO, NC, NE, NH, NJ, NY, OH, OR, PA, RI, TN, UT, VA, VT, WA, WI
Lythrum virgatum	loosestrife	VA
Macfadyena unguis-cati	cat's claw, cat's claw trumpet	FL
Maclura pomifera	osage-orange, bow-wood	AZ, GA, IL, KS, LA, MD, MO, NC, NV, OH, TN, WA, WV
Mahonia bealei		TN
Malcolmia africana	African mustard	NV, UT
Malus baccata	Siberian crabapple	IL

SCIENTIFIC NAME	COMMON NAME(S)	STATE(S) WHERE INVASIVE
Malus floribunda	Japanese crabapple, showy crabapple	IL
Malus prunifolia	plum leaved apple, crabapple	CT
Malus pumila	common apple	AL, IL, MD, MT, PA, SC, VA, WV
Malus sylvestris	apple, crabapple	OH
Malva neglecta	common mallow	NV, TN
Malva parviflora	cheeseweed mallow	CA, HI, NV
Malvaviscus penduliflorus	turk's cap	FL, GA, HI, NC
Mangifera indica	mango	FL, HI
Manilkara zapota	sapodilla	FL
Marrubium vulgare	white horehound	AZ, CA, NV, TX, UT
Marsilea quadrifolia	European water-clover; water shamrock	CT
Matricaria discoidea	pineapple weed	CA, OR, TN, WA
Medicago lupulina	black medic	CA, HI, NV, SD, VA
Medicago sativa	alfalfa	AZ, CA, HI, SD, TN, TX, UT
Melaleuca quinquenervia	broadleaf paper-bark; punktree	FL, HI
Melia azedarach	Chinaberry	AL, AR, FL, GA, HI, LA, MS, NC, OK, SC, TX, UT, VA
Melilotus indicus	sour clover	AZ, CA, HI
Melilotus officinalis	white sweet clover; yellow sweet clover	AK, AZ, CA, CO, HI, IA, ID, IL, IN, KY, MD, MI, MN, NV, NY, OK, OR, SD, TN, TX, UT, VA, WA, WI, WV, WY
Melinis repens	rose Natal grass	FL, HI
Melissa officinalis	lemon balm	OR
Mentha pulegium	pennyroyal; peppermint	CA, OR
Mentha spicata	spearmint	CA, TN
Mesembryanthemum nodiflorum	slenderleaf iceplant	AZ
Microstegium vimineum	Japanese stilt grass; Nepalese browntop	CT, DC, DE, GA, IN, KY, MD, NC, NJ, NY, PA, TN, VA, WI, WV
Mimosa pigra	catclaw mimosa	FL
Mirabilis nyctaginea	heartleaf four o'clock	OR, WA
Miscanthus sinensis	Chinese silver grass; eulalia; zebra grass	CT, DC, GA, IL, IN, KY, MD, NC, NJ, PA, SC, TN, VA, WI
Morus alba	white mulberry	AR, CT, DC, FL, GA, IA, IN, KS, KY, MD, MI, NC, NJ, NY, OK, OR, PA, SC, TN, TX, VA, VT, WA, WI
Mosla dianthera	miniature beefsteak plant	KY
Murdannia keisak	aneilima; Asian spiderwort; marsh dewflower; wart-removing herb	TN, TX, VA
Muscari botryoides	grape hyacinth	MD, TN, WV
Mycelis muralis	wall lettuce	OR, WA
Myoporum laetum	myoporum	CA
Myosotis scorpioides	true forget-me-not	CT, MI, OR, WI
Myosotis sylvatica	woodland forget-me-not	WI
Myosoton aquaticum	giant chickweed	MD, NJ, PA, VA
Myriophyllum aquaticum	parrot's-feather; parrot feather watermilfoil	CT, DE, GA, MD, NH, OR, TN, VA
Myriophyllum spicatum	Eurasian watermilfoil; spiked watermilfoil	CA, CT, DE, ID, MI, NH, NJ, NV, NY, OH, OR, PA, TN, VA,

SCIENTIFIC NAME	COMMON NAME(S)	STATE(S) WHERE INVASIVE
Myriophyllum spicatum (cont.)		VT, WA, WI
Najas minor	slender-leaved naiad	CT, NH, VT
Nandina domestica	heavenly bamboo; nandina, sacred bamboo	FL, GA, NC, TN
Nepeta cataria	catnip	MD
Nephrolepis cordifolia	tuber sword fern	FL
Nerium oleander	oleander; S.A. oleander	CA, FL, GA, LA, NV
Neyraudia reynaudiana	Burma reed; silk reed	FL
Nicotiana glauca	tree tobacco	AZ, CA, FL, HI, NV, TX
Nymphoides peltata	yellow floating heart	NH, VT
Oenothera glazioviana	red sepal evening primrose	CA
Olea europaea	olive	CA
Onopordum acanthium	Scotch thistle; Scotch cotton thistle	AZ, ID, MO, OR, UT, WA, WY
Ornithogalum nutans	nodding star-of-Bethlehem	DC, MD, PA,
Ornithogalum umbellatum	star-of-Bethlehem	CT, DC, IN, KY, MD, PA, TN, VA, WI, WV
Orobanche minor	hellroot	GA
Pachysandra terminalis	Japanese spurge; Japanese pachysandra	VA, DC
Paederia cruddasiana	sewer vine	FL
Paederia foetida	skunk vine	FL
Panicum antidotale	blue panicum	AZ
Panicum repens	torpedo grass	FL, GA, TX
Paraserianthes lophantha	plume-albizia	CA
Parentucellia viscosa	yellow glandweed	CA, HI, OR, WA
Parthenocissus tricuspidata	Boston ivy	CA
Paspalum dilatatum	dallis grass	CA, HI, MD, TN, TX
Paspalum notatum var. *latifolium* and var. *saurae*	Bahia grass	FL
Pastinaca sativa	wild parsnip	MI, OH, PA, TN, VA, WI
Paulownia tomentosa	princess tree; empress tree	CT, DC, GA, KY, LA, MD, NC, NJ, OR, PA, TN, VA, WV
Pavonia hastata	spearleaf swamp mallow	FL, GA
Pavonia spinifex	gingerbush	FL, GA
Peganum harmala	African rue	OR, WA
Pennisetum ciliare var. *ciliare*	Buffel grass	HI, TX
Pennisetum glaucum	pearl barley	AZ, CA
Pennisetum glaucum	yellow foxtail	IL, SD, WV
Pennisetum purpureum	elephant grass; Napier grass	FL, HI
Pennisetum setaceum	crimson fountain grass	AZ, CA, HI, NV
Perilla frutescens	beefsteak plant	DC, IL, MD, MO, PA, TN, VA, WV
Phalaris aquatica	Harding grass	HI, OR
Phalaris arundinacea	reed canary grass	AK, CO, CT, DE, ID, IL, IN, KY, MA, MD, MI, MO, MT, NC, NJ, NY, OH, OR, PA, TN, VA, WA, WI
Phalaris canariensis	canary grass	CA, MI
Phalaris minor	littleseed canary grass	AZ
Phellodendron amurense	Amur cork tree	IL, NY, PA, VA
Phellodendron japonicum	Japanese cork tree	NJ
Phleum pratense	Timothy grass	AZ, MD, MI, OH, OR, SD, TN, UT, VA, WA, WY
Phoenix dactylifera	date palm	CA, NV

SCIENTIFIC NAME	COMMON NAME(S)	STATE(S) WHERE INVASIVE
Phoenix reclinata	reclining date palm; Senegal date palm	FL
Phragmites australis	common reed; phragmites	CO, CT, DC, DE, GA, IN, KY, MD, MI, NC, NH, NJ, NY, OH, PA, TN, VA, VT, WI
Phyllostachys aurea	golden bamboo, running bamboo	GA, MD, PA, VA, WV
Physalis virginiana var. *virginiana*	Virginia groundcherry	CA
Picea abies	Norway spruce	HI, MD, TN
Picris hieracioides	hawkweed ox-tongue	OR, WA
Pinus pinea	Italian stone pine	CA
Pinus sylvestris	Scotch pine; scots pine	HI, IA, MA, ME, NJ, NY, OH, PA, VT, WI
Pinus thunbergiana	black pine	DE, RI, VA
Pistia stratiotes	Nile cabbage; water lettuce	DE, FL, TX
Pithecellobium dulce	blackbead; guayamochil; Madras thorn; monkeypod	FL, HI
Pittosporum undulatum	Australian cheesewood	CA
Plantago lanceolata	English plantain; lance-leaved plantain	AZ, CA, HI, MD, MI, NJ, TN, UT, VA
Plantago major	common plantain; broad-leaved plantain	AZ, CA, HI, MD, MI, NJ, TN, UT, VA
Poa annua	annual bluegrass	AZ, CA, HI, MI, TN, UT
Poa bulbosa	bulbous bluegrass	MI
Poa compressa	Canada bluegrass	CA, CT, MI, NE, OR, PA, TN, VA, WA, WI, WV
Poa pratensis	Kentucky bluegrass	AZ, CO, HI, IA, ID, KY, MD, MO, NE, OR, SD, TN, WA, WI, WY
Poa trivialis	rough bluegrass	VA
Polygonum argyrocoleon	silver-sheathed knotweed	CA, NV
Polygonum caespitosum	Oriental lady's thumb	CT, KY, MD, MI, TN, VA, WV
Polygonum convolvulus	black bindweed	AZ, HI, MI, SD
Polygonum cuspidatum	Japanese knotweed; Mexican bamboo	AK, CT, DC, DE, GA, IN, MA, MD, ME, MI, MO, NC, NH, NJ, NY, OH, OR, PA, RI, TN, VA, VT, WA, WI, WV
Polygonum lapathifolium	curlytop knotweed	TX, UT
Polygonum orientale	kiss-me-over-the-garden-gate; prince's-feather; princess-feather	MI, NJ
Polygonum perfoliatum	Asiatic tearthumb; devil's-tail tearthrumb; mile-a-minute vine; mile-a-minute-weed	CT, DC, DE, MA, MD, NJ, PA, VA, WI, WV
Polygonum persicaria	lady's-thumb; spotted lady's- thumb	KY, MD, MI, TN, UT, VA
Polygonum polystachyum	cultivated knotweed; Himalyan knotweed	OR, WA
Polygonum ramosissimum	bushy knotweed; yellow-flower knotweed	NV
Polygonum sachalinense	giant knotweed; Sakhalian knotweed	IL, MD, MI, NC, OR, RI, WA, WI
Polypogon monspeliensis	rabbitsfoot grass	AZ, NV, UT
Polypogon viridis	beardless rabbitsfoot grass; water bentgrass	AZ, CA, TX, UT
Poncirus trifoliata	trifoliate orange; hardy orange	FL, GA, LA, MS, SC, TX, WV
Populus alba	white poplar	CO, CT, DC, GA, IL, IN, KY, MA, MD, MI, MO, MT, NV, OH, OR, PA, SC, TN, VA, VT, WA, WI, WY

SCIENTIFIC NAME	COMMON NAME(S)	STATE(S) WHERE INVASIVE
Populus balsamifera	balsam poplar; balm of Gilead	TN
Populus nigra	black poplar; Lombardy poplar	MI, ND
Populus tremula	European aspen	MS
Populus × canescens	gray poplar	MS, WI
Portulaca oleracea	common purslane; little hogweed	AZ, CA, HI, IL, NV, TN, UT
Potamogeton crispus	curly-leaf pondweed	AZ, CT, NH, NJ, NV, NY, TN, VT, WI
Potentilla recta	sulfur cinquefoil	CO, ID, MD, MT, OR, WA, WY
Pouteria campechiana	canistel; eggfruit tree	FL
Prunella vulgaris	self-heal	HI, MI
Prunus avium	bird cherry	DE, MA, MD, NC, NJ, NY, OR, PA, RI, TN, VA, WA
Prunus cerasifera	cherry plum	OR
Prunus cerasus	sour cherry	CA, KY, MD, NC, NY, OR, WA, WV
Prunus domestica	garden plum; European plum	IN, MI, OR
Prunus laurocerasus	cherry-laurel	OR, WA
Prunus lusitanica	Portugal laurel	OR, WA
Prunus mahaleb	Mahaleb cherry; perfumed cherry	DC, ID, IL, MO, OR, PA, WA
Prunus padus	European bird cherry	AK, AL, PA
Prunus persica	peach	AR, CA, FL, GA, IL, KY, LA, MD, MS, NC, SC, TN, VA
Prunus spinosa	blackthorn	OR
Pseudognaphalium luteoalbum	Jersey rabbit-tobacco, Jersey cudweed	NV
Pseudosasa japonica	arrow bamboo	MD, PA, WV
Psidium cattleianum	strawberry guava	FL, HI
Psidium guajava	common guava	FL, HI
Pueraria montana lobata	kudzu-vine	AR, CT, DC, DE, FL, GA, IL, IN, KY, MD, MO, MS, NC, ND, NJ, OR, PA, SC, TN, TX, VA, WV
Punica granatum	pomegranate	CA
Pyracantha angustifolia	narrowleaf firethorn	CA, HI, OR
Pyracantha coccinea	fiery thorn; everlasting thorn; scarlet firethorn	OR
Pyrus calleryana	Bradford pear, Callery pear	IL, MD, PA
Pyrus communis	common pear	OR
Quercus acutissima	sawtooth oak	MD, SC, TN, VA
Quercus robur	English oak	WA
Quisqualis indica	Rangoon creeper	FL
Ranunculus acris	tall buttercup	MD, MI, TN, UT
Ranunculus bulbosus	bulbous buttercup	DC, MD, TN
Ranunculus ficaria	lesser celandine	CT, DC, DE, MD, NJ, OR, PA, VA, WI, WV
Ranunculus repens	creeping buttercup	OR
Raphanus raphanistrum	jointed charlock	VA
Rapistrum rugosum	annual bastard cabbage	TX
Reseda alba	white mignonette	CA
Rhamnus cathartica	common buckthorn; Hart's thorn; waythorn; Rhineberry	CO, CT, IA, IL, IN, MD, MA, MI, MN, MO, MS, ND, NH, NJ, NY, PA, RI, SD, TN, VA, VT, WI, WY
Rhamnus frangula (*Frangula alnus*)	glossy buckthorn; European alder buckthorn	CT, IL, IN, MA, MD, ME, MI, MN, MS, NH, NJ, NY, OH,

SCIENTIFIC NAME	COMMON NAME(S)	STATE(S) WHERE INVASIVE
Rhamnus frangula (cont.)		PA, RI, VA, VT, WI
Rhodomyrtus tomentosus	downy rose myrtle	FL, HI
Rhodotypos scandens	black jetbead	DE, IL, MA, MI, NY, PA, VA, WI
Ribes rubrum	garden red currant; northern red currant	NJ, OR, WA
Robinia hispida	bristly locust; rose-acacia	MI, NJ, OH, PA, WA
Robinia pseudoacacia	black locust	CA, CT, IA, IL, IN, MD, MI, MN, MO, NJ, NY, OH, OR, PA, TX, VA, VT, WA, WI
Rorippa amphibia	great watercress	VT
Rorippa austriaca	Austrian yellowcress	OR, WA
Rorippa nasturtium-aquaticum	watercress	AZ, CO, CT, KY, OR, TN, UT, WA, WI
Rosa bracteata	Macartney rose	FL, LA, MS, TX, VA
Rosa canina	dog rose	CA, IN, MD, NJ, OR, PA, VA, WA
Rosa cinnamomea	cinnamon rose	VT, WI
Rosa eglanteria	eglantine; sweetbrier	CA, IN, LA, MA, ME, NH, NY, OH, OR, PA, VA, WA, WI
Rosa gallica	French rose	GA, PA, SC, VA
Rosa micrantha	small-flower sweetbrier	NC, NY, SC, VA
Rosa multiflora	multiflora rose; rambler rose	AR, CA, CO, CT, DC, DE, GA, IL, IN, KY, LA, MA, MD, ME, MI, MO, MS, NC, NH, NJ, NY, OH, OR, PA, RI, SC, TN, VA, VT, WI, WV
Rosa rugosa	Japanese rose; rugosa rose	CT, MA, NJ, NY, PA, RI, WA
Rosa spinosissima	Scotch rose; Burnett rose	GA, IL
Rosa wichuraiana	memorial rose	KY, MS, NC, SC, TN, VA
Rosa × damascena	damask rose	NC
Rottboellia cochinchinensis	itchgrass	GA
Rubus bifrons	Himalayan-berry	GA, MS, NC, SC, TN, VA
Rubus discolor	Himalayan blackberry	AZ, CA, NJ, NV, OR, UT, WA
Rubus idaeus	European red raspberry	NY
Rubus illecebrosus	strawberry-raspberry	MD, VA
Rubus laciniatus	cut-leaf blackberry	CA, IN, NJ, OR, PA, WA, WV
Rubus macrophyllus	largeleaf blackberry	WA
Rubus phoenicolasius	wineberry	CT, CO, DC, DE, MA, MD, NC, NJ, NY, PA, TN, VA, WV
Rubus ulmifolius	elm-leaf blackberry	CA
Rubus vestitus	European blackberry	WA
Ruellia caerulea	Mexican petunia; linear-leaved wild petunia	FL
Rumex acetosella	red sorrel	AZ, CT, HI, NY, OR, TN, VA, WA, WI, WV
Rumex crispus	curly dock	AZ, CA, CT, HI, ID, MI, NE, NJ, OR, TN, TX, VA, WA, WI, WV
Rumex stenophyllus	dock	SD
Saccharum ravennae	Ravenna grass	AZ, UT
Salix alba	white willow	MI, NY, VA
Salix caprea	goat willow	NC, PA, RI
Salix cinerea	large gray willow	MD, NC, NY
Salix fragilis	crack willow	CO, IL, MA, MI, MN, NV, NY, PA, UT
Salix matsudana	corkscrew willow	MI

SCIENTIFIC NAME	COMMON NAME(S)	STATE(S) WHERE INVASIVE
Salix pentandra	bay willow	IA, MA, MD, MI, MN, PA, WI
Salix purpurea	purple willow; purple osier	CA, MA, MI, PA, WI
Salix viminalis	basket willow	MA, ME, VT, WA
Salix × *pendulina*	weeping willow	MI
Salix × *sepulcralis*	weeping willow	CT, DC, IL, NC, NY, OR, WA, WV
Salsola collina	slender Russian-thistle	CO
Salsola kali	Russian thistle; tumbleweed	AZ, CA, ID, TX, VA
Salsola paulsenii	barbwire Russian thistle	CA, NV
Salsola tragus	prickly Russian thistle	AZ, CA, CO, NV, OR, SD, UT, WA
Salvia aethiopis	Meditteranean sage	AZ, OR, UT, WA
Salvinia minima	water spangles, common salvinia	GA, TX
Salvinia molesta	giant salvinia, kariba-weed	CA, GA, HI, TX
Sansevieria hyacinthoides	iguanatail	FL
Sapium sebiferum (*Triadica sebifera*)	Chinese tallow- tree; candleberry tree; popcorn tree	AL, FL, GA, LA, MS, NC, SC, TX, VA
Saponaria officinalis	bouncing Bet; soapwort	CA, CO, IN, MD, MI, TN, WI, WV
Scabiosa atropurpurea	morningbride	TX
Scaevola sericea var. *taccada*	beach naupaka	FL
Schefflera actinophylla	schefflera; octopus tree; Queensland umbrella tree	FL, HI
Schinus molle	pepper tree	CA
Schinus terebinthifolius	Brazilian pepper	FL, HI
Schismus arabicus	Arabian schismus	AZ, CA, UT
Schismus barbatus	Meditteranean grass	AZ, CA, NV, UT
Secale cereale	cereal rye	OR, WA
Senecio jacobaea	tansy ragwort	CA, OR, WA
Senna occidentalis	coffee senna; septicweed	HI, TN
Senna pendula	climbing cassia; valamuerto	FL
Senna pendula var. *glabrata*	climbing cassia; valameurto	FL
Sesbania punicea	purple rattlebox	FL, GA
Setaria faberi	Japanese bristlegrass	IL, OH, PA, TN, VA
Setaria italica	foxtail millet	TN
Setaria pumila	yellow bristlegrass	CA, TN
Setaria viridis	green foxtail; green millet	AZ, IL, KY, SD, TN
Silene latifolia ssp. *alba*	bladder campion	MI, OR, WA
Silene vulgaris	maiden's tears	MI, WI, WY
Silybum marianum	milk thistle	CA
Sisymbrium altissimum	tall tumble-mustard	AZ, CA, CO, HI, ID, NV, OR, SD, TX, UT, WA
Sisymbrium irio	London rocket	AZ, CA, NV
Sisymbrium orientale	Indian hedge- mustard	CA
Solanum dulcamara	bittersweet nightshade; climbing nightshade	CT, MA, MD, MI, OR, PA, WA, WI
Solanum marginatum	purple African nightshade	CA
Solanum nigrum	black nightshade	CA, CT, NV, UT, VA
Solanum physalifolium	hoe nightshade	CA
Solanum rostratum	buffalobur nightshade	CA, UT
Solanum seaforthianum	Brazilian nightshade	FL
Solanum tampicense	aquatic soda apple	FL

SCIENTIFIC NAME	COMMON NAME(S)	STATE(S) WHERE INVASIVE
Solanum torvum	turkey berry	FL
Solanum triflorum	three-flowered nightshade	CA
Solanum viarum	tropical soda apple	FL, GA,TN
Sonchus arvensis	sow thistle	CO
Sonchus arvensis ssp. *arvensis*	sow thistle	OR, WA
Sonchus asper	spiny leaf sow-thistle	AZ, CA, HI, TX, UT
Sonchus oleraceus	common sow thistle	AZ, CA, HI
Sorbaria sorbifolia	false spiraea	MA, ME, MI, NH
Sorbus aucuparia	European mountain-ash	IA, IL, ME, MN, OR, WA, WI
Sorghum bicolor	broom-corn; shattercane; sorghum	NV
Sorghum bicolor drummondii	shattercane	PA
Sorghum halepense	Johnson grass	AR, AZ, CA, DE, FL, GA, HI, IL, KY, MD, MO, NC, NJ, NM, OH, OK, OR, PA, TN, TX, VA, WA, WI
Spartina alterniflora	Atlantic cordgrass; smooth cordgrass	CA, OR, WA
Spartina anglica	common cord grass	OR, WA
Spartina densiflora	denseflower cordgrass	CA
Spartina patens	salt marsh cord grass	OR, WA
Spartium junceum	Spanish broom	CA
Spergula morisonii	Morison's spurry	NJ
Sphaerophysa salsula	Swainsonpea	OR, WA
Sphagneticola trilobata	Bay Biscayne; creeping-oxeye; Singapore daisy	FL, HI
Spiraea japonica	Japanese spirea	KY, MD, NC, NJ, PA, TN, VA
Spiraea prunifolia	bridal wreath spirea	AL,TN
Spiraea thunbergii	Thunberg's meadowsweet	NC
Spirodela punctata	giant duckweed	TX
Spondias purpurea	purple mombin	FL
Stellaria media	common chickweed	HI, KY, MD, NC, NJ, PA, TN, VA, WV
Syngonium podophyllum	arrowhead vine	FL
Syringa vulgaris	common lilac	CA, WI
Syzygium cumini	jaman; Java plum	FL, HI
Syzygium jambos	jambos; Malabar plum	FL, HI
Taeniatherum caput-medusae	medusahead	CA, OR, WA
Tamarix africana	African tamarisk	SC
Tamarix aphylla	athel	AZ, CA, NV, TX
Tamarix chinensis	tamarisk; fivestamen tamarisk	AZ, CA, CO, NV, OR, UT, WA
Tamarix gallica	French tamarisk	AR, AZ, CA, CO, GA, IN, LA, NC, NM, NV, SC, TX, UT, WA, WY
Tamarix parviflora	small-flower tamarisk	CA, IN, NV, OK, OR, SD, TX
Tamarix ramosissima	saltcedar; tamarisk	AZ, CA, CO, LA, MT, NC, ND, NM, NV, OK, TX, UT, WY
Tanacetum vulgare	common tansy	MD, ID, OR, WA, WI, WY
Taraxacum laevigatum	red-seed dandelion	NJ
Taraxacum officinale	common dandelion	AZ, CA, HI, ID, MD, MI, NJ, OH, PA, TX, UT, VA, WY
Taxus cuspidata	Japanese yew	NJ, VA
Tectaria incisa	incised halberd fern	FL
Terminalia catappa	tropical almond; India-almond	FL, HI
Thespesia populnea	seaside mahoe; portia tree	FL

SCIENTIFIC NAME	COMMON NAME(S)	STATE(S) WHERE INVASIVE
Thinopyrum intermedium	intermediate wheatgrass	ID, OR
Thinopyrum ponticum	rush wheatgrass	UT
Thlaspi arvense	field cress; penny cress	ID, TN
Torilis arvensis	spreading hedge- parsley	OR, TN, WA, WI
Torilis japonica	erect hedge-parsley	WI
Tradescantia fluminensis	green wandering Jew	FL
Tradescantia spathacea	boat-lily; oyster plant	FL
Tragopogon dubius	yellow goat's beard; yellow salsify	AK, ID, NE, NV, OR, SD, TN, UT, WA
Tragopogon porrifolius	salsify; vegetable oyster	SD
Tragopogon pratensis	meadow salsify; yellow goatsbeard	MD, OR, SD, TN, WA
Trapa natans	water chestnut	CT, DE, MA, NH, NY, PA, VA, VT, WI
Tribulus terrestris	caltrop; cat's head; devil's thorn; puncturevine	AZ, CA, NE, NV, OR, SD, TX, UT, WA
Trifolium aureum	hop clover	VA
Trifolium campestre	low hop-clover; field clover	MD, TN
Trifolium dubium	suckling clover	HI, MD, SD, TN
Trifolium hybridum	alsike clover	SD, TN
Trifolium pratense	red clover	HI, MD, MI, TN, VA, WI
Trifolium repens	white clover	AZ, CA, HI, MD, MI, TN, WI
Tripleurospermum maritimum subsp. *inodorum* (*Matricaria perforata*)	scentless false mayweed	OR, WA
Triticum aestivum	common wheat	CA
Tussilago farfara	coltsfoot	CT, ME, NC, NJ, TN
Ulex europaeus	European gorse; furze; whin	CA, HI, OR, WA
Ulmus parvifolia	Chinese elm	DC, NC, NE, NJ, VA, WI
Ulmus procera	English elm	CA
Ulmus pumila	Siberian elm; dwarf elm; littleleaf elm;	AZ, IA, ID, IL, IN, KS, KY, MA, MD, MI, MN, MO, NE, NM, NV, OH, OK, OR, PA, TX, UT, VA, WA, WI, WV
Umbellularia californica	California laurel	OR
Urena lobata	Caesarweed	FL, HI
Urochloa maxima	green panic grass; Guinea grass	HI, TX
Urochloa mutica	buffalo grass; Dutch grass; para grass	FL, HI
Urtica dioica	European stinging nettle	DC, MD, OH, PA, WV
Valeriana officinalis	garden heliotrope	CT, IL, WI
Vallisneria americana	American eel-grass; tape-grass	NV
Verbascum blattaria	moth mullein	NJ, OR, WA
Verbascum thapsus	common mullein; flannel-leaved mullein	AZ, CA, CO, CT, HI, ID, IL, MO, NJ, NV, OH, OR, PA, SD, TN, VA, WA, WI, WV, WY
Verbena bonariensis	tall vervain	GA, OR
Vernicia fordii	tung-oil tree	FL
Veronica anagallis-aquatica	water- speedwell	CA, UT
Veronica arvensis	corn speedwell	HI, SD
Veronica beccabunga	European speedwell; brooklime	CT, NJ
Veronica biloba	bilobed speedwell; two-lobe speedwell	WY
Veronica hederifolia	ivy-leaved speedwell	MD, NJ, TN, VA, WV
Veronica serpyllifolia	speedwell	MD, TN

SCIENTIFIC NAME	COMMON NAME(S)	STATE(S) WHERE INVASIVE
Viburnum dilatatum	linden viburnum	DC, VA
Viburnum lantana	wayfaring-tree	IL, PA, WI
Viburnum opulus	European cranberry	KY, IL, MI, MO, NH, NY, OH, VT
Viburnum opulus var. *opulus*	Guelder rose; cranberrybush viburnum	IN, PA, WI
Viburnum plicatum	Japanese snowball	DC
Viburnum sieboldii	Siebold viburnum	NY, PA
Vicia cracca	bird vetch	AK, OR, WA
Vicia sativa	common vetch	HI, TN
Vicia villosa	hairy vetch	MI, OR, WA
Vinca major	bigleaf periwinkle	AZ, CA, GA, LA, MD, OR, NC, NM, TN, UT, WA
Vinca minor	common periwinkle	CA, CT, DC, DE, GA, IA, IL, IN, KY, MD, MI, NC, NJ, NY, OH, OR, PA, RI, SC, TN, TX, VA, WA, WI, WV
Vitex agnus-castus	lilac chaste-tree	FL, LA, NC, NY, SC, TX
Vitex rotundifolia	beach vitex	SC
Vitex trifolia	simpleleaf chastetree	FL
Vitis vinifera	European grape	CA, WA
Vulpia myuros	annual fescue; foxtail fescue; red-tail fescue	HI, OR, WA
Wisteria floribunda	Japanese wisteria	DC, MD, NC, NJ, PA, SC, TN, VA
Wisteria sinensis	Chinese wisteria	DC, FL, GA, HI, IL, KY, LA, MA, MD, NC, NJ, NY, PA, SC, TN, VA
Youngia japonica	Oriental false hawks-beard; Japanese hawk's beard	DC, HI, VA
Zygophyllum fabago	Syrian bean-caper	OR, WA

Index of Invasive Plants

INDEX OF INVASIVE PLANTS

Index of Native Plants

INDEX OF NATIVE PLANTS

INDEX OF NATIVE PLANTS

Find Out More About Invasive Plants in North America

Invasive Plants: Weeds of the Global Garden, originally published in 1996, was the first comprehensive publication to identify the worst invasive plants in North America and discuss how they endanger the future of our remaining wild landscapes. Still cited as an invaluable resource by land managers and ecologists as well as gardeners, this handbook redefines the weed to include escaped garden plants: Almost half of the most invasive plant species in the United States and Canada were brought here intentionally for horticultural use. It identifies the worst invasives in every North American region and tells readers what to do about them to help keep the native plants, and the wildlife they support, from disappearing from our land and lives.

Brooklyn Botanic Garden All-Region Guides

World renowned for pioneering gardening information, Brooklyn Botanic Garden's award-winning guides provide practical advice in a compact format for gardeners in every region of North America. To order other fine titles, call 718-623-7286 or shop online at shop.bbg.org. For additional information about Brooklyn Botanic Garden, call 718-623-7200 or visit bbg.org.

Providing expert gardening advice for over 60 years

Join Brooklyn Botanic Garden as an annual Subscriber Member and receive our next three gardening handbooks delivered directly to you, plus *Plants & Gardens News, BBG Members News,* and reciprocal privileges at many botanic gardens across the country. Visit bbg.org/subscribe for details.